Teaching Through The Ill Body

TRANSGRESSIONS: CULTURAL STUDIES AND EDUCATION

Scope
Cultural studies provides an analytical toolbox for both making sense of educational practice and extending the insights of educational professionals into their labors. In this context *Transgressions: Cultural Studies and Education* provides a collection of books in the domain that specify this assertion. Crafted for an audience of teachers, teacher educators, scholars and students of cultural studies and others interested in cultural studies and pedagogy, the series documents both the possibilities of and the controversies surrounding the intersection of cultural studies and education. The editors and the authors of this series do not assume that the interaction of cultural studies and education devalues other types of knowledge and analytical forms. Rather the intersection of these knowledge disciplines offers a rejuvenating, optimistic, and positive perspective on education and educational institutions. Some might describe its contribution as democratic, emancipatory, and transformative. The editors and authors maintain that cultural studies helps free educators from sterile, monolithic analyses that have for too long undermined efforts to think of educational practices by providing other words, new languages, and fresh metaphors. Operating in an interdisciplinary cosmos, Transgressions: Cultural Studies and Education is dedicated to exploring the ways cultural studies enhances the study and practice of education. With this in mind the series focuses in a non-exclusive way on popular culture as well as other dimensions of cultural studies including social theory, social justice and positionality, cultural dimensions of technological innovation, new media and media literacy, new forms of oppression emerging in an electronic hyperreality, and postcolonial global concerns. With these concerns in mind cultural studies scholars often argue that the realm of popular culture is the most powerful educational force in contemporary culture. Indeed, in the twenty-first century this pedagogical dynamic is sweeping through the entire world. Educators, they believe, must understand these emerging realities in order to gain an important voice in the pedagogical conversation.

Without an understanding of cultural pedagogy's (education that takes place outside of formal schooling) role in the shaping of individual identity–youth identity in particular–the role educators play in the lives of their students will continue to fade. Why do so many of our students feel that life is incomprehensible and devoid of meaning? What does it mean, teachers wonder, when young people are unable to describe their moods, their affective affiliation to the society around them. Meanings provided young people by mainstream institutions often do little to help them deal with their affective complexity, their difficulty negotiating the rift between meaning and affect. School knowledge and educational expectations seem as anachronistic as a ditto machine, not that learning ways of rational thought and making sense of the world are unimportant.

But school knowledge and educational expectations often have little to offer students about making sense of the way they feel, the way their affective lives are shaped. In no way do we argue that analysis of the production of youth in an electronic mediated world demands some "touchy-feely" educational superficiality. What is needed in this context is a rigorous analysis of the interrelationship between pedagogy, popular culture, meaning making, and youth subjectivity. In an era marked by youth depression, violence, and suicide such insights become extremely important, even life saving. Pessimism about the future is the common sense of many contemporary youth with its concomitant feeling that no one can make a difference.

If affective production can be shaped to reflect these perspectives, then it can be reshaped to lay the groundwork for optimism, passionate commitment, and transformative educational and political activity. In these ways cultural studies adds a dimension to the work of education unfilled by any other sub-discipline. This is what Transgressions: Cultural Studies and Education seeks to produce—literature on these issues that makes a difference. It seeks to publish studies that help those who work with young people, those individuals involved in the disciplines that study children and youth, and young people themselves improve their lives in these bizarre times.

TEACHING THROUGH THE ILL BODY

A Spiritual and Aesthetic Approach to Pedagogy and Illness

Marla Morris
Georgia Southern University

SENSE PUBLISHERS
ROTTERDAM / NEW YORK/TAIPEI

A C.I.P. record for this book is available from the Library of Congress.

ISBN 978-90-8790-429-6 (paperback)
ISBN 978-90-8790-430-2 (hardback)
ISBN 978-90-8790-431-9 (e-book)

Published by: Sense Publishers,
P.O. Box 21858, 3001 AW
Rotterdam, The Netherlands
http://www.sensepublishers.com

Printed on acid-free paper

This Book is Dedicated To Delese Wear

TABLE OF CONTENTS

ACKNOWLEDGMENTS

I would like to thank Mary Aswell Doll, my loving partner, who has supported me like a rock throughout this ordeal. The Jungian turn taken in this book is due to Mary's influence. Thank you for introducing me to the Jungians. I would like to thank Mary also for her ongoing encouragment to publish this book. I would like to thank Naomi Rucker who listened to my craziness throughout the worst of times. I would like to thank my doctors, Joe Christian, William Keith Fackler and Joseph Hathaway. Without my doctors I would not be here today. I dedicated this book to Delese Wear. It was Delese who suggested that I tell my story. I can't thank her enough for sparking the idea for the book. I would like to thank Delese also for introducing me to the medical humanities field. I would like to thank William F. Pinar who helped me understand curriculum studies and who gave me a home in academe. I would also like to thank Shirley Steinberg and Michel Lokhorst for believing in my project.

TEACHING THROUGH THE ILL BODY
A PHENOMENOLOGICAL EXPLORATION

I begin in the company of Eve Sedgwick (2003) who tells us that "whatever else we know, we know there isn't time for bullshit" (p. 149). There isn't time for bullshit when you are faced with serious illness. Julia Kristeva (1989) writes of the "black sun" of depression. When one faces serious illness one inevitably has to face this back sun. Illness breaks the psyche. Arthur Frank (1991) says,

> When the body breaks down, so does the life. Even when medicine can fix the body, that doesn't always put the life back together again. . . . At those times the experience of illness goes beyond the limits of medicine. (p. 8)

When facing serious illness one tends to fall to pieces. A certain amount of falling to pieces, though, is necessary in order to get into that black sun. One must go down into the underworld in order to survive the ordeal of illness. If one pushes away the inevitable depression associated with illness trouble looms. At some time in life one faces mortality of course. But serious illness forces one to face mortality with a sense of urgency. Illness of any sort is a form of psychic paralysis. The shock of a serious diagnosis stuns psyche into stillness and horror. Rafael J. Tamargo (2001) states that 'paresis' is Greek for "a letting go" (xiv). A letting go. Is letting go the beginning of dying? Paresis, a letting go, a breaking down, a form of psychic death. How to begin to understand what physical and psychic transformations are at hand. How to begin to comprehend the dreadful. But dread and comprehension are a start toward psychic repair. Paradoxically, people do live in states of psychic repair even while they might be chronically or even terminally ill. It is nihilistic to do otherwise. Coming to terms with illness--as difficult as it may be--is a start toward the road of reparation. Psyche needs repair. Deborah Britzman (2003) claims that education is "the wavering between breakdowns in meaning and our urge for their reparation" (p. 9). To educate about illness is key. Learning about illness and the course the illness might take are necessary steps along the difficult path of life's way. Whatever else illness is, it is certainly a breakdown in meaning. Nothing makes sense any longer. But some people do make sense of what seems senseless and manage to live productive lives even if they are facing the unthinkable. If one refuses the call to educate oneself about one's condition (by repressing what is wrong) the return of the repressed is at hand.

What does the ill body teach? What does the teacher do through the ill body? Arthur Frank (1995) suggests that when one is ill one engages in what he calls "the pedagogy of suffering" (p. 145). Frank explains that "The "pedagogy of suffering" is the phrase I have used in my own earlier writing to describe what the ill have to teach society" (p. 145). A pedagogy of suffering might allow for exploration of physical as well as psychological woundedness. That woundedness is the site of vulnerability. The ill body teaches through this wounded vulnerability. The ill body teaches through brokenness and heartache. If anything, the ill body teaches that going into the woundedness rather than thwarting it is a key to getting through it. Going psychically into painful sites is not easy. Delving deeply into troubled waters means being in touch with that which is nearly unrepresentable. How to represent one's dying?

Many scholars of various backgrounds call for an ethics of the body, an ethics of writing about the ill body so as to teach others what illness is (Frank, 1991; 1995; Hawkins, 1993; Nettles, 2001). It was my reading of Saundra Nettles' (2001) moving account of her brain tumor that got me-to-thinking. Nettles' poetic and beautifully written narrative of illness and recovery moved me. Reading Nettles' account allowed me to enter what she called 'crazy visitations.' Brain tumors are extremely frightening because as Nettles points out they can alter personality. Brain tumors can also kill.

Even if an incurable illness strikes psychic shock does fade over time and the decision must be made to move on. My point here is that even though illness happens life can be made meaningful. What other choice does one have? One can succumb to the tragedy. But what kind of choice is this?

One of the most difficult types of illness to get a handle on is chronic illness. One can be well--or at least appear to be well--even though one suffers from a chronic illness. Experiencing chronic illness is living in a constant state of Otherness. (Chronically ill people have a sense that those who are well do not understand what it means to live with a chronic condition.) Living on the edge of chronicity-- if you will-- is not easy. Always lurking in the backdrop are relapses, remissions and recurrences. People who are well may not understand what it is like to live like this--always on the alert for something to go wrong. But those who are ill can certainly share their conditions with the well. The well, then, are introduced into a strange world of the ill. And what a strange world it is. Entering the world of the ill, however, does not mean that the well person suddenly gets it, or understands it. People who are well and enter into the world of the ill-- by reading pathographies or simply talking with those who suffer from chronic illness-- might become a little more empathetic with those who are ill. Yet having empathy for the Other does not mean that one fully understands the life that ill people have to live. The most important thing here is that well people allow the ill to tell their stories and be heard.

Listening to life stories or autobiographies is what psychoanalysts do daily. But those who are not analysts or depth psychologists are not trained to listen. When people become ill, friends often turn away. When animals get hurt, members of their pack sometimes abandon them. Fear of the Other and fear of death underlie these turnings. The problem is that people are afraid of what is Other, of what they do not understand and of what makes them afraid to face their own mortality. William F. Pinar (2000) has repeatedly reminded us of the importance of what he terms "an autobiographic of alterity" (p. 30). Pinar explains,

Pinar *autobiography of alterity*

Curriculum understood as currere [is] a form of social psychoanalysis, a complicated conversation with myself and others, the point of which is movement: autobiographic, political, cultural. (p. 30)

Curriculum is meant here in the sense of curriculum vita, or life story. The telling of a life story is both psychic and political--this is Pinar's point. Critics of autobiography--especially those of the Marxist bent--argue that autobiography is narcissistic. But isn't narcissism necessary in order to understand the Other within the self as well as the self within the Other? How else do you understand Others if not through understanding yourself? Because we are situated in a social nexus communications between self and Other are political. As feminists taught us years ago, the personal is political. The point of autobiography--or in this case pathography--is to point to our eccentricities and the ways in which illness makes us strange and strangers to ourselves.

Illness is often thought of as an alien thing that enters into the body like a parasite. How to live with the parasite of illness, how to live with an alien force inside of the body? This is the strange thing about getting sick. Suddenly you are not yourself!! 'I don't feel myself today' is what people say when they are not feeling well. If you feel that you are not yourself then who are you? This book is an autobiography of alterity. After experiencing a serious illness, certainty about self vanishes.

In some cases, the easiest way to approach the illness of another is to blame the victim. 'It must be your fault, you did it to yourself.' People who get AIDS are blamed because of promiscuity. People who have cancer get blamed for sunbathing too much. People who break bones are blamed for their clumsiness. Those of us who suffer from stomach problems are called hysterical. Arthur Frank (1991) tells us that "people can't give up the idea that the ill person is responsible for the disease" (p. 123). The ill person is so used to hearing this blame the victim mentality that they internalize it and start blaming themselves too: 'If only I had worked out in the gym. If only I had been more active this would not have happened to me.' 'Maybe I shouldn't read so much and stay in the house so much. Is that what has made me ill.? More fresh air maybe?' Susan Sontag (1977) put it this way:

> Psychological themes of illness are powerful means of placing the blame on the ill. Patients who are instructed that they have, unwittingly, caused their disease are also being made to feel that they have deserved it. (p. 57).

People who suffer from stomach ailments or migraine headaches are often blamed for their over-excited, nervous personalities. The phrase 'nervous stomach' suggests that neurosis caused stomach trouble. But there are many things that can go wrong with the stomach that have little to do with psychological issues. Viruses are often the cause of stomach disorders. Parkinson's can be an underlying cause of stomach problems. Is one to blame for picking up a virus or getting Parkinson's? I don't think so.

And yet there is a connection between psyche and soma--in fact these are inextricably connected. You cannot separate out psyche from soma. But still, this

3

does not mean that one can blame the victim or suggest that the victim deserves to be ill. Joyce McDougall (1989) says that when one is ill the "body has gone mad" (p. 18). Is there a tight connection between the psyche and the soma? Is my illness partly psycho-somatic? McDougall explains psycho-somatic illness is real; it is not something made up. Psycho-somatic connections are real and alter the real body. McDougall refers to psycho-somatic illnesses as "psychosomatosis" (p. 18). Here, the psyche that is out of whack can cause real physiological problems that might even be deadly. McDougall (1989) points out that "although many psychosomatic symptoms may rapidly lead to death. . . paradoxically, they too represent an attempt to survive" (p. 30). It is a paradox that getting sick is the way the body/ psyche attempts cure. In order to cure oneself of something, one must go under; one must journey to Hades in order to function. The symptoms are sending messages from the underworld. What message is the psyche-soma trying to send? Perhaps the term cure misleads however. Chronically ill people are not cured. They live with chronic illness always. Perhaps, then, getting sick is the psyche's way of telling a story that does not want to be told.

Illness and vulnerability make insults seem worse. Before the onset of illness, one might take insults with a grain of salt. But illness changes everything. One becomes hypersensitive to negativities. In the early days of my illness, I was teaching doctoral students the work of John Dewey. On the first night of teaching Dewey's (1989) *On Education*, students started complaining. 'Dewey rambles, Dewey is too hard, Dewey is irrelevant, what is the point, why are we reading this, what does this have to do with anything' and so forth. In the old days-- before I got sick--I would have shrugged these remarks off. But because I did not feel well, because I felt especially vulnerable, I felt that the attack on Dewey was also an attack on me. Being affronted while sick, makes the illness worse. I felt like students were ganging up on me. Is this not a symptom of paranoia? I am reminded of Deborah Britzman's (2003) comments about the experience she had teaching the work of Freud. She said that one student called Sigmund Freud a 'pig.' Britzman talks about how she was hurt and how she confronted her student. Britzman chalks up the refusal to learn as a fear of the new. This is generally true. People do not like what is new because it threatens what is old. Although my students did not call Dewey a pig, they really hurt my feelings. Their comments devastated. It was a late class, I was tired. I felt sick. Feeling sick makes it all seem worse than it is.

Emmanuel Levinas (2000) says "[s]ickness is already a gap between those expressive movements and the biological ones. It is already a call for medication" (p. 11). To medicate is to pathologize. How to live in a world of pathology? How to keep psyche from becoming pathological? Or is psyche always already pathological when the body gets ill? Every medicine has a side effect. The side effects sometimes are worse than the disease. What are the side effects of psyche being tamped down with medicine? Does psyche split off, become paranoid, become psychotic? Some medicines that are meant to treat the disease can inadvertently induce psychosis. Visual or auditory hallucinations can be the result of side effects. Psyche is made sick because of the treatment. Every drug has side effects. What is the effect of the side, or what Eve Sedgwick (2003) calls the "beside" (p. 8)? Isn't it enough to have to deal with the illness? But once treatment has begun one has to deal with the "beside" of the treatment, the side effects of treatment. This might not seem to be a big deal but it is. When medicines interfere with healthy parts of the body the accompanying frustration makes everything worse. Then there is the fear that the negative effect of medicine could damage the body. Sometimes the damage is irreversible. Reglan causes facial tics. They could become permanent.

Finding out what medicines work and what medicines do not work takes time. The patient must be patient. And yet it is as if the world has turned upside down and little is recognizable anymore. Can patience be a virtue in an unrecognizable world? Anxiety overshadows patience. Emmanuel Levinas (1987) declares "[w]here something absolutely unknowable appears [fear sets in]. Absolutely unknowable means foreign to all light, rendering every assumption of possibility impossible, but where we ourselves are seized" (p. 71). [Serious illness is the unknowable and unthinkable. Illness is like Orpheus descending. Going down under is like being kidnapped and taken (or seized) into the underworld. One must go down in order to come back up.] *repeated - going into the underworld*

Like an old car, once the body starts breaking down, it seems like everything starts to fall apart. A stroke leads to paralysis which in turn leads to other problems. Heart problems can lead to lung problems which can lead to death. Even acid reflux disease can lead to lung problems which in turn can lead to pneumonia and possibly death. Arthur Kleinman (1988) says, "[t]he undercurrent of chronic illness is like the volcano: it does not go away. It menaces. It erupts. It is out of control. One damned thing follows another" (p. 44). One damn thing follows another! Kleinman's got it right. Psychologically managing the ongoing crisis troubles. The psychoanalytic question might be of what use do we put our illness? Can we make use out of something that is terrible? The psyche needs to do something with illness. If psyche represses the illness, she crumbles. If psyche expresses illness— through talking or writing about it--a certain amount of healing takes place. Or not. Psychic healing is possible if one uses the illness in such a way as to help psyche explore what has gone wrong. Making use of an illness does not mean simply complaining about it, although a certain amount of complaining can serve to empty out psychic trash. Making use of an illness means working the illness psychically so that a productive life is possible. One simply must make the best of a bad job. What is the alternative? Continual rumination on suicide as a way out is cowardly. Making the best of illness means making meaning out of it. Making the best of illness means writing about it so that others might learn about what it means to be sick. Everybody gets sick at some time. Reading about sickness helps one get through it. Reading about sickness is a way of having company.

Sometimes the medical community is slow to respond to complaints. Or perhaps it is just that medical tests take time. Diagnoses take time. But in the meantime, the patient has little patience for the length of time some diagnoses take. Not knowing what is wrong frightens. The psyche can only take so much unknowing. It is not as if giving a name to the disease will make it better, but naming the problem helps. Once the problem is named, moving on can happen. Now, moving on does not mean denying the seriousness of the illness. Moving on in the early stages does not even mean accepting the illness. Moving on at early stages means figuring out a way to stay sane. Moving on means making use of illness. Turning something awful into something creative is a first step.

Doctors are scientists and will not name what is wrong until their machines and measurements prove that something is wrong. This can be very frustrating for the patient who wants a quick answer. The reporting of symptoms is not enough. Some doctors might not believe patients. Female patents are treated differently by some doctors than male patients because--let's face it--we live in a patriarchal culture. Men are more likely to feel that when a woman complains of pain that she is merely hysterical. When Jacqueline du Pre—one of the greatest cellists of the twentieth century—complained of numbness, double vision and exhaustion her doctors dismissed her complaints as mere hysteria (Wilson, 1998; Easton, 1989). The fact of the matter is that Du Pre had multiple sclerosis and became completely and utterly debilitated and died from complications of the disease. She was only twenty-seven when she had to give up playing the cello because of the devastating effects of MS. Terrible things happen to people. Unspeakable. Du Pre's story is heartbreaking.

David Morris (2000) suggests that no matter what gender,

> What the patient reports is subjective (and untrustworthy), what the lab reports is objective (and true). Numbers are objective (and serious); stories are subjective (and trivial). Doctors are authorities on disease, while patients remain the more or less unreliable narrators of their own unruly illnesses. (p. 38)

sad - but very... true!

John Weaver (2001) writes similarly about what happens to testimonies of Holocaust survivors in the field of history. Historians, with few exceptions, feel that survivor testimony is unreliable and so the survivors get written out of their own history. They get invisibled from the text of their stories. The narratives that historians write are not based on survivor stories but on written documents like train schedules and newspaper articles. But these written documents are also stories, narratives.

The narratives that sick people tell—especially stories that women tell-- tend to be discounted by the medical community. It is thought that the sick are unreliable narrators. How to trust a patient's narrative? Is she making it up? Does she just want pain medicine? Is she looking for attention? Hysteria? It frustrates patients to know that doctors may not believe them. This pain is real! How to express this and get a doctor to take it seriously! Perhaps male patients do not have to struggle so much because when they complain doctors listen. But for women, the situation differs.

It is difficult for patients to describe to doctors what the problem is. Doctors have little clinical understanding of pain so a report of pain could mean a million different things. Eve Sedgwick (2003), in her book on affect and pedagogy, explores experiences that do have not 'propositions'. Are there pains without propositions? Are there symptoms without propositions? Sedgwick fleshes out experiences that are hard to articulate. How to put in words what is beyond language? Getting sick throws you into a whirlwind of chaos. Can one describe being thrown? Heidegger's (1935) notion of thrownness is useful here. Being thrown into an illness--or so it seems--troubles. How to avoid vertigo? When one has vertigo walking without falling becomes nearly impossible. Everything comes up from the ground and swirls around. Space and time are out of joint. Distances cannot be measured. Perspective is out of joint because suffering occurs under the shadow of fear. Fear alters perception. Perception alters language. Is there any other way to express illness beside language? Or does illness wish to express something somatically which it cannot express via language? Joyce McDougall (1989) says,

> But not all communications use language. In attempting to attack any awareness of certain thoughts, fantasies or conflictual situations apt to stir up strong feelings of either a painful or an overexciting nature, a patient may, for example, produce a somatic explosion instead of a thought, a fantasy or a dream. (p. 11)

Somatic explosions can be the body's way of speaking for a blocked psyche. Migraines are somatic explosions. The sick body is sending a message to psyche to explore that archaic part of self that is wounded. Or maybe the headaches are caused simply because of too much reading. Perhaps the somatic explosion forces one into a state of invalidism so that time --as gift or curse-- is given in order to think on the past. When one thinks on the past, old childhood wounds come up from the underworld. When these wounds come up psyche has a chance to catch up with itself and deal with that which has been neglected. A neglected wound only grows worse. The introduction of a physical ailment in life may force one to deal with a horrific past that has been conveniently repressed or forgotten. The body--as Alice Miller (2005) tells us--never lies. Thomas Moore (1992) points out that Jungian psychologist Robert Sardello

> recommends that if our hearts are attacking us or if cancer is immersing us in fantasies of death, then we should listen to these symptoms and adjust life accordingly. Rather than blame, we could respond. Listening to the message of the body is not the same as blaming the patient. (p. 159)

Listening to the body is also listening to an archaic past. The body--as we learn from Jung and Freud--is built on archaeological layers of debris. The debris needs to be dealt with or it will deal with us. Psyche will deal with you if you haven't dealt with her. Like Medusa, she will take you by surprise and torment you. Ongoing depression could be symptomatic of an unthought past. Debris tends to pile up. When the pile gets too high it has to be emptied or psyche breaks. A broken psyche clutters and clatters. What message is the body sending? What message is heard? Messages can be sent but psyche might not be ready to hear them.

Maybe the message is to be found in dreams. Repetitive dreams are important because they are definitely sending a message. Dreams tell much about what we conveniently forget. Dreaming of an ill body might be a foreshadowing of an illness-to-come. Jung--as we know--did not shy away from the idea that dreams could predict future events. Dreams also point backwards toward our mothers. We *pathographies- stories of illness*

are born of our mothers so our dreams tend to be remnants of the mother. We might not literally dream of our mothers, but the symbols and images might point back to the mother, to the phantasized mother that is. Dreams never get us back to our real mothers. But what of the mother and illness? Most often, illnesses are genetic or a result of exposure to a toxic chemical of some sort. Sometimes, however, they are caused by an ongoing internal psychic trauma. Dreams tell the tale.

If mother was bad, dreams are symptomatic of an internalization of that badness. Joyce McDougall (1989) says, "[t]he physically attacked body is at the same time a way of attacking the body of the internalized mother. . ." (p. 29). The internalized bad object is attacking the body. The message is the mother? Is the phantasized mother attacking me? Is my phantasy of my mother doing this to me? We do not want to blame our mothers of course. But repressed hostility toward the bad mother can lead to physical illness. We know the psychic toll repression takes. But it can also take a physical toll. What am I to do? Internalized bad objects don't just go away, they get worse. Can child abuse lead to adulthood disease? It is this question that I am getting at here. Some suggest that many suffer from stomach and other abdominal ailments especially if they were abused as children. Is it that child abuse weakens the immune system because so much strain is put on one's defence mechanisms? Are victims of childhood abuse more prone to infections or skin disorders? Or is illness all genetics or environmental toxins?

What happens when the body betrays? A sense of chaos sets in. How to live in perpetual chaos? The stable, ordered life is over. Anne Hunsaker Hawkins (1993) tells us that pathographies (stories of illness) describe more often than not the chaos into which the sick get thrown. She remarks,

> Pathographical narratives offer us a disquieting glimpse of what it is like to live in the absence of order and coherence. They show us the drastic interruption of a life of meaning and purpose by an illness that often seems arbitrary, cruel, and senseless. . . . (p. 2)

chaos, narrative Like Hawkins, Arthur Frank (1995) comments that illness may result in what he calls "chaos narratives." A chaos narrative is not really a narrative at all. Frank suggests that when life is overshadowed by chaos the story telling gets interrupted by the chaos. When one lives under the shadow of chaos, stories are impossible to tell. Living a life of chaos is worsened when the illness is incurable and or terminal. Here, one lives under "the threat of disintegration" (Frank, 2005, p. 171). Frank comments that "The chaos narrative is overwhelmed by this threat; disintegration has become the teller's encompassing reality" (p. 171). To know that at any time one could "deteriorate" is frightening to say the least. Deterioration is the body's betrayal. How to continue, how to go on when one knows that things will only get worse? This opens one up to a terrible sense of vulnerability. To admit that one feels vulnerable is not acceptable in American society. Vulnerability and illness in American culture are simply not acceptable. Illness is viewed by many as signs of weakness. Weakness is not acceptable in American life. This is the culture of macho.

Sander Gilman (1995) points out that illness is associated with the abnormal. He says

> [s]ince the early 19th century being ill meant being subhuman: . . . illness is understood in the medical (and pathological) literature of the 19th century as dependent in its definition of the normal. The healthy are the baseline for any definition of the acceptable human being, as if the changes of the body, labelled as illness or aging or disability, were foreign to the definition of the 'real' human being. (1995, p. 53)

And yet when we think about the high rate of cancer or AIDS in this country, do we also think that all of these victims are 'abnormal?' So many people have cancer that it is not abnormal but rather seems to be a normal state of affairs. That is, cancer is so prevalent that it has become the norm rather than the exception. And because cancer has become part and parcel of life in America—every other person seems to have some sort of cancer-- that it is also simultaneously unthinkable. AIDS sufferers not only have to deal with this horrific immune deficiency but also have to deal with the stigma of having a disease related to sexuality. AIDS victims are shunned and blamed. AIDS victims are unlike cancer patients in that they have to cope with the social stigma that goes along with having this disease. This causes unbearable psychic pain not to mention the inevitable loss of friendships and unsympathetic family.

There are two paths toward grappling with illness. One can choose to integrate illness into the personality or one can have a psychic meltdown. Perhaps at some stage during illness psychic meltdown becomes necessary. The only way to integrate the illness into the personality is to break open psyche. But if one stays in psychic meltdown mode, life is over. If one is not capable of integrating illness into the personality, psychic splitting, dissociation or even death become inevitable. Sometimes, though, dissociation serves as a defence mechanism. Dissociation—if it is limited—can help protect ego from crumbling. Arthur Frank (1995) comments,

> The body is so degraded by an over determination of disease and social mistreatment that survival depends on the self's dissociation from the body. . . . . A person who has recently started to experience pain speaks of "it" hurting "me" and can dissociate from "it" (p. 103)

Dissociation can be useful at times. It can also be damaging. It depends on how one uses it. I tend to be a little dissociated from time to time naturally. I don't mean that I'm completely split off, but I often drift, especially during mundane tasks like grocery shopping. It feels as if an alien force drives dissociation. For one Georg Groddeck (1961/1923), the 'IT' (a more mystical Id than Freud's) has a mind of its own and drives psyche with or without its consent. Certainly the notion of the 'It' drives home the point that human beings are not the masters of their own house. Groddeck (1961/1923) declares,

> I hold the view that man is animated by the unknown, that there is within him an "Es," an "It," some wondrous force which directs both what he himself

does, and what happens to him. The affirmation "I live" is only conditionally correct, it expresses only a small and superficial part of the fundamental principle, "Man is lived by the It. "(p. 11)

If the 'It' is living in me, if 'It' is me, what is 'It' trying to say? What is the message? Is there a message at all? Is there is no meaning? Is there nothing to be learned?

The body is bound to fall to pieces eventually. That's all there is to it. It's just a matter of time, a matter of when, not if. Susan Sontag (1977) says,

> Illness is the night-side of life, a more onerous citizenship. Everyone who is born holds dual citizenship, in the Kingdom of the well and in the Kingdom of the Sick. Although we all prefer to use only the good passport, sooner or later each of us is obliged, at least for a spell, to identify ourselves as citizens of that other place. (p. 3)

Most people, at some time in their lives experience illness of one kind or another. If that illness lasts for any duration of time, one begins to enter into what Sontag calls "the Kingdom of the Sick." That Kingdom is more like Kafka's Castle where strange things happen, where reason becomes null and void, where doors are opened and shut without knowledge or understanding. The castle that is the body is a vast labyrinth that is not really understood. Nobody really knows why we get sick to begin with, we just do. Some are luckier than others and avoid major illness. But others are not so lucky.

Commonsense attitudes about illness make the illness confusing to deal with. 'Oh, it will get better.' 'Or, don't worry things always have a way of working out.' Well, it won't get better if it's chronic, the illness morphs, and sometimes things only go down hill. The illness changes in the way that it manifests itself, but it doesn't necessarily get better because it changes. And to compound things, Americans tend to have a happy-go-lucky attitude about everything. There is a pot of gold over every rainbow; from darkness into light. These hope-filled metanarratives only serve to cover over, mask and whitewash the seriousness of some illnesses. Notions like hope cloud the real situation. How can you hope that a child with terminal cancer will get better when she will not? Or, more perversely how can you hope that when the child dies she will float into heaven and finally be happy? This way of thinking prevails. I for one have never understood the notion of heaven or hope. When death comes people say ridiculous things like 'it was all for the best or it was better that she died sooner than later.' 'God has a master plan that we just do not understand. It was his will.' What kind of God allows a five year old child to die a painful death? Audre Lorde (1997) addresses these problems as she states,

> Like superficial spirituality, looking on the bright side of things is a euphemism used for obscuring certain realities of life, open consideration of which might prove threatening or dangerous to the status quo. (p. 76)

There is no bright side to terminal cancer. And it seems a most cruel thing when a child dies from cancer or any other hideous disease. Childhood terminal illness seems the cruellest of all. Illness does not lead to rainbows. It leads to nothing but more illness, chronicity means just that. It doesn't go away, it won't go away and that's the way it is. Arthur Frank (1991) suggests, "[b]eing ill is just another way of living, but by the time we have lived through illness we are living differently" (p. 3). There are many ways of 'living differently.' Illness can make you bitter, morbidly depressed, anxious and filled with a sense of dread. This is certainly an awful way to live. One must get used to new psychic companions. One must "make room"--as Michael Eigen (2005, p.52) puts it-- for psychic difficulties. Making room for illness means allowing it to be there. Making light of it or dismissing it will only make things worse. Making room for illness means that one does not repress it but acknowledge that it is there. Not only that, making use of the illness is a key to living with dignity. Making use of an illness means making meaning out of it. Writing about it. Thinking through it. Turning the illness into some sort of creative task. Turning the illness into something else that might be of some use to somebody else. It is all about the turning. Turning what is bad into something useful. Painting perhaps. Poetry. Music, Writing. Storytelling.

The patient who crosses over to the other side of illness lives in the land of the white coats. Just as one thinks the tests are over, more are ordered and more white coats are consulted. You are never done with the white coats if you are chronically ill. There seems to be a great divide between the white coats and the patients. The white coats take on a sort of godlike status. The doctor is godlike. The patient—on the other hand-- gets more and more Medusa--like. The patient feels dirty, broken, ugly. Snake hair is ratty; meanness has settled in, and the unrelenting feeling of deterioration and rotting is on the horizon. The patient may feel gritty next to her doctor as he or she becomes or represents the angel-in-white, the god-of-insight, Apollo. Apollo-doctor seems to know what to do. But the patient remains in the dark. Anatole Broyard (1992) tells us that, "[a]s he lay dying, Tolstoy said, "I don't understand what I'm supposed to do" (p. 76). Tolstoy's is a profound statement. When the doctor does not know what to do, What AM I to do? When one is so sick what is to be done? Eigen (2005) teaches that no matter what storm we suffer we should embrace it and go with it. 'Going with it' is meant in a sort of Buddhist sense. Eigen tells us that his "portrayals are concerned with letting feeling storms speak [here I would add storms of physical as well as psychic illness], letting them have their say, seeing where they lead" (p. 9). Still, just because you embrace your illness does not mean that you won't psychically collapse. You just might collapse and if you do, then go with that too. Allow yourself to breakdown and then you might begin to put the pieces back together.

Other detrimental commonsense ideas on being sick are these: suffering makes you a better person. Not. Suffering is noble. Audre Lorde says no way. Lorde comments "[p]ain does not mellow you, nor does it ennoble" (p. 49). There is little that is noble about suffering pain. Pain is pain. Pain is the unthinkable. And doctors often do not treat pain. Doctors are afraid that people will abuse pain pills and become addicted to them. But some people really need pain pills in order to get through the day. But suffering does not make you a better person.

Another commonsense response to illness is that it makes us interesting. Get that!! Susan Sontag (1977) straightens us out on this one for sure. She remarks that it used to be thought that

> [s]ickness was a way of making people "interesting"--which is how "romantic" was originally defined. (Schlegel, in his essay "On the Study of Greek Poetry" [1795], offers "the interesting" as the ideal of modern--that is, romantic poetry.) "The ideal of perfect health, Novalis wrote in a fragment from the period 1799—1800 "is only scientifically interesting"; what is really interesting is sickness. . . ." (p.31)

There is nothing interesting in and of itself about being sick. Being sick is awful. Feeling awful is not interesting-- it just is. If we say that it is interesting to feel awful are we not then glorifying suffering? Suffering should never be glorified. How can something that negatively interrupts one's life be glorified? Is Hollywood at fault here? Does Hollywood romanticize illness? American film tends to glorify illness. Americans love the movie disease. Whatever that is!

Whatever illness is, it is socially constructed, as many scholars of medicine point out. We frame illness with culturally constructed lenses. There is no other way of seeing it. David Morris (2000) explains.

> In a culture dominated by the vision of utopian bodies, illnesses that twist and distort the human figure will register as vaguely disreputable signs of personal defeat, too often met with silence and denial. Western biomedicine, with its objectifying materializing, clinical gaze, contributes to shaping a culture in which substandard bodies are relegated to institutions or to the marginal social spaces . . . . (p. 159)

Being sick makes one feel like a failure. The body has failed. The failed body is the failed person. Being sick means you are a failure--at least some think this way. Of course we know from a psychoanalytic perspective that people who are full of self-loathing to begin with will probably amplify this personality trait as they move through their illness. Negative personality traits tend to become pronounced when dealing with serious issues like illness. Getting sick is a psychic disfiguring. The psychic house of cards begins to crumble and cave in. What to do with this cave in? Some turn to suicidal ideation; others turn to creative outlets.

Whatever illness is, it changes you. Period. After the onset of my illness, I changed. I am a different person now. Not better, not wiser, not more enlightened, not more noble. I am just different. I am different because I am chronically ill. One thing illness has done for me is that it has freed me to do what I want. It has, in a way, freed me to do certain things I would have never done when I was well because I did not see the urgency in doing these things. I have returned to my music after not playing for 20 years. Twenty years ago I had plans of becoming a professional classical pianist but these dreams were dashed because of a hand injury. Since then, however, I've healed—somewhat—from the injury and have embraced music in ways that I never would have 20 years ago. The body has a memory and my hand reminds me when I push too much and the pain begins again. I am teaching myself the guitar and the cello and would like to become accomplished in both. These new loves would have been unthinkable 20 years ago. Certainly in the classical music world, it is taboo to play more than one instrument. But I'm not in that world anymore. I'm in my own world. I feel suddenly freed from disciplinary shackles. When you suffer from a serious illness you do crazy things because you think 'what the hell.' When you face your own mortality--in a way-- you have a new found freedom. Isaiah Berlin (1997), hammers out the relation between realizing one's own mortality and the freedom accompanying that realization.

> Then what is it that I am now freer to do? I may seek to reconcile myself to what has occurred, not kick against the pricks, arrange my affairs, make my will, refrain from a display of sorrow or indignation inappropriate when facing the inevitable--that is what stoicism or taking things philosophically has historically come to mean. (p. 115)

Seneca-- a well known Stoic-- advised that if you are going to 'go out' (e.g. die), you simply must go out in style. Seneca (1969) declared, "[a]s it is with a play, so it is with life--what matters is not how long the acting lasts, but how good it is. It is not important at what point you stop. Stop where you will--only make sure you round it off with a good ending" (p. 130). What will be my good ending? Hopefully, I will have little regret when all is said and done. I have a few regrets of course. Never finishing music school is one of them. Living a good death--or as Camus (1972) might put it a 'happy death'-- is to die knowing that one has lived. Really lived. I often ask myself if I am really living. Living with intensity. Not just passing time waiting for the conductor to call.

POST (SCRIPT)

I write this post (script) to chapter one several years after having written the bulk of this book. As the book progresses I will tell more and more of my story. I offer these small snippets of memory after each chapter to situate myself within the larger theoretical narrative. I write now looking back and thinking about what happened and how I dealt with being struck down by a terrible illness. These post(scripts) explore issues that turn on memory.

It all started with a candy bar.

My partner and I--Mary--just came back from Prague. In the airport in Prague, I had eaten a chocolate candy bar. Almost immediately I knew something was wrong. I thought it was just heartburn. But days after we arrived back in the States I started getting chest pains. I had never experienced this before so of course I was freaked out. And then I could not eat. I would be full after eating almost nothing. A handful of chips felt like eating a seven course meal. I experienced what is called early satiety. The fullness seemed never to go away. Then the trips to the doctor began and everything just kept getting worse. As I was deteriorating--still undiagnosed--I continued to teach and continued to lose weight. In the back of my mind was the worry that something was terribly wrong. Seriously wrong. The whirlwind of confusion and chaos was only just beginning. My doctor put me on an acid reflux medication thinking that's that, it's acid reflux. But then I started getting pains in my back and down my arms. I even went to the emergency room thinking I was having a heart attack. They had no clue what was wrong with me. An emergency room visit ran up a cost of $ 5,000.00. Imagine the cost of being hospitalized!! American health care troubles. It is easy to go bankrupt, lose your home and your mind under this system. While all this was going on I was still teaching. At my university we have a heavy teaching load. I was teaching three or four classes every semester. My semesters seemed nightmarish. I wondered whether I could continue working at all. And then I thought about the dreaded tenure clock. That clock doesn't stop if you get sick. It just keeps on ticking. So I kept teaching. Looking back, I do not know how I did it. Some inner drive pushed me to keep teaching, writing and studying. I could have just collapsed but I did not.

Teaching through the ill body means feeling whatever it feels like to be ill. The teacher who is ill might choose to tell her students about her condition or not. Not telling might be better for those who carefully guard their private lives. But teaching is a public affair and the private seeps into the public no matter how guarded one tends to be. During the early days of my illness--I suffer from a condition called gastroparesis--I did not confide in my students. I did not think that that was appropriate. They probably sensed that something was wrong, anyway. My weight dropped by thirty pounds and I was in much pain which I tried to hide. It was hard for me to stand up. It was hard to lecture. It was even hard to walk. I recall going to the American Educational Research Association (AERA) conference in Chicago when I was very sick. I could barely walk across the bridge from one hotel to the other to attend sessions. I recall having to sit down at the book exhibit because walking was just too painful. I was suffering from a lot of chest pain at the time. I distinctly remember running into Patti Lather on a bridge in Chicago. She immediately knew that I was sick. That she noticed that I did not look well struck me partly because nobody pays attention to anybody—especially in academe. Patti was not so much in a hurry not to notice that I looked terrible. I appreciated very much Patti's concern. As much as I did not want people to know that I was sick, the body never lies (Miller, 2005). During the early days of the illness it crossed my mind that I might have to quit teaching and drop out of academe. In my early twenties I had to drop of out music school because of my hand injury—all of these memories started flooding back. I felt like such a failure and again I thought I would have to drop out. A compounded sense of failure overwhelmed. The simplest things were so difficult for me that I spent most of my time on the couch. Getting in the car and driving an hour to school, lecturing was nearly impossible. Every word was accompanied by pain.

The most frightening thing about the onset of illness is not knowing what it is. It took about three months of tests to get diagnosed. I almost felt a sense of relief when they told me what I had. Gastroparesis is a very serious condition if it is severe. Gastroparesis is a disease of the stomach. Here, the stomach has been damaged in such a way that it does not work right. I could hardly eat. If I ate grits I got chest pains. If I ate baby food I could not digest it. It would sit in my stomach until I got chest pains. I would be full for hours after eating half a jar of baby food. I began to become repulsed by food. Food was enemy number one.

Teaching requires a great amount of energy. Food is fuel. Without fuel teaching becomes nearly impossible. I kept on going though, I don't know how. That inner drive and life force kept me going.

While at that AERA in Chicago I roomed with Delese Wear. Delese has worked for years on medical education and suggested that I read pathographies. She suggested that I write a book about my experience. It never crossed my mind to do so before Delese suggested it. So this book came about because of Delese's suggestion. Delese told me that pathographies interest people. They are of interest to people because they are personal and phenomenological. Lay people turn to pathographies rather than other kinds of medical literatures because they can better relate to the personal than to the technical. Most of the medical literatures on disease is technical in nature and is only really written for other medical people. After finishing this book, I soon found out that no one--in academic publishing-- wanted to hear about my illness. Illness is taboo in academe. Academic presses are very reluctant to publish books that are autobiographical. Talking about sickness is not considered academic enough. The patient's side of the story is not welcomed. Trade presses, however, publish many pathographies. But academic publishers are very hesitant to do so. This publisher SENSE is different though. I thank the forward--looking people at SENSE for the opportunity to share my story. SENSE is one of the few academic publishers to take storytelling and pathography seriously.

As I began studying the pathography literature I felt a bit of relief psychologically. I also studied illness from the narrative perspective of the physician. The literatures— especially if they turned on narrative-- were all fascinating to me. I became engrossed with my studies and I think that it was this that helped me get through those early days. I found much solace in my books. Gradually I found solace in teaching, even though I felt awful. Teaching helped me get my mind off of my body at least for a while.

Listening to the music of *Yes* also helped me get through those early days. Something about the music of my youth helped me get it together. Every day, though, I fell apart. Listening to Cat Stevens somehow transported me back to my childhood and out of the present. I did not want to be in the present. I wanted to be elsewhere. Music transported me backwards psychically. For some reason I wanted to go backward in time to escape the now. I wanted to return to a childhood that never was I suppose. I wanted to return to the days of going to the Civic Arena to see my favourite groups like *Yes* and *Genesis*. I wanted to return to that rural aspect of my childhood. I wanted to return to those Pennsylvania woods where I would swing on vines across shallow creeks. I wanted to return to that mythological childhood of made up places like Hang Man's Hollow. I wanted to get out of the present and get back into a nostalgic mode. I wanted to get back to a time that never was. I did not see a future, I could not see a future time. Memory sustained me. Memory fabricated, fantasized. Memory as defence mechanism.

As time passes, memory fades. It was important that I wrote the bulk of this book when I did because while the experiences were still fresh I was able to write about them with much detail. If I would have waited, the book would have been very different. Memory is a particular kind of experience that is hard to grasp. But it is to these felt experiences that I turn. I wanted somehow to get at experience through symbol and image. Yi- Fu Tuan (1977) talks about the idea of experience in an interesting way. Tuan states,

> Experience is the overcoming of perils. The word "experience" shares a common root (per) with "experiment," "expert," and "perilous." To experience in the active sense requires that one venture forth into the unfamiliar and experiment with the elusive and uncertain. (p. 9)

experience

What strikes me in Tuan's passage is the connection between experience and peril. Getting sick can feel perilous--especially when the illness is serious. A common reaction to the early days of illness is disbelief. I do recall saying to myself, this isn't happening to me. And then I would ruminate on that thought. Or, I would say to myself, I can't believe that this is happening. The more weight I lost the more perilous the experience. My worry was that I would have a heart attack from losing so much weight so quickly. To live in a perilous situation is anxiety making to say the least. The question is-- what does one do with that anxiety? Did my teaching become anxious I wonder? Were my lectures meaningless in the face of the gravity of my situation? I remember feeling extremely isolated even though I had a network of support. But still I felt terribly alone. I kept saying to myself, nobody gets this. Nobody ever even heard of this disease. Even today I feel like nobody gets this. People look at me—I imagine--and think I'm just fine. But I am not. I know that there are people out there who know what gastroparesis is but I have never met them. Having a disease that is not well known is also a strange experience. Today I don't even bother telling people what is wrong with me unless they have some time to listen. Even if they do listen, I feel as if they just don't get it. How could they? I tell them I have gastroparesis and they kind of look at me funny and say, oh. I have a chronic illness, yet today I am well. I am as well as I am going to get. That is the twist with chronicity. Being sick and well at the same time is the postmodern condition. As long as I take my meds, I'm as well as I am going to get. Without the meds, I would die.

Memory is a funny thing. As I think back to the beginning of my illness and try to make sense of what happened chronologically, I can't do it. I am having trouble putting the pieces together in order. The problem is trying to think chronologically. Memory does not work that way. The more chronologically I try to think, the less I can remember and the less I can write. So what I have decided to do in these post(scripts) is to reflect back as the memories come back. Memory tends to take on its own life. Things appear, then disappear. Some of the memories repeat over and over again. The nature of memory is repetition and forgetting. Memories come back in spotted ways. Memories come back in messy ways. Memories come back completely out of order. Some of the memories that come back now--some five years after the diagnosis--are those that strike me, those that stand out.

Experience is about ground, horizon, background. Experience as remembered is about messy and fuzzy ground, horizon, background. It is this fuzzy quality of memory that historians do not like. Testimony does not get at the Truth with a capital T. Storytelling might not get the tale exactly as it unfolded. Historians want precision, so they distrust memory. And this is why patients' testimonies are left out of medical literature. Memory is constructed. It-is -what- it -becomes as time moves forward. Memory is not straightforward.

My aim in the book is to record two differing time-zones-of-memory. Time-zone-1 was written during the very early days of my illness. Time zone 1 archives the worst days of my condition. Time-zone-1 includes the beginning of each chapter up until the subhead called post (script). Time-zone-2 is the time of the now—five years later-- found after the subheadings I call post (scripts). These are the afterwards-of-the-pre (script) ions. In these post (scripts) I look back from a different horizon, from the horizon-of-the-now in order to better understand what transpired. Two competing times. Two competing fields of memories. Freud tells us that every experience stays with us for the rest of our lives. Everything we go through in life gets sedimented in the psyche. It's all there, we just have to pull it out. The memories that fade might be those mundane ones that did not really make an impact; or, they might be the extremely traumatic memories with which one cannot deal. Even though memories might fade, they are always buried in the psyche forever.

Serious illnesses are all very different from one another. So the experience of one illness may not be anything like the experience of another illness. However, there are some common themes that emerge no matter what the illness. Some of the experiences I have had can be generalized to other kinds of conditions. And yet, two cases of the same illness manifest differently, even though the symptoms might be similar. Gastroparesis has no cure. In this respect it is like other conditions that are incurable. And so my despair over this incurability might resonate with others who suffer from incurable disease. On the other hand, the experience of pain and despair are intensely private and difficult to put into words. At the end of the day, I cannot, in words, explain what my pain feels like to someone else. And yet, all we have is language so we do the best we can.

There is no cure for gastroparesis, but with medicine some of the lucky ones— like me-- function. Some people with this condition have to be put on feeding tubes and are continually in and out of the hospital. My case never got to that point. I am one of the lucky ones as I said. I am lucky too that I was diagnosed within three months and put on the right medicines. Some people are not diagnosed until it is too late. I am lucky that I have good medical care. I owe a debt of gratitude to all of my doctors.

The point of writing a pathography is to get one's story heard. There are not enough patients who are heard. The story of disease is mostly told from the experts' position, from the position of the physician. There are plenty of scholarly books on disease. This book is a scholarly pathography. I tell my story and theorize. I am primarily interested in exploring the teaching life lived in a state of chronic illness. This is what makes my contribution different from many other pathographies. One can always read scholarly medical journals of course, but what is said in them often eludes the lay person. This book is written for lay people and scholars and it is written especially for teachers. Teachers get sick, students get sick. Monographs on teachers teaching while ill are few and far between. I wanted to fill that gap with this book. This book is an attempt to teach through the ill body.

KNOWING AND BELIEVING

During the first three months of my illness--before diagnosis--I did not know what was happening to me. The doctor probably had certain clues but before the tests were done he did not know for sure either. As I said earlier it is the not knowing that causes anxiety and excessive rumination. One tends to ruminate on the worst case scenario. I thought I had stomach cancer. I thought I was going to die. I looked in the mirror and saw a disappearing body. When I saw my sister three months into the illness she looked at me in utter disbelief and horror. Her first response was, 'oh my God.' I was pale as a ghost and skinny as a rail. I remember sitting in Starbucks thinking, I am going to die. On that I ruminated secretly. I had my mini-breakdowns daily. To whom would I give my books when I died? Flipping out. Ruminating on death. As the disease progresses, one feels a slipping down a slope of no return. A terrifying realization. Something is happening. I knew I was sliding into unknown waters; I was sliding into the unthinkable. In curriculum studies, many of us write about the unthinkable without really thinking about what that means. But now I was feeling the unthinkable. These were all very private thoughts at the time. I certainly did not want to tell people that I thought I was dying. Part of me knew that that thought was irrational. I felt my world closing in on me and a terrible urgency to get things done. I felt like I was losing a grip on reality. At the time, I had no way of articulating this insanity. Yet, I did manage to hold it together.

I was diagnosed three months into my illness. Finally! I said to myself. Now they can quit thinking that I am an hysterical woman. This is what I thought they thought. I felt as if nobody believed me when I said, I can't eat. The medical tests proved that I have a real physical, neuromuscular problem with my stomach. Gastroparesis means a paralysis of the stomach. For some, the stomach stops working altogether. My stomach works—but at a very low level. With medicine, I can eat. Without medicine I cannot eat. To be so dependent on medicine unmoors.

At any rate, it is one thing to know you have an illness; it is another thing to believe it. It takes time to believe. There is always the lingering disbelief. There is always the denial. After a long time, one begins to believe that what has happened has happened. And then there is the false hope of recovery. At one point, I stopped taking my stomach medicine because I felt much better and thought to myself I don't need this stuff, I'm fine. It didn't take long to get really sick again. I started having chest pains, back pains and food was getting to be impossible to digest. Taking myself off the medicine was a real lesson to me. It was at that juncture that I began to believe that I really had a serious problem. It was then that I began to believe I was sick. I knew that I was sick before--on an intellectual level--but now I believed it--on an emotional level. Finally realizing that there was something wrong changed me. I changed. That change was profound. Wittgenstein (1958) talks about "the dawning of an aspect" (p. 194e). When an aspect dawns, its realization is made concrete. But this dawning is slow-to-come. It is like the slowness of the dawn. Understanding the gravity of a serious illness takes time. It certainly does not happen over night. Even now, sometimes I am in utter disbelief. And sometimes I do wonder if--when I get older--I will deteriorate. I have been holding steady for a few years and hope that things stay this way. But the thing about the body is that it has a mind of its own (Mary Doll, personal communication). The body does what it wants without your consent.

To complicate matters, my mother was recently diagnosed with Parkinson's Plus. This disease is also called multiple systems atrophy. The prognosis couldn't be worse. Her rapid deterioration shocks. Five years ago—at the exact time I got ill, she began to have symptoms. First there was the fall, the dizziness. Then the change in gait and speech. Now she cannot get out of a chair by herself and she can hardly walk. By the time this book is published she could be dead. The average life expectancy for her condition is about six years. Her diagnosis has in some ways made me feel guilty for writing this book because my condition is not nearly as serious as hers because my condition can be managed with meds. Hers cannot. She is the one with the big story, not me. I am surviving. She will not survive much longer in her state. Dementia, dysphagia, possible pulmonary embolism and the collapse occurs swiftly and certainly within only a matter of a few years. It is hard for children to watch their parents get sick. My mother can hardly walk, she cannot use her arms, she falls down and hits her head, her speech is slowed and she is getting worse. It is a devastating disease. Of course the common reaction to this devastation is--once again-- this is not happening. Why is this happening to my family? Why is there so much sickness in my family? One of my nieces has cerebral palsy, another has cystic fibrosis and yet another has anorexia. Are we like the Kennedy's? Are we cursed?

Although over the past five years I have experienced the ups and downs, the denials, the breakdowns associated with my own illness, witnessing the progressive deterioration of my mother is somehow worse. I wake up with dread every day. Again I am in a state of disbelief about what is happening. This happens to other peoples' mothers, not mine, I think to myself. Other people—strangers on the internet-- get Parkinson's Plus. My mother cannot live a normal life any longer. She is no longer independent and eventually she will probably be bed ridden. From a walker to a wheelchair to a bed. This is an awful thing to have to go through. When your own mother gets terribly ill, it kills something inside of you. I'm on the verge of breaking down everyday. It is as if I am starting all over again! I am in the beginning stages of disbelief all over again. I am in the beginning stages of devastation all over again. The lesson I have learned is that even though you may work through psychological stages of coping with your own illness, when a parent or relative gets sick, you have to go through the stages of coping all over again. My grief seems endless. Teaching through the ill body means teaching through the web of others who are ill as well. Sickness happens in a web of relations. We do not live in a vacuum. My illness is connected to others' illnesses. I see my condition, then, in relation to others who also suffer. It is in these complex relations that we attempt to make sense of the unthinkable.

Language is limited especially when expressing pain. Words simply cannot express complex emotions. Language is so limited. Wittgenstein (1958) asks profound questions related to meaning and the significance of feeling. His message --in his late work-- is that feeling cannot be represented in language. He explains.

> What does it mean to say, "what is happening now has significance"? What is a deep feeling? Could someone have a feeling of ardent love or hope for the space of a second? (p. 153e)

Wittgenstein suggests that deep feeling cannot be put into words. Fleeting feelings cannot be captured in language. What would it be to put into words a significant event? Can words capture that significance? Wittgenstein ultimately says no. Getting sick is significant. But that significance is hard to express. Things change after one gets sick. But those changes are impossible to put into language because they are deeply psychical. The psyche eludes.

Back in the classroom, all of these disturbing and elusive feelings about my mother swirl around. I am distracted. How to focus on the lecture at hand when it feels as if my world is crumbling? Being pulled back down into Hades once again. Is there ever a time in life when things are not chaotic and dark? How to teach in the midst of ongoing chaos and darkness? Maxine Greene many years ago wrote about light in dark times. But I am not seeing the light here. What I am seeing is what Unamuno called 'the tragic sense of life'. Living as tragedy unfolds. Teaching as tragedy. Ilya Prigogine (1997) -- in his book titled *The End of Certainty: Time, Chaos, and the New Laws of Nature*--writes about chaos from a cosmological and scientific perspective. Chaos accompanies order in the universe. That is just the way it is. Living in chaos is living with serious illness. But unlike chaos theorists, I am not finding any order in my universe. Or, maybe the order is found in studying, teaching and writing. Still, my universe feels much more chaotic than it does orderly.

Teaching through the ill body is about much more than teaching or the ill body. The body teaches that life is more fragile than one would like to think. Life hangs on a thread it seems. What kind of a teacher can one be when confronted with life threatening situations? Teaching during periods of great stress and crisis troubles. What do I have to teach, I wonder? Teaching is a public act. To what extent does the private merge with the public? If these two realms cannot be separated-- which I think they cannot-- what impact does the private have on one's teaching life? This is the stuff that nobody talks about. The taboo subject of teaching under-the-sign-of- illness is not dealt with in the curriculum literature to any great extent. So much of what is private eludes. Dread runs deep. The drive to live-on gets thwarted. What kind of teaching really matters? I mean what are we teaching when we teach? Are we teaching trivia or are we grappling with the profound? The body teaches profound lessons about living and dying. Are we able to listen to what the body has to teach? Sickness is such an intimate experience that it is at once beyond language and yet it permeates everything that we do. Yi-Fu Tuan (1977) says that "[i]ntimate experiences lie buried in our innermost being so that not only do we lack the words to give them form but often we are not even aware of them" (p. 136). Is there unconscious suffering? Is this what Tuan proposes? How to put the feeling of unconscious dread into words? It is just not possible. And yet we put dread in words. I feel dreadful. But this statement means nothing to someone else. I feel dreadful and I am teaching tonight. This statement sounds flat, without feeling and means little to others. But if we are to examine the teaching life, we must examine dread, death, and illness. Teaching is serious.

I began this chapter talking about exploring illness phenomenologically. Phenomenology, generally speaking, deals with private things, it deals with feeling states. The problem of phenomenology is that one cannot translate a private experience to somebody else. All private experiences--especially when we talk about pain--remain private. And yet the scholar's task is to make the private public; the scholar's task is to try to translate the untranslatable so as to help others live-on.

CURRICULUM AS THE SITE OF VULNERABILITY

When I first became ill, I spent the entire summer on the couch. I bought a small CD player and listened to music I remember growing up. I disappeared into the sounds of *Yes.* That took me back. I spent the entire summer on the couch waiting. Waiting for the doctor to call. Waiting for test results, waiting for more procedures, waiting for a diagnosis. The summer seemed interminable. Waiting. When I thought one procedure was finished they began yet another one. I thought after the endoscopy that all I had was reflux. But I continued to get worse. My symptoms changed, I had pain in my back, in my chest, down my arms. Back to the white coats. More tests. Losing weight. I kept having dreams of my father who died in 1999. He was there with me through the whole ordeal. But I began to wonder if he was sending me messages. I was glad to see him but worried that this was a sign of death. What a tangled web we weave. Christmas came and went and more tests. Blood tests, tests for diabetes, tests for the small intestine. Nothing. They pretend to be in control. White coats and sterile hand shakes. The patient-- doctor relationship is a funny one. When you are feeling so vulnerable, the doctor becomes all. The doctor becomes a god, an Apollo, a Zeus. The doctor becomes a wise sage, a Socrates. As symptoms worsen the patient becomes more vulnerable and more dependent on the doctor. The doctor looms larger and larger. Now he becomes a healer, a Christ figure, a prophet, Isaiah. But when he disappoints and no answers come, the images crash into the underworld and the doctor becomes the devil. The doctor is a complex figure in the imagination of the patient. He is now janus-faced. Dual. The double. He is both Gilgamesh and Einkadu; he is both Persephone and Demeter. And when he doesn't act up to your expectations he becomes the bad breast, the mother who is not good enough, the mother who is incapable of being a container. In the down times, the patient feels abandoned. Eric Cassell (1991) explains.

As the sick get sicker, their need to bond--to be a part of others--increases. The doctor. . . is the person to whom they may be the most open. The origin of the attachment in the human condition is invisible--sick persons do not know that what they are feeling about their doctor arose because of something called the doctor--patient relationship; it feels to them simply like affection-- sometimes very strong affection, which may become possessive. . . . The doctor's smile elates them, the doctor's frown casts them down, and they become desperately afraid the doctor will abandon them. (p. 72)

In January my doctor moved to Macon and I felt abandoned. Silly as it sounds, I became quite attached to him and when he left I felt completely and utterly crushed. I had a difficult time making the transition to the next doctor. The next doctor had to convince me that he was taking me seriously. I betrayed him, I suppose, by getting a second opinion from somebody else. This second opinion doctor was a complete madman. His was the office of Dr. Tarr and Professor Fether (Poe, 1976). I could see misdiagnoses coming down the pike so I fled and returned to the doctor who replaced my first gastroenterologist. I confessed to him that I fled and he spent much time with me convincing me that he did take me seriously and studied my case carefully. That was all I needed to hear. I needed the human connection. And finally I didn't feel abandoned. It is amazing how vulnerable one can feel in the midst of turmoil. Now, I feel connected to this doctor just as I did my first gastroenterologist.

I look up at the blue sky here in Savannah and wonder if I'll live till retirement. What's the point of having retirement money when you think you are expiring? I called TIAA-CREFF (retirement fund for university professors) and asked for all my money. They said for what? I said to pay off my Steinway. They said no way. It's my money!! Why are they hoarding it? I'm not going to make it till retirement age anyway. Facing mortality makes you do crazy things. David Morris (2000) suggests that whatever else illness is, it alters one's sense of identity and makes one more aware of mortality. He tells us that,

> Illness threatens to undo our sense of who we are. Its darkest power lies in showing us a picture of ourselves--false, damaged, unreliable, and inescapably mortal—that we desperately do not want to see. A serious and protracted illness constitutes an immersion in an alien reality where almost everything changes. (p. 38)

Every day I wonder whether I will I wake up tomorrow. Will I pass out while driving? Will I be able to eat today? Will I be able to teach my class without feeling dizzy? Will my students detect my illness? Should I tell them? What difference would that make in the classroom? I walked into my doctoral seminar with a heart monitor machine attached to me. They were horrified. Or perhaps it is me who is horrified. Why is it that the moment I make it in academe I get sick? Is academe making me sick? Or was I doomed since childhood? Is this illness some archaic remnant of a childhood gone badly? But back to teaching. Teaching becomes a nearly impossible task when one is seriously ill. Pain, weakness and embarrassment loom large. But one must carry on I suppose. During the worst days of my illness I kept teaching. Was I a fool or a madwoman to do so? Looking back, I am glad I stayed in the classroom during those dark days because my students held me together psychologically. They were the glue to my sanity. Thank god for students.

What kind of teacher is the ill teacher? Derrida (2002) talks about the teacher as one who delivers signs. He says,

> . . . the semiotic structure of teaching, the practically semiotic interpretation of the pedagogical relation: Teaching delivers signs. The teaching body produces

(shows and puts forward) signs or, more precisely, signifiers supposing the knowledge of a prior signified. (p. 81)

What kind of knowledge is it that signifies the ill body? The ill teaching body? The body not without organs as Deleuze or Schreber might say, but the body with sick organs. The wounded teaching body. What can a wounded teaching body teach students? Vulnerability while teaching Dewey. Dewey tells us that those who seek certainty are simpletons. When one is ill one wants clear-cut answers. One speculates. But no answers come. I will give the doctors one week to find an answer (I want to know for certain what the diagnosis is). But I fear that these tests will go on interminably and they won't find anything or maybe they will tell me I'm dying. The tests do continue for many months to come. They still do not know the diagnosis. The body deteriorates, shrinks and psyche goes into a state of shock and denial. And then it sinks in. The patient, after a few months, begins to realize that she is really sick. This is an awful realization.

Arthur Frank (1995) suggests that writing the story of illness makes us active witnesses in our own dramas. The passive patient (and patient means, passive) is the one who sits by quietly and listens to the doctor's orders. One mustn't be noncompliant or one might end up 'circling the drain'. (Delese Wear, personal communication) At any rate, Frank (1995) says,

> Seriously ill people are wounded not just in body but in voice. They need to become storytellers in order to recover the voices that illness and its treatment often take away. (xii)

Have I become Frank's storyteller?

I never thought of myself as a storyteller. I've always thought of myself as a theorist. Never a storyteller. But I am telling my story now, so I guess that makes me a storyteller. It is difficult when telling a story of the ill teaching body to recall exactly and precisely how events have unfolded. I suppose it isn't important to get an exact likeness of the memories of the first days of illness. What is more important is to express a sort of phenomenology of the illness, to get the gist of what it is like to FEEL ill among the healthy.

Anne Hunsaker Hawkins (1993) explains the genre of pathography.

> Pathography is an immensely rich reservoir of the metaphors and models that surround illness in contemporary culture. These books are of value to us not because they record "what happened"-- . . . but precisely because they are interpretations of experience. (p. 25)

What I am offering here is an interpretation of experience. My experience has been an utter shock to me. I have been healthy my whole life until recently and then I was struck down by debilitating illness. It is that I cannot eat. It is that I need to take medicine to help me eat just a little. Without the medicine I cannot eat. People who are worse off than me have to have feeding tubes inserted in their bodies, or have gastric pace makers installed. If I had to have a feeding tube inserted I think I would have to call it quits. There comes a point when life is not worth living. My beloved Stoics believed this. At what point does one pull the plug on life; when is life is not worth living? I haven't reached that place but I know many chronic sufferers of illness do.

I continually try to figure out what led up to this crisis. It all started with chocolate. The heartburn started in the Prague airport. I stupidly packed my Gaviscon. On the all-night flight home I couldn't sleep and couldn't eat. We were bumped up to first class. I remember looking around at all these rich fat people thinking, how can they eat like that? Look at all that food they are consuming. That's disgusting, I thought. Are they all in the Mafia? They can eat as much as Tony Soprano!! At any rate, the next day more heartburn, the day after that more heartburn and then the chest pains started. Then the doctor, then the ER and then the gastroenterologist. Then the barium swallows, the endoscopy, the CAT scans, the PH Study and menometry, the radioactivated egg test, the intestine test, the EEG, the heart monitor, the test for diabetes, the ultrasounds, the x-rays, the throat scans. You name it, I had the test. Later, there were strictures, rings and the inability to swallow, more stretching of the esophagus, more sickness. Not being able to eat. How we take eating for granted. We don't even give it a second thought because it is so primal.

As I write this, I am trying to put my life back together. I am trying to get some sense of order in such a chaotic and crazy time. Poststructuralism doesn't help me here. A poststructural world is a chaotic world. When you are sick, chaos is not what you need. Order is greatly needed. Making sense of the unthinkable is difficult. Even though I can recount all these procedures and tests, nothing makes sense to me. I am trying to order the dis-order of my life. I am trying to re-count what I cannot understand, to make sense out of events that are completely and utterly chaotic. Linda Hunt (2000) tells us that,

> examination of people's long -term adaptations to chronic illness reveals that the initial phase of disruption is often followed by a period of reorganization and reconstruction of the self and one's place in the world. (p. 88)

I am trying to re-organize my life and figure out my new identity. I have become the ill teaching body. I can never be the same in the classroom as I was before I got sick. I am now the ill teaching body and things have changed. Being chronically ill is now part of who I am. I worry that my colleagues think that I am unreliable because I've had to cancel some classes. I wonder if they will hold this against me when I go up for tenure. I know that they can't, but they might. Will my students respect me less or see me as less than human because of my illness? Students-- especially the young ones--do not like to see weakness.

I was so exhausted after Spring semester-- teaching through the ill body-- that I spent what seemed to be months falling asleep in my green chair. The sleep was so intense and so heavy. The world just seemed to be passing by and I was sitting in my green chair falling asleep all the time from pure and utter exhaustion. I thought to myself what on earth is happening to me? I am no longer part of this world.

Mary and I took a trip to Vermont over the summer and stayed in restful places with lovely green lawns and Vermontish chairs and beautiful countryside. I thought the rest would rejuvenate me. It was a perfectly peaceful rest. Upon return home, though, I spent what seemed like day after day after day falling asleep in my green chair again--the world passing by--my life passing by. Virginia Woolf (2002/1930) speaks to my condition.

> Sunk deep among pillows in one chair, we raise our feet even an inch above the ground on another, we cease to be soldiers in the army of the upright; we become deserters. They march to battle; we float with sticks on the stream; helter-skelter with the dead leaves on the lawn, irresponsible and disinterested rabble, perhaps for the first time for years, to look round, to look up--to look, for example, at the sky. (p. 12)

Being sick does make you have a new appreciation for things green, things blue. The sky. A moment of happiness. A single tear. A phone call from an old friend. A student who tells you she enjoyed your class. An email from a colleague. An old song on the radio. The sounds of the keyboard while typing up a paper. Illness gives you a certain ear for hearing the mundane all over again in a new way. I appreciate the trivial, my puppy, the smell of the autumn, and even the smell of the paper factory. At least I am alive, as difficult as the days have been. I do have a life. And I am fighting to make it worth something. I have seen the black sky; I have felt death in my heart of hearts. As crazy as it sounds. The horses are running toward the black sky. The Dali Lama (2002) tells us, in his book titled *Advice on Dying and Living a Better Life*, that when one is preparing to die, different phenomena are experienced. One of those phenomena is what he terms "vivid black mind-sky" (p. 120). When I had brain zaps or what I thought were seizures or whatever they were I saw exactly what the Dali Lama describes above: 'A vivid-black mind sky.' I did not, however black out. The world just turned black. I cannot put it more simply. I felt no pain, just an electrical shock charging through my head and a jolt that seemed to throw me across the room. A vivid-black mind sky. Okay, maybe neurons are going nuts, or short-circuiting. A vivid-black mind sky. I don't know what it was. An aura, they called it. A poetic emptiness. A draining of the life force. A lighting bolt. A horse running through my brain. A train wreck. A jagged awakening. A conversion experience. A conversion to what? A reminder that I do not walk among the 'upright' as Virginia Woolf put it. No matter what face I put on during the day the face of death hovers. Everything seems funny and terribly sad at once. I am tormented by thoughts of death.

I am attempting to speak the unspeakable and I turn to Audre Lorde (1997) to help me. "What are the words you do not yet have? What do you need to say? What are the tyrannies you swallow day by day and attempt to make your own?" (p. 19). The tyrannies of living with chronic illness are many. There is no going back now. What's done cannot be undone. The damage is there. The body has a memory and continually reminds me that I am teaching through the ill body. My chest feels as if someone poured battery acid down it. I've got a golf ball in my throat. My stomach is filled with knives. Metaphors of pain help I suppose. Images

27

help I suppose. But all along, still hoping I will return to health. In the back of my mind I know I will return to the world of the upright. I will get better. Or will I?

Arthur Frank (1995) calls thoughts like these a "restitution narrative" (p. 90) whereby the ill person thinks she will "return to just before the beginning: good as new". . . (p. 90). But after a while, I figured that I would never return to 'as good as new', to before this whole mess started. Illness changes and shifts. It comes in waves and cycles. Some days are better than others, some days are really bad. Illness rarely stays in a steady state. David Morris (2000) remarks,

> Illness, however, is not strictly speaking an object. It is not something we can know inside and out, through an inventing of its material properties, like a moon rock. Even when caused by a toxin, by a microbe, or by a dysfunction of an organ, illness is a fluid process that changes as we change. . . . (p. 5)

Some days it hurts to eat an apple. Apples are hard to swallow. Some days it hurts to eat bread. Bread is very difficult to digest. I can only eat part of a peanut butter sandwich, never the whole thing. Too much food in my stomach is painful. The worst thing I can be is full. Being full is pain-ful. It hurts to drink Gatorade. Like pouring acid down my throat. Forget about grits. Certainly no broccoli. After eating Chinese food one night, I thought I'd die from the pain of broccoli. Or how about coleslaw? The pain of coleslaw. I can't even put it in words. Some days I'm full on a nut, other days I can eat a piece of cake and be okay. Some days I'm dizzy other days I'm fine. Some days I 'm so tired I can hardly walk, other days I'm dancing in the streets, jagged up. The medicines make me feel both agitated and dragged out, fogbrained and dead- headed, confused and contented all at once. This body is no longer mine. That is clear. This is the drugged body. Derrida (1991) says that the pharmakon "can worsen the ill instead of remedy it" (p. 126). The pharmakon is both poison and cure. I can't tell which it is, poison or cure. I am able to eat, but now am having brain zaps. I am able to function but have tics; I am able to walk, but having generalized spasms in my legs and arms. Oh my God I'm a mess!! Derrida (1991) tells us that Plato is

> suspicious of the pharmakon in general, even in the case of drugs used exclusively for therapeutic ends, even when they are wielded with good intentions, and even when they are as such effective. There is no such thing as a harmless remedy. The pharmakon can never be simply beneficial. (p. 128)

Both poison and cure. These drugs have both helped and poisoned. While watching *The Exorcist* one late night I looked in the bathroom mirror and thought I saw my face moving by itself. I though to myself, no, it's just *The Exorcist* rubbing off. But the next day, while teaching, my face was doing very weird things. My God, I had tics! It was terrible. My students wanted to talk to me after class and my face was ticcing-out!! A medication called reglan had caused these tics. That stuff was poison. I had to get off that for sure. Plato was right: all medicines are suspect.

Managed symptoms. Making my life at least liveable, no matter at what subhuman level. How long can the body tolerate foreign substances? What does the body do with toxins? What is the message of toxins? If I stop taking the medicines, I die. If I continue to take the medicines I may die. In ten years, we might see commercials on TV saying, 'people who have been taking blah blah blah will grow two heads. If one morning you wake up with two heads, call this number now, 1-800-TWOHEADS.' Everything is funny and sad at once. Oliver Sacks (1992) tells us that Anatole Broyard

> writes of how little we can bear the thought of an anonymous illness, how we need to make illness metaphorical, to make them our own, and how we need always to be ill, and to die, with style. And how people, if they become ill, must become storytellers. (xiii)

Being ill with style. I like that. Shopping is a must. In the past year I bought 7 professorial jackets, a new black leather coat, $325 Italian shoes, Italian silk shirts plural. Yesterday I bought a pair of black shoes, $125. I thought about buying a hat. I thought about buying a Mercedes so I can look smart, intimidating and well. Of course, on a teacher's salary there is no way I can afford a Mercedes. Okay, how about a second hand one? That I did buy. How about 7 guitars? I bought 7 guitars. Mary can't keep count. There is also a small Mercedes sitting in our sun room, namely the Steinway M Grand. Now, some may accuse me of being a consumer capitalist. I buy things that make me feel better. Instruments have given me back my soul. Clothes make the woman. I will die in style and I will become a storyteller!! What I am glad about is that I still have desire. When there is no more desire-- even if it is material-- there is no more life as far as I'm concerned. When I lose the desire to write, to play, even to shop, my life is over.

In the meanwhile, I'm living in the house of the pharmakon, living in the drugged body which is no longer my own. The desire to desire is the gift of life. But perhaps the gift of life is indeed connected with the "gift of death" about which Derrida (1992) waxes eloquently. I have only begun to understand Derrida's point about the "gift" of death through experiencing this illness. Derrida (1992) remarks that,

> Philosophy isn't something that comes to the soul by accident, for it is nothing other than this vigil over death that watches out for death and watches over death, as if over the very life of the soul. The psyche as life, as breath of life, as pneuma, only appears out of this concerned anticipation of dying. (p. 15)

In many ways, being ill makes one more alive. Illness makes one think more intensely of mortality. Illness brings you face-to-face with the idea of death, or with thoughts that one might die at any moment. As irrational as the thoughts may seem--if death is not imminent-- these thoughts are part and parcel of the process of illness. Thinking about death abstractly, through philosophical concepts, is very different from being directly confronted with death in reality. The gift about which Derrida speaks is not a simple romanticism of death, but rather a suggestion that death allows one to be more open to life; to the gift that is life. Embracing death as a possibility allows one to get things done, to do things one might not have done before, to call old friends, to finish up projects, to write one's guts out. Thoughts of death make one naked before Being. The realization of death allows one to cut through to the core of one's life, to focus on what is important and not on what is trivial, on what is meaningful and not on what is meaningless. Death makes one fiercely protective of one's time because time is limited. I tell my graduate students NOT to read people with whom they do not want to keep company. Keep company only with those you want to, otherwise you will clutter up your psychc and soul. I don't waste time reading books that are second rate. I only keep company with the great ones, like Thoreau, Havel, Bradbury, Arendt, Jung, Hillman, von Franz. Freud.

Things change, things become contradictory and confusing as life descends into the spiral of chaos. Virginia Woolf (2002/1930) remarks,

> how the world has changed its shape; the tools of business grown remote; the sounds of festival become romantic like a merry-go-round heard across far fields; and friends have changed, some putting on a strange beauty, others deformed to the squatness of toads, while the whole landscape of life lies remote and fair, like the shape seen from a ship far out at sea. . . . (p. 8)

Life does change. Focus shifts. Smells become more intense. My tendency to drift becomes more intense. My energy is easily sapped. It all seems so silly. The bickering in faculty meetings over how much money we will or will not get for travel, where to put new faculty offices, what to do when lines are cut, how the budget only gets worse, how we are in hard times-- all of this now seems so silly and so stupid.

I'll tell you about hard times. I am living a Dickensian nightmare. How many times have I stood at my kitchen sink doing dishes with pain roaring down my back. How many times have I taken a walk in the park and had to stop and sit on the curb from chest pains. Emmanuel Levinas (1987) says,

> In suffering there is an absence of all refuge. It is the fact of being directly exposed to being. It is made up of the impossibility of fleeting or retreating. The whole acuity of suffering lies in the impossibility of retreat. (p. 69)

How can one retreat from one's own body? There is nowhere to go. One can go inside or dissociate. But even in dissociation the body is still there as a reminder. There simply is no getting around the wounded body. Maybe I drank too much coffee. Maybe I shouldn't have worked night shift for ten years. Maybe I work too hard now. Maybe I worry too much. Is this my fault? And here we go again. I am talking through the thoughts running through my head like horses running down the fret board of a Taylor guitar. What am I doing? Arthur Frank (1991) suggests I am seizing the situation.

> To seize the opportunity offered by illness, we must live illness actively; we must think a lot talk a lot, and some, like me, must write a lot. (p. 3)

In a way, writing is a way of expelling toxins. The writing just pours out over the keyboard as if my body is writing its own story in its own time. A sort of automatic writing at that. The body has a story to tell and it is telling it. But after the writing is over, there is only more writing to do, says the body. The dissociated body. This is not my body, my reliable body, the one I could count on to make sense of experience. We take sense-making for granted. Anymore, I cannot make sense of things, although this narrative is an attempt to make sense of what is non-sense. But not nonsense at all. This narrative is one of exposure. In "Echographies of Television" Jacques Derrida and Bernard Stiegler (2002) argue that,

> We see, here, how our present divides itself: the living present is itself divided. From now on, it bears death within itself and reinscribes in its own immediacy what ought as it were to survive it. It divides itself, in its life, between its life and its after life, without which there would be no image, no recording. (p. 51)

The image of the death within life--installed within the archive of lived experience-- moves one to do strange things. The image and recording of the image. The image and the idea, the clouds and the sky, the sick and the well, the dread and the pharmacy. These are images and ideas, feelings and thoughts that never end until the end. Illness narratives create an archive for the ill and for the well. But the well do not often read narratives of the ill. The well have no reason to go into the realm of Hades.

I dreamt I had tuberculosis and I awoke with a terrible cough. I dreamt of being wounded with everyone walking around me as if not seeing me. I dreamt of being castrated. Can a woman be castrated? Psychologically speaking—yes. These were probably all precursors. James Hillman (1979c) writes,

> Concerning sickness in dreams, whatever appears wounded, sick, or dying may be understood as that content leading the dreamer into the House of Hades. (Sick animals and children in folklore are occasioned by a death demon.) These are contents with the most psychological importance, having been singled out by the dream-work as its material for its opus contranaturam. These are the images that are bringing about a change in us (rather than our trying to change them), and so they are doing the work of the psychopompos. (p. 146)

For years I have had a repetitive dream of pulling stuff out of my mouth. I can never get rid of it; it just keeps coming and coming. The inability to expel toxins. The dream was perhaps trying to tell me that something was very wrong. Something oral, something with the entire oral system. From digestion to neural impulses. Everything moves backwards. My psyche, through these dreams, has been trying to tell me that something is out of alignment. I have a motility disorder. My swallowing is too slow. My stomach is too slow. Everything moves backwards. What is in the stomach, since it cannot go down, comes up as acid. Enough acid on the esophagus and you've got a case of cancer. Five years is the life expectancy for esophageal cancer. I have had acid pouring out over my esophagus as long as I can remember. So these problems are old, archaic and perhaps even genetic.

Downward. Into Hades. The bolt that shocked Paul at the crossroads. But I did not have a conversion. What I had was the shock of my life. The question is how to capture that shock phenomenologically, poetically. And is it a sin to turn illness into poesis? Does a poetic rendering of illness trivialize or romanticize it? I hope not. I draw on George Batille (1988) to help me articulate that moment in time when my entire life turned on its head.

> For at the moment when the lightning strike blinds me, I am the flash of a broken life, and this life--anguish and vertigo--opening itself up to an infinite void, is ruptured. . . (p. 77)

It was an electrical bolt dashing through my head. Psyche has cracked opened to the void of nothingness, to the void of the underworld. Sometimes I don't know whether I want to break down and cry or laugh hysterically or go shopping. The only thing I can do is "bear witness," as Derrida (2002, p. 136) puts it. Bearing witness is the mark of responsibility. Witnessing this illness is an ethical imperative for me, since it is something I can leave behind when my body finally fails. I would feel guilty if I hadn't archived this experience for others. It is important that we tell our stories. So many of us think our stories aren't worth telling. But to tell one's story is to educate others. This is the task at hand. To educate is to bear witness! And one must be, as Derrida (2002) puts it, vigilant about articulating experience. "To take a position" (p. 136) on illness is to educate responsibly. Derrida (2002) remarks,

> The citizen, in the present form of citizenship, in his current situation, must doubtless be vigilant: this is what we do, for example, when we take a position, engage in a discourse, act in order to convince, in order to exert pressure, in order to bear witness, when we go out into the streets, vote, or sign a text. (p. 136)

We must be vigilant not only when we vote, but when we express our ill state, the state of the ill, the state of the sick. In becoming ever more vigilant, one moves toward capturing in dense texture what it feels like to teach through the ill body. Vigilance means detail as well. Lived experience captured in the moment is full of detail, nuance and fleeting unknowables.

A phenomenology of the ill body. What might that look like? And how can one continue to be vigilant in its expression? Bearing witness to one's own demise. Bearing witness to the broken body. Vulnerability. To tell you the tale. But to tell the tale vigilantly without blinders, without comfort, without false hope, without sanitization. Vulnerability in the telling. And the hardest time is when the writing stops and I am left alone with my crazy thoughts rambling in my brain. How much can I tell? The never ending monologue of death tormenting me. Maybe I am like Schreber, vomit mouth, cannot stop talking, cannot write enough about the illness that has colonized my body. I am reminded of Tolstoy's (1886) character Ivan Ilych. One day well, the next day deathly ill. The narrator in the story says,

[handwritten margin note: telling the story ...]

He would go to his study, lie down, and again be alone with it: face to face with It. And nothing could be done with it except to look at it and shudder. (p. 134)

I think now not only of my own death but of the death of others. I think of my father's death, of the last time I saw him. How ill he looked. How old he looked. How sorry I was to be saying goodbye in the parking lot at a Baton Rouge restaurant. How I turned around and saw him limping away with my books under his arm. I knew he wasn't well, but I didn't know he was that unwell. I should have said goodbye better. Why didn't I know he was dying? A week after I saw him, he died. As Levinas (2000) says that "[m]y relation with death is also made up of the emotional and intellectual repercussions of the knowledge of the death of others" (p. 10). Thoughts of my own death point me toward thinking about the death of my father. Could I have been closer to him? What did I not say to him that I wanted to? Couldn't he have just waited until I got my Ph.D.? Why did he have to go before I began playing again? There are so many things I want to tell him now. He comes to me in my dreams often. He once said to me in a dream that I will get bored and it will be time to move on. I don't know what he was trying to tell me. But I have some ideas. At any rate, Levinas (2000) raises some interesting questions about the death of others and our relations with these others.

[D]oes the relationship to death of the other not deliver its meaning, does it not articulate it by the depth of affection [la profounder de l'affection] from the dread that is felt before the death of the other? (p. 13)

When my father died my whole world crumbled. I lost the person to whom I felt closest on the planet. I felt completely abandoned. But I continued to teach. The day after the dreadful phone call came about his death I stepped into the classroom and my students held me together. I didn't want to stop teaching because I felt that I would fall apart without the theater of the classroom.

There was no funeral. There were no services. There was no gathering. Only a gathering storm of my own emotions. Only a lot of regret. My father was heretical. He did not believe in anything, not even himself. He did not believe in any institutions. He used to say, "when the conductor calls, you have to get off the train." He did not believe even in John Lennon. He donated his body to medical science. And so he became a cadaver for medical students. At first this horrified me. But later on I thought this was a generous offering. He was a generous man, generous to a fault. As Delese Wear points out there is nothing more generous than the donation of one's body to medical science. (personal communication) I suppose he believed in the medical community enough to do this. Well, I still miss him terribly and wish I could call him. I still hear his voice and see his smile. I still remember his drunken frenzies and his anger too. When I was a child he dropped me on my head in the driveway of our suburban house. He must have been drunk. Drunk or not my love for him never faltered. Levinas (2000) says that death is "[a] departure toward the unknown, a departure without return, a departure with no forwarding address" (p. 9). No forwarding address. No voice heard anymore. Just the chill of the air. I look in my phone book and see his old telephone number and think what if I were to call? Is his number finally and forever disconnected? Is it finally not ringing? Did the train conductor really call him? When I graduated from LSU I imagined that he was sitting up in the stands cheering me on. And I saw someone there who looked like him. As a matter of fact, I often see people who look like him. Graduation was bittersweet because he died just four weeks before I took my Ph.D. If he could have just held on. But what a stupidly selfish thought that is. It was his time to go. As he would have said, the conductor called, he had to de-train. Arthur Frank (1995) might suggest that this detour through the death of my father is part of the illness narrative. He says,

> If chaos stories are told on the edge of a wound, they are also told on the edges of speech. Ultimately, chaos is told in the silences that speech cannot penetrate or illuminate. (p. 101)

On the edge of my wounded psyche is the death of my father and his illness. I have never been able to integrate the death of my father into my lifestory. How can one finally and forever cope with the death of a parent? Perhaps I am stuck in melancholic dis-repair. But how can one achieve mourning and completely expel the loved object? I don't think mourning in the Freudian sense is ever possible to complete. If I am stuck in the object of my father, if I am in the shadow of my father, then so be it. So what. The death of the father is perhaps one of the most negatively profound events of a life. Freud knew this was so. James Hillman (1979a) remarks,

> Freud's underworld experience, like Jung's own descent later, was the touchstone of his entire life. So, Freud wrote of his Traumdeutung: "Insight such as this falls to one's lot but once in a lifetime." And the reason for this personal significance against the myths of the underworld. Freud writes: " It [the book] was, I found, a portion of my own self-analysis my reaction to my father's death-- that is to say, to the most important event, the most poignant loss, of a man's life." (p. 21)

I suppose this book is, in part, a reaction to my father's death as well as a reaction to my illness. The illness has made me respond more to thinking through my father's death. We were emotionally bonded even though we hardly saw each other. I see him in me all the time. His hands are mine, my musicality is his, my intellect is his. And yet I am not him, not at all. But he was my flesh and blood and I loved him. My testimony of illness is also, then, a testimony of my love for my father. For it is to my father that I address my work. I write mostly for my father.

Chronicity. Chronos. Time. Time is limited on this earth and we must do what we must do. Illness writes the body. Rafael Campo (1997) poetically suggests,

> Just as the body could be made legible by violence, I also came to learn that the body itself would write upon the world. It could remake its very form. (17)

The body can write upon the world. The body is writing this world. As Oliver Sacks (1996) suggests, "Any disease introduces a doubleness into life--an "it" with its own needs, demands and limitations" (p. 77). The 'it' in my case is the body writing its own story, the body writing automatically the tale that needs telling. The body spewing forth its toxins. But now I must prepare for my class on Dewey again. I must give my body a rest and return tomorrow to write the body's curriculum.

POST (SCRIPT)

What is a post (script)? It is an afterwards, it is the script that comes after. But there is no script when it comes to illness narratives. There are pre (scriptions), yes, but no scripted narratives. In a post (script) one deals with memories that fade, memories that come as flash backs, with traumatic memories. Memory work--as Freud taught--becomes crucial when dealing with illness. Edward Casey (1991) talks of the seriousness with which we should treat memory work. He states

> In short, I am calling for a return to memory as more than mere mental "flotsam"--as more than a mere engrammatic inscription [emphasis mine] of the left-overs, the rags and tatters, of our lives. Remembering, rather, is soul-making, is its very basis. As such, remembering needs itself to be remembered--just as soul itself needs to be remembered in this soulless time of ours. (p. 179)

Trivial or petty remembrances are the left-over inscriptions. Why waste time on the trivial and that which is left over? This is Casey's point. Some thrive on petty memories. But memory-work that is profound explores turning points in life, times of tremendous grief or happiness. Some of us focus on grief; some forget the grief. What gets remembered gets remembered for a reason. Selective memory. We pick and choose unconsciously. Casey is calling for a working on memory. That differs from 'merely remembering'. 'Merely remembering' does not do the work that psyche needs. Working on memory means finding meaning in one's past so that the now can also be meaningful. Memory work is also soulful work, Casey tells us. Soul and memory are inextricably tied. Soul-making--a topic I will explore in greater detail later--is mystical. How to make a soul? One must work at having a soul and keeping that soul. For me, soul is a symbol of deep interiority; it is not a literal thing. Going down deep into the site of interiority allows the mystic to ask strange questions.

Memory that goes down deep digs up strange artefacts. And these artefacts may not be clear. Memory is strange. Memory is stranger than fiction because it is partly fiction, partly fantasy, partly reality, and partly a mystery. There are days when memories seem blocked out; there are other days when the past crowds in on the present. When memory, soul, deep interiority, mysticism and soul-making are tied to illness, the illness gets worked through. A worked through illness is one that is integrated into a life. The longer the illness lasts, the more serious the nature of the illness, the more one is forced to move inward, to look deep into that interior space of memory and perhaps even the void. Dealing with illness opens out into the void, into that nothingness of being. For Buddhists nothingness is all there is. It is our true state. Working on memory, the soul, the void and nothingness all lead toward the path of the mystical. When I talk about illness and its connection to spirituality in this book what I am talking about are these things. I will continue to flesh these out later. Going deeper into interior spaces to explore voids, gaps, holes, blocks, and blanks means going deeper into a mystical spirituality. For some spirituality means searching for a transcendent god. That is not what I mean here. For me, spirituality means going down and into the mystery that is the soul. For me, the sacred is right here in my heart, in my soul. The sacred is not transcendent. My position would be called pantheism and so I join Spinoza and ecopsychologists and Native Americans who believe that souls are everywhere, that the earth is sacred.

When one gets ill, spiritual questions become important. Why am I here? Why did this happen to me? How can I make meaning out of a bad situation? Is there any meaning in it? What is to become of me? How do I go on? What kind of character will I reveal during the worst times of my illness? These are all deeply spiritual questions. I am not arguing, however, that we romanticize illness by linking it with spirituality. I am not suggesting that you have to get sick to become spiritual. I think that the spiritual questions will come if one is already spiritual to begin with.

Memory work is not easy because it is work. Looking back at the early days of an illness pains. And these pains must be worked through or they will keep psyche imprisoned. Memories come at the most peculiar times. While teaching a foundations class, I suddenly remembered a medical procedure that went wrong. As they began to put me under a local anaesthesia, I started coughing violently. Whatever they injected into me felt like poison. I felt like I could not breathe. I thought I was going to die. Once again. Back in class, my students were watching *Bowling for Columbine*--the controversial film by Michael Moore-- while I was drifting off into the memory of the procedure gone wrong. What an inappropriate time to be drifting. But that is the way memory works. It comes upon you whenever it likes. We have little control over the power of memory.

Memory fades. I am taken aback by how much of what I had written five years ago I had forgotten. Sometimes I wonder if there is something wrong with my memory. Or, is this continual fading part of the human condition? If life continually fades away, what do we leave behind? If memory is all we really have, what if it fades too much? What if we cannot remember at all? When I re-read my book I am actually surprised at how much of what I initially archived had been forgotten. I am surprised that I am surprised. It is as if now I am another person reading this text. Wittgenstein (1958) talks to these issues in an interesting way. He asks the curious question about being surprised or being taken up with what seems novel. How can an old text--one that was written years ago and hammered out with intense thoughtfulness--be forgotten? How can one's own writing be surprising? How quickly that feeling of surprise passes as I re-acquaint myself with what I had written several years ago. Wittgenstein (1958) addresses the issue of surprise.

> I should like to say that what dawns here [the surprise] lasts only as long as I am occupied with the object in a particular way. . . . Ask yourself "For how long am I struck by a thing?"--For how long do I find it new? (p. 210e)

Upon a second re-reading of my text, it all comes back. The novelty fades quickly. The surprise vanishes.

How long does the memory of the beginning of an illness seem surprising? When does it dawn on a person that life has changed forever? And how long does that feeling last? This transformation is a negative one. How long can one live in the space of the negative? How to make use of the negative? When illness drags on and on it gets tiresome and depressing. How long can one be tired? Does the depression that is associated with the illness last for the duration, does it last forever?

As I return to this text years later and re-read-- I am struck by several things. Firstly, I am struck by the amount of detail I was able to capture during those early years of sickness. All of the medical procedures now have faded and some of them I have completely forgotten about--probably because they were so hideous. If I were to have written the book now--years later--there is no way I could have captured all the detail that I did back then. This is why it is important to write where we are. To continue to archive a life as it happens. Leaving texts behind. This is the teaching that is left. It is what matters most. Some scholars wait and wait to write that one perfect book. And then death catches them short and the book never gets written. Illness has taught me that you have to live for the now because that is all there is. If you wait until the future to write, you will never do it or it will be too foggy to capture in words.

I have always been interested in notions of the archive, memory and forgetting. Most of my scholarly work has turned on these ideas in one way or another. Archiving a life can be done in pictures, family albums, streaming video, You Tube. But archiving a life in words is different. Words can only say so much--and yet words can say a lot. And yet words say nothing. Forgetting makes us particularly vulnerable. Too much forgetting wipes out an entire life.

Vulnerability was the key to the first part of this chapter. What did I mean when I wrote this? How did I feel writing this? Did the writing leave me too open to public inspection? When does the private become embarrassing? What should we keep secret? Why is vulnerability perceived as a negative trait? What did I mean by a curriculum of vulnerability? Curriculum vita means lived experience. Vulnerability means to talk of lived experience when one is on the edge or when one feels as if one has fallen off the edge. Vulnerability is to admit regret and despair. Vulnerability means to be able to be open to others. Scrutiny by others about the most private of affairs leaves us vulnerable. Traditional scholarship is not about vulnerability. It is about the argument, the position statement, the data and the research. But who made up these rules? If scholarship is to reflect one's curriculum vita, one's lived experience, then vulnerability is certainly part of it. Or, maybe traditional scholars believe that scholarship should have nothing to do with the self. How is that possible? No matter what you write--let's face it--you are always already writing about yourself. And what is wrong with that? Well, many academic presses say no to "I" statements. To talk in the first person is still considered anathema by some. This is reactionary.

Vulnerability also means situating one's lived experience in nests of others' who are also vulnerable. I had forgotten that I talked about my father's death in the first part of the chapter. When I re-read this chapter, quite frankly, I was stunned by my personal admissions of regret. A death in the family certainly makes one feel vulnerable. I remember clearly the phone call. I remember also trying to teach under the shadow of death. I would go into my office, close the door and cry. And then I would go on and teach. I shared with my students the bad news and they became a network of support for me. It is amazing how the community of the classroom can become so human if the teacher allows it to become human.

And this death reminds me of yet another one. Last year, my grandmother died. It was another hard year. I felt close to my grandmother as she had been a big part of my life. On Friday nights when I was growing up we would go to her apartment on North Negley Avenue and leave the door open for Elijah. I loved my grandmother. She had a bright aura around her. She held our family together during chaotic times. At any rate, the funeral was held on a cold, dark, snowy day. Standing at the grave I recall feeling snow flakes falling on my face. It was a dignified service as the Rabbi spoke words I did not understand. It didn't matter what he said, just the sound of his voice gave the event some coherence even though I felt that my world had just completely shattered. In the distance, I remember seeing a headstone that read 'Morris.' That could have been the headstone of my paternal grandfather or paternal grandmother as all of my family is buried in the same Jewish cemetery in Pittsburgh. Death is a family affair. And then I had a crazy thought. As the snowflakes fell on my face and I looked in the distance at that headstone I thought to myself, that headstone is a warning, a sign. That headstone is me.

And back in the classroom I went. Right after the funeral. There is never time to grieve when one is a teacher. Death is part of life and the classroom is about both. How off track this country has gotten when I think about education. What do high stakes testing have to do with anything that matters? American education is a tragedy. I am speaking to the chorus here I know. But America has lost its way. The aim of American education has little to do with profound issues of life and death. Build more bombs and teach the art of colonization. What kind of monsters are we creating? I fear to think what the future of America will look like.

John Miller (2000) writes about soul and the classroom. He believes, like Edward Casey, that this is a soulless society. We live in mean times. The question Miller raises is how to inject the soul back into the classroom. He talks about the importance of having "an authentic presence" (p. 121) in the classroom. What does this mean in light of illness? How can the teacher be authentic if the illness is something that she does not want to share with her students? Students do not like to see teachers vulnerable. Sometimes they will go after a vulnerable teacher by acting out in class. Is illness something that should be made public? This is question I think about a lot because it is much like the question of queers coming out in the classroom. Yet another problem that I have had to deal with.

Like being queer, illness is taboo in American culture. A teacher who tells her students that she is sick could backfire on her. Coming out as queer can also backfire. Coming out as queer in the classroom has backfired on me many times. Perhaps this backfire is the root of my hesitation with authenticity. To be authentic at what price? If a teacher has AIDS and tells her students, she will be shunned. AIDS is still a taboo illness. Perhaps it is more noble to be honest with students and tell them the truth or at least address some of the issues as they naturally come up in class.

I have had classes where I have talked to my students honestly about my condition, but in the early days I felt that my illness must not be used as some kind of pedagogic tool. In a way I felt like that would trivialize my situation. Moreover, I was so sick that there was no way I could deal with discussing it with students because I couldn't even deal with it myself. Sometimes authenticity is not the royal road to good teaching. Sometimes secrets need to be kept. During the early days of my illness I felt that it should not to be made public because it would serve only to fetishize.

Illnesses that are invisible-- like gastroparesis-- are especially hard for other people to understand. If people do not see you as being ill--that is, if you do not look ill-- they will not understand why the situation is so grave. It is a myth that illness has a certain look about it. Sometimes people can have rosy cheeks and look healthy but have terminal cancer. Illnesses deceive. Serious illness and gravity go hand in hand. Simone Weil (2006) tells us that "[t]wo forces rule the universe: light and gravity" (p. 1). But I see no light in grave illness. Grave illness weighs on memory.

The flash of a memory can destroy the whole day. For some, the memory of the day of diagnosis is devastating. Cancer, Parkinson's, cystic fibrosis, cerebral palsy, multiple sclerosis, schizophrenia--all devastating diseases. A psychological response to these diseases is projection. These are the diseases that other people get. Somebody else gets diseases like that, not me. Projection in this sense serves to protect the ego from shattering. When we think that the world is made of us (the healthy) versus them (the sick), it is easier to deal with disease because it is their problem, not ours. But when disease strikes home, this mindset collapses.

A niece of one of my doctoral students--a small child of no more than six years old--struggled with terminal cancer for what seemed like forever. The family's ups and downs and discussions were shared with close friends. I was an outsider to this, but I witnessed how the death of this child devastated this family. My doctoral student struggled with this and I suggested that she write about it in her dissertation to work through it. She plans to defend soon and has written a moving, sensitive narrative of struggling with the terminal cancer and death of her little niece. Freud tells us that when we are struck by a problem to write it out, write it out, write it out. I do not know how the writing of the dissertation helped my student. She can only know that.

Terminal illness strikes young children too. And perhaps this is the biggest tragedy of all. My doctoral student was remarkably brave about the whole ordeal. She somehow managed to finish her dissertation and defend. How people move on in the midst of chaos amazes. At times, thanatos can be over-ridden by Eros. Leigh's strong life force kept her moving-on in the midst of death and despair.

Teachers and students do share illness narratives when the time seems appropriate to bring them out into the open. I think the sharing of these stories helps educate others who know little about dealing with things of this nature. Educating others means making meaning. Making meaning means dwelling, thinking, remembering. Teaching changes under the sign of disease and meaning making takes disturbing detours. Dennis Patrick Slattery (2004) teaches that woundedness and communion go hand in hand. He says, "[w]ounds connected all of us at the deepest level of being" (p. 74). The wound of Parkinson's Plus allows an otherwise estranged family to become connected because of this terrible tragedy. Witnessing this debilitating disease manifest and worsen deeply saddens. The sadness builds communion but also destroys people at the same time. The sadness of coping with disease is beyond language. The overwhelming feeling of deep grief is unspeakable.

As I try to teach my classes and focus on whatever text we are reading, coming up from below my gut is that feeling of dread about my mother's rapid deterioration. I look around the room and think all these people are fine, why did this have to happen to my mother? Teaching is complex because feelings like this come out of the blue and disrupt whatever is going on in the classroom. In the next moment my mind drifts to the death of a small child--to Leigh's niece-- and the evening lecture seems pointless and hopelessly out of touch. Teaching is a complex art because memory invades, possesses and consumes. How to continue teaching? What to teach? What really matters? What kind of education really matters? This question becomes more urgent and more pointed if faced with horrible situations. The aim of education is to ask the big philosophical and spiritual questions. What knowledge will allow the student to live-on? From the living-through-of-diagnosis to the realization-of-no-cure, what can a teacher possibly teach her students? How to get out from under day to day trivia? Living through the death of a parent or a child or a friend changes the psyche. It does not change it for the better, it just changes it. Psyche grows tired. But out of a sense of tiredness wisdom may come. A wisdom guide is that teacher who acknowledges her tiredness, her world weariness and sadness. I think if these things are acknowledged at a deeply soulful level, teaching will become directed toward the existential questions of life, the questions that matter, the questions that question our very being. Abraham Joshua Heschel (2004) talks about having *A Passion for Truth* --as the title of his book suggests. A passion for truth means not glossing over what fate brings. There are many ways to deny reality. What does it mean to teach truth? For what purpose does one teach? Does one teach to escape from hard questions? It is easy to get lost in a text that has little to do with important issues. It is easy to get lost in abstractions without making any connection to lived experience. Does one teach to explore a passion for truth? And if so, what kind of truth would that be? How to commune with students in this search for truth? Truth is not the eternal Idea around which Plato built his philosophy. Truth means that we are born, we live, we get sick and die. What do people make of despair? How do they use that despair? Is there any way of building an educated community around what Kierkegaard called from 'sickness unto death'? Is this a community concern? Should this be one of the aims of education? It is interesting that in most college core curricula, courses on death and dying or disease are not taught. These subjects are taught only to medical students. Shouldn't these kinds of courses be integrated into the core curriculum? I think we are under-educating students and doing them a great disservice by not dealing head on with these profound issues around which everybody must deal. I am not talking here about 'how to' courses either. I am not talking about teaching strategies to deal with an ailing parent. What I am suggesting, rather, is that we invent courses that ask the big spiritual, philosophical and psychological questions that really matter in a life. Isn't that the core of life? And shouldn't that be part of the core curriculum? When I see that students take courses in bowling as one of the core curriculum classes at a university my stomach turns. Courses like this make a mockery of education and trivialize the purpose of going to a university.

The memories come back hauntingly. Standing in the driveway in front of our house, I recall saying to Mary, my partner, that the gastroparesis was cured. A doctor who I'd never seen before ran a test on my stomach and told me that my stomach emptied as it should have. And I thought 'oh, I am better now, I'm glad that's over with.' I slammed the car door thinking, 'well that's that.' But this doctor who I'd never seen before obviously knew very little about gastroparesis. He was dead wrong. My stomach was just as bad as ever. Upon returning to my regular gastroenterologist, he said to me 'you are not well.' Running through my head were sentences like these: 'You are telling me that I am not better? How long is this going to go on? I want to get back to my normal life.' So I asked around. I asked my pharmacist if I would have to take domperidone (a stomach medicine) for the rest of my life. He said yes. I did not believe him. I asked the nurse, 'does this ever go away'? She said no. I could not believe what I was hearing. Denial happens in degrees and stages. I took myself off the medicine and thought, I don't need this any more, I feel fine. As I said earlier this was my wakeup call. Taking myself off the medicine proved to me once and for all that without the medicine I would die. If you can't eat you die. That is the reality of gastroparesis. And I am one of the lucky ones though. All of these memories jumble up together and come back time and time again. The slamming of the car door symbolized my being finished with my disease--or so I thought. I wanted to shut it out of my life. My psyche slammed shut in denial.

Teaching through the ill body is about much more than simply lecturing. The memories keep coming back unbidden through the lectures. One is subject to mind drift when memory invades. Edward Casey (1991) talks to the issue of memory and its returns. He states that,

> [t]here is a peculiar steadiness in our absorption in memories which contrast with the flightiness of imagining, whose mercurial character may even rule over our rumination. And when this ruminative steadiness is combined with the emotions of reminiscence, we find ourselves in that ruminescent state which remembering alone can induce. (p. 165)

Rumination takes on more rumination. Memories take on their own memories. Nothing comes back in any particular order. Memory does not obey the laws of time. Time is out of joint. The steadiness of the absorption of memory about which Casey speaks rings so true in my case. And there is also a steadiness in the absorption of forgetting. I am more concerned with the forgetting than the remembering. It is in the forgetting that we are made most vulnerable. What is there if you cannot remember? Nothing. The void. Teaching goes on while underneath, psyche ruminates, anxieties rumble, the void opens. Can one teach anything with all of this psychic noise going on? The complexities of teaching cannot be made more apparent when psyche is preoccupied or invaded with unwanted memories. The words that come out of the mouth are overshadowed by the ongoing inner monologue, the ongoing cries and whispers, the ongoing chaos, the ongoing shattering of the soul.

PSYCHE AND ILLNESS

THE TECHNICIAN spoke to me in a very matter of fact way and said, "Yea, the morgue is right down the hall. They wheel bodies down there all day long. People die every day in the hospital." He said this as he was preparing my head for the electrodes. I kept thinking about the word paresis as he put goop on my head and began wrapping it up in a turban. I could see my head wrapped up in the reflection of the glass from the window in front of me. Let go. Okay let go. Just let go, it is as simple as that, just go with it. If you are ill you are ill, just let go. I had a horrific headache during the whole procedure, probably from not having any coffee beforehand. Why do people have EEG'S? I asked the technician. He said, "well some people are brain-dead. Babies 7 days old have EEG's and victims of car accidents have them to see what is still working--hey, I would be real upset if there was somethin' wrong with my noodle!" My 'noodle'? I began drifting once the test began, I thought of Groddeck's (1977) comments on illness. What is it that makes people ill? Groddeck says, the It. "[T]he It makes people ill, because it is pursuing some purpose which it finds useful" (p. 40). What purpose is there in illness? What purpose could 'it' serve? I don't think there is any purpose in illness. Is the unconscious sending me messages? If it is, it sure is sadistic. Where is the unconscious driving me? Why is it driving me into the ground? Groddeck argues that illness saves us from something. "The illness, be it acute or chronic, infectious or not, makes the individual rest, protects him from being hurt by the outside world or from well-known phenomena which are unbearable" (Groddeck, 1977, p. 117). I suppose what Groddeck is suggesting is that illness, in some ways, can be reparative. Working to repair the damaged psyche. What does that mean? That repair is limited and fleeting. Coping mechanisms help repair but there is never total repair. There is little good that comes from bad. Nothing good that comes out of illness. The only thing that comes out of illness is more illness. There is no light at the end of the tunnel. Illness is a dystopic condition. To believe that there is some good end that comes as a result of illness is dangerously naive. I don't think there is a good end to illness. There are no happy endings to illness. The optimists' dis-ease manifests when people say things like 'Oh don't worry, you'll get better, maybe it's for a reason, everything is God's will, it will make you a stronger person, it's all for the best." Simpleton statements outrage. All of these trite expressions are ways of not dealing with the seriousness of the situation at hand. Trite expressions like these are ways of whitewashing, denying, and trivializing. I say hogwash. If you suffer from a chronic illness or terminal cancer or 5th stage Parkinson's or AIDS it is not God's will, it will not work out, and there is plenty about which to worry. No worries? Plenty of worries. Illness does not happen for a reason, it is not in some divine plan. And if illness were God's will, what kind of evil God would will such things? Who needs an evil God? When people say things like 'try to be happy with what you have', I sink. Making use of an illness—turning toward artistic expression or writing poems about it for example-- does not mean being happy about it. Isaiah Berlin (1997) explains that the idea of happiness is dangerous.

> Happy are those who live under a discipline which they accept without question, who freely obey the orders of leaders, spiritual or temporal, whose word is fully accepted as unbreakable law; or those who have, by their own methods, arrived at clear and unshakable conviction about what to do and what to be and brook no possible doubts. I can only say that those who rest on such comfortable beds of dogma are victims of forms of self-induced myopia, blinkers that may make for contentment, but not for understanding of what it is to be human. (Berlin, 1977, p. 11)

Understanding what it is to be human means facing the truth. Patients who have to undergo medical tests (like the test I endured when they stuck electrodes to my head) have to face the truth of test results. These test results may make you very unhappy.

My chart read "cerebral dysfunction." They never did figure out what this cerebral dysfunction was. Regardless, the experience of that cerebral dysfunction terrified. A blackness, total. A darkened mind. A jolt. Thrown across the room. An alien invasion. Frozen and then thrown. The mind is a terrible thing when it has a mind of its own. To fire and misfire—the neuroscience of the brain. Brain dead. Brain alive.

To be human is to confront one's mortality---which can be horrifying--and that is not happiness making. A cerebral dysfunction is nothing to make light of. Why it happened, I will never know. What caused it, I will never know. Not knowing or understanding why something happens to the body makes one paranoid and fearful. Did I just have a bad dream? For a moment in time, everything went black. I could not move and yet I felt as if I had been thrown across the room. Was it a hallucination? I will never know. Is my brain acting out a Deleuzian 'line of flight'? Is my brain a Derridean archive overload? Is there such a thing as an overloaded brain? Must one cross the threshold of dys-function in order to function fluidly? For answers, we might turn to our dreams for clues. Freud acknowledged that dreams signal illness. Freud (1961) tells us that,

> So early as a writer as Aristotle regarded it as quite possible that the beginnings of an illness might make themselves felt in dreams before anything will be noticed of it in waking life. . . (pp. 33-34)

Dreams reveal secrets of psyche. But do they reveal secrets of illness? Doubting Thomas here. What of dreams of drowning? Dreams of falling? Dreams of being lost? Dreams of pulling stuff out of the mouth? Being devoured? Archetypal. Symptoms. Is there a connection between pulling stuff out of the mouth--in a dream-- and suffering a motility disorder? In dysmotility, everything moves backwards. Dreams signal the inability to express the what-is-to-come. Signs. symbols and clues. Messages. But messages make little sense at the time they are delivered. Perhaps the postman delivered messages to the wrong address? The addressee has moved. Does the body know in advance that things will go wrong? Can genetic weakness speak through dreams? Do genes speak? Are there early warning signs?

When I first became ill, I refused to believe it. I thought after a week of taking nexium I could go back to my old life. The nurse said, 'you can't stop taking that!' My response was, 'oh come on, what medical school did you go to?' Well, it turns out she was right. The stomach medicine too I thought was temporary. When the pharmacist told me that I had to take it forever, I was horrified. I still had not acknowledged the chronic nature of what was-to-come. Chronic was not a word in my vocabulary. When the doctor said the word chronic I just couldn't believe it. One day my doctor said, 'You are not well.' That sentence stunned me. And he said, 'if you deteriorate. . . .' I stopped listening after the word 'deteriorate.' I drove around in my car mindlessly, shocked. It amazes how psyche defends itself through denial. Anatole Broyard (1992) tells us that,

> You don't really know that you're ill until the doctor tells you so. When he tells you you're ill, this is not the same as giving you permission to be ill. You eke out your illness. (p. 37)

What does eking out an illness mean? Do you create the way you want to be ill? Do you construct your image, your self-representation as ill? Is illness performative? I suppose it is performative. Drama. The drama of illness. Illness as theater. These thoughts repulse. They romanticize. There is nothing romantic about being ill. There is a lot of head shaking. No. This is not happening. This happens to other people. Looking on the internet, desperate to find out the facts--if there are facts--- misleading information abounds. Some websites say things like gastroparesis is a common condition that over time gets better. Or, gastroparesis is not really serious. And then you read websites that talk about people dying from gastroparesis. Dying from it!! What is the truth? Gastroparesis is a terribly misunderstood condition that too often is made light of. People can become completely disabled from this disease or die. Is it serious or not?

What did my 'cerebral dysfunction' have to do with gastroparesis? Probably nothing. But like an old car, when one part of the body breaks, others break as well. Rumination sets in when everything seems to be going wrong. Speculation is the mind's worst enemy. What if it is incurable? What if it happens again? Why am I getting headaches? For how long will I endure chest pains? Will I ever be able to eat more than donuts? What if this condition kills? What if I imagined all of this? What difference does knowledge make? Why can't I find the truth? Is anybody out there? I never met anyone with gastroparesis and most people never heard of it. Who can I talk to? I have no one to talk to. Ongoing rumination, obsessive speculation. Insanity. What is wrong. What to do. Where to turn. I want to know why. Isaiah Berlin (1997) claims, my knowledge that a disease, for which no cure has been discovered, is destroying me or my friend, may well sap my particular creative capacity, and inhibit me in this or that way; and to be inhibited--whatever its long-term advantages--is not to be rendered more free. It may be replied to this that if I am suffering from a disease and do not know it, I am less free than one who knows, and can at least try to take steps to check it, even if the disease has so far proved to be incurable. (pp. 114-115)

Does knowing the cause of a disease set you free? Free from what? Free to do what? Knowing the cause might depress even more. What if there is no known cause? Does that make you free or not? It is not always clear what the diagnosis or cause of illness means, even if it has a name. Rumination. Rumination. On and on. Rumination is a most private affair. Ongoing inner monologue dismantles psyche.

If anything, illness tires. Too tired to walk, to eat, even to sleep. Even sleep makes you tired. The more sleep you get the more sleep you need the more tired you get. And the world goes on. It goes on without you. The mundane world continues as the electrodes are being stuck to your head. The mundane world goes on without you as you hold your hand to your chest as it throbs in pain. On TV Dr. Phil rambles. Morning shows continue even when you are lying in a hospital bed with wires stuck to your head. People talk about football games and hurricanes as if nothing is happening. They are just glad it isn't their 'noodle' that has gone haywire. When you tell someone that you are sick, they are secretly glad it isn't their problem. Cynicism.

Speaking of illness. Illness speaking. A ruminating voice urgently rattles. What message is at hand? Words overtake psyche. The words keep coming. Invading words. I cannot stop the words. Words demand to be written, to find a home. The unconscious sends a message but I cannot yet read it. People who get sick often remain silent. But one must never remain silent. Audre Lorde (1997) contends that "it is not difference which immobilizes us, but silence. And there are so many silences to be broken" (p. 22). Stigmas and taboos. Illness stigmatizes. It is taboo to be sick in a culture that prizes youth, ultra white teeth and perfect hair. Don't tell people how sick you are or you'll lose your job. They will think you are unreliable. Paranoia. Don't tell people that you are sick because they will walk on egg shells when they are around you. Don't tell people you are sick because they will avoid you like the plague. People can't deal with sickness, it threatens. Vulnerability wounds. Sick people live in the margins and are marginalized. How can educators change this? Is this not our responsibility to see that we undo marginalization of the subjugated? The ill are subjugated. Nobody wants to be around them. Abandoning people when they are ill is all too common. Don't abandon me. If the sick person talks of her sickness she is accused of languishing in self-pity. There is no self- pity on this front. I certainly do not pity myself. Don't pity me. But try to understand me. This testimony is a document meant for others to try to understand the situation of being ill. Understanding might allow for at least a little empathy.

Deterioration, disgust vulnerability and anguish. Images of a bruised brain. Images of a stomach bubbling up with acid like a volcano. Gastric pace makers.

Blood brain barrier. My chest hurts. Rumination. When does rumination become insanity? Never so aware of the organs until they get sick. Maybe my organs are sick of me. Body in revolt. The body-mind is not split in two of course. And throughout this narrative I struggle to talk about psyche and body without separating out one from the other but it is hard not to do so. Psychebody is one thing, but when illness strikes, body and mind feel as if they are two. Can a person live as a double? Psyche. Body. Is this what analysts call splitting? The Cartesian split is at hand. Is this the beginning of a psychic breakdown? This is not my body. Reader's Digest: This is Paul's body. Yes, that's it. This body belongs to somebody else named Paul, or Peter or Mary. It is not my body. My body does not act like this. How to get my own body back? Am I losing it? Michael Eigen (1998) addresses psychic disintegration.

> Disintegration is real. There are times environmental impingement breaks us down. We disintegrate under traumatic impacts and need recovery time. Sometimes we recover in deformed ways. We harden and refuse to disintegrate, or partially harden around pockets of disintegration or can not stop it. We fear life that has horror of disintegration built into it. (p.21)

Does psyche disintegrate alongside bodily organs? Does psyche crack open to the big blue sky? Does psyche stay intact enough to witness organ deterioration? The psychoanalytic response suggests that psyche pulls the organs in the direction of deterioration. Psyche makes body ill. Or is it that the body makes psyche ill? How to talk about both as one!! It is not very postmodern of me to think of psyche and body as two things. I try to think them together but the illness has driven a wedge between them as if I were a double.

Symptoms of psychic crashes. Not showering. Spending heaps and heaps of money. Driving aimlessly around in the car. Ignoring phone calls. Staring into space all day long. Stuck on the couch. Can't move. Falling to pieces. What difference does anything make when the whole world is falling to pieces? Who cares. The not-knowing what is wrong, the knowing the cause, the not-knowing the cause, the no-cause, the they don't know mentality. It's enough to drive anyone mad.

I wanted to ask the technician (who was doing the brain test) if he watched the TV show *Six Feet Under*. I forget what he said. Forgetting. It as if the mind just blanks out. When will I break? When will it hit me that something is seriously wrong? I must cancel my classes this week. But I cannot just sit at home and do nothing. I must get back to work. My mind begins to drift. Stupid music plays as they do the EEG. I begin thinking of my father when he was in the hospital after his stroke. My sister and I took the train through the alligator swamps of Louisiana to see him in some weird outbackish state hospital in the middle of nowhere. He tried to put on a good face; he even tried to eat a meal like a normal person but proceeded to throw it up violently. The doctor pulled us into a room to tell us the gravity of his condition. It seemed like TV. Was this the TV show *Six Feet Under*? Surreal. It was not a real moment in time. My father cried and said he would be back to work soon. Seeing a parent cry devastates. He could hardly walk. He had a pronounced limp, talked out of one side of his mouth. Slurred his words. I heard my father's voice in my own when I emailed my department chair and told her I would be back to work soon come hell or high water. She said what about the seizures, what about driving. I told her I would be okay, not to worry. Maybe I will crash my car while having a seizure, but I refuse to give in to this illness--I thought. This illness creates its own identity through me. Now my colleagues see me as sickly. Not a transient illness, but an ongoing problem that defines. I am a sick teacher and teach through the ill body. What does the ill body teach? Everyday I wake up and I wonder what surprises my body has in store for me. David Morris (2000) explains,

> Illness somehow defines us. It tells us who we are. It informs us; in a sense Nietzsche understood in his bones, that we are creatures marked by a uniquely unstable relation to health. Unlike robots or rabbits, humans possess a tendency toward repeated and often protracted illnesses that seem finally less a flaw in our design than a mysterious signature. (p.1)

The signature of the illness, what might that mean? The signature that has ravaged my body. What is it that is writing the body? Sickness as inscription. The mystic writing pad sickens. Does writing about the illness make it worse? To what does this signature address? What has happened to the well body and the well signature, the signature before the illness? Do those two signatures differ? What is the aim of the sick inscription? Am I two different persons? The double. The archetype of the double. Bion's Twins! Or am I performing two different pieces? Who is doing the writing? The body that writes is not my body anymore; it belongs to the medical community, the community of doctors and technicians. The lie of identity. Identity as (non) signature. Derrida (1991) talks much about the notion of the signature. If anything, he complexifies what it means to have a signature. In *Signature Event Context* Derrida (1991) remarks,

> The effects of signature are the most ordinary things in the world. The condition of possibility for these effects is simultaneously, once again, the condition of their impossibility, of the impossibility of their rigorous purity. In order to function, that is, in order to be legible, a signature must have a repeatable, iterable, imitatable form; it must be able to detach itself from the present and singular intention of its production. It is its sameness which, in altering its identity and singularity, divides the seal. (p. 107)

The effect of a signature does two things. It tells us who the signature belongs to and yet that 'who' puzzles. Hence the signature is never pure but always doubled. My signature signifies who I am but not who I am--simultaneously--because I am ever changing. My signature before the illness differed from the signature of the now because my illness has now become my signature. I would rather it not be that way. I am who I am-- but my illness is not me. And yet it is. The alien body. Alienation from self. The illness wraps its head around me; I cannot get my head around it. It is wrapped around my head like a cobra. I walk the hallways in a fog, not knowing who I am, not knowing where I am. I suffer a snake bite in the mind.

While in the hospital yesterday, walking down a long hallway toward the technician's testing area, I felt like I was in the twilight zone and yet the hospital was eerily familiar. I had been down similar hallways just last year when they did a million tests on my stomach. But what also alarmingly came to mind was that this hospital is much like the Education building where I teach. This hospital reminds me of the academy, it is the academy. The academy of illness. I am being schooled in the academy of the sick. I am being schooled in the world of doctors and technicians. My psyche is schooling me in the ways of the unknown, in the ways of the deep unconscious. Cryptic messages. Groddeck (1977) suggests the 'It' (the unconscious) tells a tale to which we must listen. Psyche

> allows it to continue in narrower confines as a chronic condition, or destroys the fight of the factions with death. In the illness we hear the It's commanding voice ordering soul and body, organs, tissues, and cells, and all its creatures: 'Go far and no further!' I gave you far reaching independence; since you want to abuse it in internecine quarters I shall restrict it, and if that does not stop you I shall destroy it and you.' (p. 199)

Narrowed existence. Narrowed in food, drink. walk. Narrowed emotionality. Only depression, anxiety. My life has been narrowed by tiredness, by eyes darting wildly in fastshifting motion, in zoning out, in the wish to disappear. To write it all down and disappear into the text of the signature. The signature that is not mine. I don't know whose signature this is or whose illness this is. It isn't mine. It is the illness of a culture where illness is not a signature at all. It is the illness of a culture where illness is shunned. It is the illness of a world gone mad and a body gone dead. Is there something in me that wants me dead? Do internal, unconscious bad objects want me dead? Is there something in all of us that wants us dead? Is Freud's death instinct real? All of the speculation in the world won't make you better, in fact, it could make you worse. Then why bother writing the signature of illness? Why bother at all? Hell as inscription.

The technician finally turned the lights back on. My head was killing me. I should have had coffee before doing this test. No coffee=big headache. Or maybe the EEG gave me a headache. As he removed the electrodes from my head, I heard once again the blasting TV set with Dr. Phil rambling about weight loss. The mundane of the everyday pushed its way into my psyche. The technician told me that he does three or four of these tests every day. What kind of life must that be? Sticking electrodes on heads and watching brain waves on a computer screen day in and day out—what kind of life must that be? I guess that is his signature. When I stood up from the EEG I felt exhausted emotionally. How many more tests, how long will it be before I know? When will they refer me to the neurologist? How serious is this? Am I going to die? Will I have a stroke like my father?

And thoughts of teaching Dewey through the ill body were on my mind. I must get back to the classroom where life seems normal and everything makes sense. The classroom has its own signature, it is the world, it is my world and I miss teaching while sitting at home waiting for the technicians to relay the message to the neurologist who relays the message to the nurse who relays the message to the first doctor who relays the message back to the nurse who calls me to tell me there is nothing wrong.

Psyche is a funny thing. She puts you through it, but for what? Psyche is a muse. Psyche is a devil. Psyche is the double. Psyche pulls you through it or puts you in the ground. Psyche maddens. Psyche terrifies. Jung (1977) puts it this way, "[l]ife is crazy and meaningful at once" (p. 31). Schizoid-ness is an ontological state of all Being. Psyche expresses illness in symbols and images. Jung always teaches us to go to the images. But even if I go to the images, they tell me little. And yet the dream images do tell me a little something. Images and psychic symbols con-fuse. Images and symbols give clues as to what needs to be done. Jung (1977) helps here. In his book titled *The Archetypes and the Collective Unconscious* he states that,

> The symbolic process is an experience in images and of images. Its deve-lopment usually shows an enantiodromian structure the text of the I Ching, and so presents a rhythm of negative and positive, loss and gain, dark and light. Its beginning is almost invariably characterized by getting stuck in some impossible situation. . . . the initial situation is overcome on a higher level. (pp. 38- 39)

Jung stuns. Intense experience is of a schizoid character. It con-fuses to feel both dark and light at once. It con-fuses to feel that everything is funny and sad at once. It con-fuses to tell the tale. One feels "stuck in some impossible situation" as Jung puts it. There seems no way out, no passage through the darkness. Psyche gets stuck and sinks. Floats and drifts off. Psyche dreams of both falling and flying. Like Groddeck, Jung argues that psyche has a mind of her own! Jung (1983) states that "there are things in the psyche which I do not produce, but which produce themselves and have their own life" (p. 120). Psyche produces illness, I do not produce it. Again the double. Psyche has an alternative agenda. Psyche has a hidden curriculum. But who am I? Am I the receptacle of psyche who lives her life through me? Psyche is alterity. Psyche is the strangeness within. Psyche is an archaic remnant. She was there long before I was born. Psyche is a Zen Koan: What was your face before you were born?

Isolation of Psyche. If one suffers from a rare disease, isolation is heightened because you cannot find anyone with whom to share stories. If you suffer from terminal illness, isolation is heightened because you are alone with the terrible anticipation of your own death. What is it to know that you are going to die? What is it to know that your illness will only get worse? No matter what you do, things will turn only darker. Isolation. Feeling isolated depresses. Jung, however, has a remedy for this. In his book called *The Symbolic Life* Jung (1976) says,

> But if he [the patient] is shown that his particular ailment is not his ailment only, but a general ailment --even a god's ailment--he is in the company of men and gods, and this knowledge produces a healing effect. (p. 103)

Jung suggests that if you suffer from a snake bite, for example, go to the fairy tales and myths and find others who suffer similarly. There you will find your company and solace. The snake bite is archetypal. If we follow Jung's teachings we might find solace in studying ancient texts. This takes time. Books are the scholar's companions. Digging through texts heals. Even if answers aren't found, the digging is healing in and of itself. Digging in texts is also digging into Psyche. The deeper the dig the stranger things get. The deeper the dig the more disturbing things get! And yet the digging is healing. Freud believed that it is all about the archaeology of the mind. But if psyche is hellbent on destruction what does that say about her? Is she a monster? Partly yes. Jung (1983) reminds us that,

> Even enlightened psychologists like Freud give us an extremely unpleasant picture of what lies slumbering in the depths of the human psyche. (p. 196)

One wonders how long serious illness "slumbers" in psyche. Serious illness may seem to happen all of a sudden, because it seems to burst on the scene abruptly. But perhaps it has always already been there waiting in the wings. But why is it waiting in the wings to begin with? If psyche has a mind of her own, what kind of mind is it that sickens? As Hegel said, history has no happy peoples. Psyche is the site of torment, grief. Psyche is the site of depression, anxiety and angst. Psyche is the storehouse of the negative. Psyche is from dark to dark. Psyche is through the looking glass darkly. Psyche is death or points-toward-death. Marie-Louise von Franz (1980b) declares,

> Then one thinks of the old descriptions of the godhead of death, as for instance in the Graeco-Roman religion where death is Jupiter or Zeus of the Underworld, the god of the infinite and the treasure keeper. The land of the dead is like a treasury and the god of death like the keeper of an enormous treasury. . . . (p. 31)

What treasure is there in the land of the dead? Isn't the land of the dead barren? A wasteland. Let us go then to the land of the dead. Isle of the dead. Isn't the land of the dead from dust to dust? Psyche actively imagines death in order to bring to life symbols that give clues. These clues are meant to help, to edify, to teach. Death is a 'treasure' [Derrida calls death a gift] to imagine because it allows psyche space to open out. This vast opening tends toward a horizon of nothingness. Psyche symbolizes nothingness and somethingness. The somethingness of Zeus and Jupiter. Psyche is space. Opening that space is key.

Psyche tends to repeat. Psyche is repetition. She is mostly repetition- compulsion. She wants to get her message across. Illness forces one to think about mortality over and over again. Obsession with mortality becomes the mantra, the ongoing repetition, the ongoing compulsion. There is great value, however, in repetition compulsion. Von Franz (1980a) explains.

> By repetition a shock is assimilated, and therefore if you have had a psychological shock you tend to digest it by repetition till you have integrated all aspects and then you get your balance back. (p. 205)

Obsessing about mortality can be overwhelming and quite frankly depressing. Von Franz teaches that we "digest by repetition." Psyche can--with work--digest even the most indigestible stuff. To escape the chaos of illness—this is what ego wants. The great escape. But the unconscious forbids escape. No Houdini allowed in the dreamworld. Chaos must be something that is integrated, not something from which one must escape. Psyche discovers order, as von Franz points out, when death--chaos is "integrated" into life. When one integrates death into life, obsessions stop. Or at least that is the hope. When one integrates illness into life, a release opens out. Getting stuck and getting unstuck in cycles of chaos and order mirror the madness of the cosmos. Chaos and order are the two governing principles of the cosmos. The point is not to get stuck in a chaotic state forever. People who get stuck in chaos forever go stark raving mad. Making meaning out of chaos is what psychoanalysis is all about. The point is not to wipe away the chaos but to go into it. To dive into the well. To sink into the abyss.

Balance and companionship are key to getting unstuck. But achieving these things doesn't mean that everything is fine, because it is not. Finding balance when a life is out of balance challenges. Struggles ensue daily. Collapse threatens. The funny thing about psyche is that at bottom she is unbalanced. In psyche the center will not hold because she has no center. Jung--in an almost postmodern fashion--teaches that psyche has no center. There is no at-bottom, there is no acorn as James Hillman (2007) puts it. Truth has it that psychic chaos and the foundationlessness of lived experience reign. Jung (1983) explains.

> You will naturally ask whether the unconscious [which is psyche] possesses a centre too. I would hardly venture to assume that there is in the unconscious a ruling principle analogous to the ego. As a matter of fact, everything points to the contrary. If there were such a centre, we could expect almost regular signs of its existence. . . . As a rule, unconscious phenomena manifest themselves in fairly chaotic and unsystematic form. (p. 213)

If psyche has no center, no bottom, no system, no order, how then to find balance in chaos? When seriously ill the last thing one wants to think about is being thrown into an ever more chaotic state--but this is exactly what psyche does. She throws you back into the primal muck. Dreams--or rather nightmares--tell the tale. After the death of my grandmother, I repeatedly had dreams that she was alive and well. Or, I repeatedly dreamt that she died all over again. I dreamt of her apartment on Negley Avenue. I was a child again going to visit her on Friday night when we opened to door for the prophet Elijah. When I woke up from my dream, it took a few moments for me to figure out who was dead and who was alive. I would awaken totally confused. It would take me a few minutes to realize that she had died. The dreams echoed back to childhood as if no time had elapsed at all between then and now. The unconscious knows no time. Dreams mix everything up. Time(s) blur together. They make no sense. Yet they make perfect sense. If waking life were like the dreaming one we would be psychotic. Dreaming is psychotic.

Trying to make sense of illness alters the dream world and the dream world in turn alters waking life. Like those dreams of my grandmother, in the early days of my illness I often dreamt that I was well. I would awaken only to be utterly confused. It would again take me a few minutes to sort out the truth of the matter.

Was I really sick? Or not? Maybe it is all just a bad dream. How to work through chaos? An ordered life, then, is a chaotic one.

A chaotic life is an ordered one. Or is there order to chaos? Jung talks of wholeness in relation to mandalas. Buddhists paint mandalas in sand only to blow them away. In the wholeness of the mandala is also the nothingness of Being. We are but sand. Wholeness too is found in symmetry and disorder. Mandalas are symmetrical, but their dissolution is not. When the Buddhist monks blow away the sand, it goes in every which way. We too go in every which way. Jung (1977) explains that "[t]he Sanskrit word mandala means 'circle' "(p. 355). He explains that in Tibetan Buddhism the mandala

> is known in ritual usage as a yantra, an instrument of contemplation. It is meant to aid concentration by narrowing the psychic field of vision and restricting it to the centre. (p. 356)

Perhaps concentration on the center of a circle ironically allows one to let go of that center when the mandala is finally destroyed. Focusing on something, like repetition compulsion, allows one to also let go of it. Naming the problem allows one to let it go. Focusing seriously on one's illness is a way to find a center and yet to allow that center to vanish. To center on the illness is a way to de-center it. The work of psyche is done always in aporetic or dialectical movements. Psyche tells us that it is 'this' and it is 'not this' all at once. The center of illness might be what it is; it is a stomach illness or head injury or a neurological dysfunction. But there is no center to any of these signifiers. There is no center because the brain is always changing. This is part of the reason that we do not understand it.

Illness alters the human person in her entirety. Illness spreads psychically throughout the vast labyrinths of the bodymind. At the end of the day, the bodymind is nothingness-- at least this is what the Buddhists teach. Yet while we are alive we are something, we do have a bodymind but underneath all something is nothing-- the Buddhists tell us. Again, we have these strange aporias with which to grapple. Psyche is con-fusing. Psyche tells us a tale of doubles. Psyche is twinned. Psyche can be cruel or kind. There is a darkness about psyche that one can never grasp. This is what Freud and Jung studied so intently. They seemed to be interested not so much in what makes us well so much as what makes us ill-- whether that illness is psychic or physical or both. As Jung (1963, p. 234) points out it is to the "disturbances" we should turn. Jung teaches too that these disturbances are not only intrapsychic but they are also interpsychic. It is to our inter-relations with the world and the collective unconscious that we need to focus. The object-relations theorists--although they do not talk of a collective unconscious--also point to the importance of studying inter-relations as well as intrapsychic phenomena. Object-relations theorists are not simply concerned with studying communications between one conscious mind to another; rather, they are mostly concerned with the study of relations between one *unconscious* mind to another. The unconscious mind speaks without speaking and communicates at a pre-verbal level. Speaking without words. Thinking without the use of language. Curious non-thoughts. Non-thoughts as well as thoughts are not only private but also social, collective. Jung suggests that we not only study the interiority of psyche but also the connections to the collective psyche, the collective unconscious and the larger social 'sphere' in which we live our lives. Jung (1963) explains,

> The personal sphere is indeed disturbed, but such disturbances need not be primary; they may well be secondary, the consequence of an insupportable change in the social atmosphere. The cause of disturbance is, therefore, not to be sought in the personal surroundings, but rather in the collective situation. (p. 234)

What in our collective surroundings make us ill? Living in this culture of fear is enough to make anyone sick. Toxic waste. Pesticides. Viruses. E-coli. Fear. What is it that makes us physically ill? Weak genes? The mother? Not dealing with archaic psychological issues? Is it bad luck? Well, we do know that the high rates of cancer in America are not accidental. I am reminded of Rachel Carson's (1990/1962) whistle blowing book *Silent Spring*. Here she tells us about DDT and how deadly it is. The scientific community did not take her seriously because a) she was a woman and b) she did not have a Ph.D. Carson, however, proved the scientific community to be dead wrong. DDT is deadly and has been banned from use. The problem, however, is that DDT stays in the soil no matter how much clean up is done. Here in Savannah, Oatland Island is the place where DDT was first made. I have recently learned that all the alligators at Oatland Island have mysteriously died. DDT? Toxic waste? A virus? Water pollution? Many of the other insecticides Carson talks about in her book are still used today. The bug companies just change the names of the toxins to make them seem safe. In the South, one can see mosquito spray trucks spraying poison as if it were nothing as people walk by playing with their children in the park. The spray is thick and lots of it is dumped everywhere: on playgrounds, in backyards. High cancer rates should come as little surprise. In the United States, we also have a high rate of autism and Parkinson's disease. Pesticides are part of the problem. Our social collective is highly contaminated. Our food is also filled with toxins. Asbestos is in our schools and in our homes. Cows are injected with hormones and antibiotics. What kind of milk are we drinking? God only knows what it is that we are eating. Even candy bars have a small amount of rat by-products in them!! It is no wonder that one can get sick from eating. The social collective causes illness. What is to be done? The collective psyche, the private psyche, the inherited psyche, the transgenerational psyche all contribute to dis-ease formation. The complications are endless.

POST (SCRIPT) : OTHER BODIES, OTHER ROOMS

This book is disturbing. I would have it no other way. All of my books are disturbing. Why would anyone write on happiness? What's to write about? As I re-read what I had written in the above section some five years ago, I understand that my issues are also the issues of others. Speaking about myself is a way to speak to the Other. Autobiography is always already social. Speaking to the Other within and the Other in the Other person. David Smith (2006) puts it this way. He states that, "[i]dentity is never a stand-alone phenomenon; it is always constructed through the scaffolding of Others. . ." (pp. 31-32). A continual criticism especially by Marxists is that autobiographical writing is narcissistic and beside the point. Who cares about you! Yet as Smith points out, the self becomes a self through studying the self in relation to others. I only learned how to articulate my feelings by studying the pathographies of others. It was through the work of others that I learned to speak of myself. My issues--as personal as they may be--are also the issues of others. People get sick. The issue of sickness is everybody's issue. Everybody gets sick at one time or another. Studying other pathographies helped me to better understand what I was going through. Studying the Other teaches about the self. I would have been completely at a loss to articulate my own struggles if I hadn't read the work of others. To say ' know thyself' is not enough however. The only way one comes to the self is through the study of the Other. The self is a self only through the other.

On a new reading of this chapter, I see patterns of thought found in the work of two other educational theorists. I am not the first one to talk about teaching in bad times, or teachers who are not well—even though my twist differs. I am thinking of two books that gave me the courage to explore bad times. Mary Aswell Doll's (1995) *To the Lighthouse and Back: Writings on Teaching and Living* and Paula Salvio's (2007) book called *Anne Sexton: Teacher of Weird Abundance* deal with some of the issues I have raised here. Mary's book deals with two tragic events of her life: the deaths of her mother and brother. She talks openly about her experience teaching while trying to cope. The book is a painfully honest autobiography that explores the place of suffering in the classroom. Doll (1995) eloquently talks about the ways in which teaching becomes surreal while coping with her brother's illness and death.

> When AIDS became a reality in his life and his death was now something sure that we would wait for, my brother became more real to me than ever. His death was so real to me that my life activities, particularly teaching, became unreal. The classroom structure, curriculum, texts, chairs, desks--all seemed outside the bounds of what matters in life, as if life is not the subject of the classroom, not at all. (p.141)

When tragedy first strikes--as with a diagnosis of AIDS--psyche goes into a state of shock. Patients and care givers both experience this state of shock as the diagnosis becomes more real. The surreal nature of the classroom that Doll describes is that shock. Everything changes. Later in the book, Doll talks about how she began to think her teaching "inauthentic" (p. 142) because she was not integrating the lessons of dying into her classroom. She was trying to split off the trauma from the classroom. This does not work because the classroom is life, she suggests. Doll realized that it was okay to explore her suffering in the classroom. She says,

> Suffering, relating, and conversing have been the themes of my remarks. I believe these--ings have a valid place in the classroom, especially as we face a faceless society. (p. 38).

When I teach Doll's book, I find that students are overwhelmed by these deeply moving, and very sad stories. Students find the book --ironically--a relief. Here is a real person talking about real issues. Students are used to reading academic books that do not speak to them, that do not connect to them in any way. In Doll's book they find a voice in the wilderness and wonder why so many books in academe miss the point altogether. Focusing on methods and classroom management just don't get it. Doll's book has been a real ice breaker for students. The community of the classroom becomes more open, dialogue flows and the classroom dynamics change. How can suffering not be part of classroom life when so much of life is suffering? How do we manage to teach everything but suffering? And why do educators presuppose that teaching is always happy making?

As I moved through the different stages of my own illness, I too began to open up to my students more and more. I no longer feel that I needed to keep my illness a secret. This move, however, was gradual. Over time, I began sharing my stories with my students and I found that classroom dynamics changed. The willingness to be more open on my part turned the classroom into a real community. The relations that I was able to build with my students changed everything. These student-teacher relations became much more meaningful. I found that as I began to be more open and honest with them, stronger bonds were built. Before my illness, I tended to be a rather aloof teacher. Perhaps that is a part of my personality. I also felt the need to keep my distance because I teach in the deep South and Jews and Queers are not exactly welcomed here. Being Jewish, queer and ill presents many peda-gogical problems! Teaching in the deep South is highly problematic for minorities especially. Many of my students come from fundamentalist, ultra right wing families. Knowing this-- I kept my distance. But I found that after I got ill, sharing stories with my students broke down barriers that I never thought possible.

Like Doll's (1995) book, Salvio's (2007) book on Anne Sexton deals with teaching in dark times. Salvio suggests that teacher biographies might explore the less than perfect teacher. This is not a trend in educational literature. Teacher biographies tend to be stories of teacher-heros. Salvio suggests that perhaps we should look at teacher unheros. Anne Sexton--the less than perfect teacher-- had no boundaries. She did a lot of things in the classroom that would raise eyebrows, to say the least. And this is in part why Salvio's book is important to read. Sexton's poetry and her teaching of that poetry broke ground for women of her generation. What she taught changed the lives of many people. If anything Sexton taught people to be more authentic about their problems, about mental illness and bodily decay. Salvio (2007) explains.

> Given Sexton's subjects--abortion, adultery, cancer, suicide, mental anguish, and addictions--all unspeakable topics for a female poet [and I would add a teacher] of her time, Sexton's poetic project might be cast as one that creates openings into what lies outside of the cognitively accessible. (p. 5)

When I think about our work as curriculum scholars, I think of pushing boundaries. I think of transgressions. I think our task is to teach that which is unthinkable. Might we follow Sexton's lead? In what classes do we deal with subjects of the body, of the ill body? What kind of teachings leave marks on students? What sorts of courses really impact their lives? All of the subjects around which Sexton mused broke the rules. Can we not dare to break more rules? How do we get at the 'cognitively inaccessible?' I think of Wittgenstein's late work and how he asked very strange questions. He tried to get at the inaccessible. He tried to think through the unthinkable. But like so many other philosophers of his generation, the body was a taboo subject. His duck-rabbit was dis-embodied! One wonders whether his radical change from logician to mystic was brought about because of changes in his body? Mere speculation here. But scholars must speculate. Did his sexuality change his philosophy? If philosophy comes from the body how can it not be altered by the body? If teaching comes from the body how can it not be changed by that body? We do teach through the body. Teaching through the ill body brings with it certain problems. Did Sexton become a beloved teacher because she dared to share her transgressions and bodily excesses with her students? Did she become a beloved teacher because she dared to speak the unspeakable? She talked of the body and through the body. Her poetry was through and through embodied. And it was this that her male colleagues did not like. Salvio (2007) tells us that

> Not all critics were enamored of Sexton's autobiographical writing [and she also taught autobiographically]. Anne Sexton has often been criticized for using writing, specifically the confessional genre, to act out her personal problems, her own "small wounds," resorting to what Robert Boyers describes as "excessive self-dramatization, even spilling into the undertones of self-pity" (1974, 207). As noted, the criticisms lodged at Sexton for using the confessional genre to air family secrets provoke long-contested questions about the place of self-disclosure in the classroom. (p. 3)

Some potential criticisms of my book may also turn on the issue of self-disclosure. Is self-disclosure academic? Who defines what counts as academic? Many male academics typically criticize women who talk about their bodies. Many males write from the male gaze of no-body, pretending that the body is irrelevant to the work of teaching and scholarship. Let the critics blather their blather. I follow in a tradition of honoring autobiography and honoring the body. Greek myth, to Wicca, to ecofeminism all honor the body. In curriculum studies, I follow the lead of both Doll and Salvio. I take courage from both of these writers to speak honestly about topics that are clearly not acceptable in academe. The body is not always beautiful. In fact, most often it is decaying. Perhaps it is this decay that threatens men. Or maybe it threatens all of us. Is that why fake teeth are so popular in the States? It costs around 30 thousand dollars to get white, fake teeth installed. If this isn't the most absurd mark of American lust for perfection and beauty I don't know what is. But somehow these fake white teeth look somehow wrong. They look fake. Why do we want to look fake? The body decays. Teeth rot. Why can't we deal with this? This is exactly what Sexton was trying to get at in her poetry. But the formalists like T.S. Eliot and company would have no truck with female bodies. Did Eliot not institutionalize his wife? One might speculate why he did that. It seems to me that many men hate women who talk openly about their decaying bodies. Let us go then you and I to the fake tooth doctor and get faked up.

Other bodies, other rooms. When the body is treated as a site of extreme alterity, one must enter other rooms of thought. Modernist thought--[and much scholarship is still written in this mode] tends to be sterile, without emotion; modernist thought pretends to be transparent in language and meaning. The body as a site of Otherness is one that leaks. Ugliness and decay. This is the body that we do not want to think about. The body as a site of Otherness is the body that breaks down. The haunted body. Torments. Scholarship should haunt. And it is to the haunting we should turn.

In the first part of this chapter, I spun a pathographic narrative around a single event. Why this particular event stood out more to me than others is unclear. The ground and horizon of being elude. The ground and horizon of being become meaningful only if made concrete. Abstractions need to be concretized. The body is not an abstraction, it is concrete. We must think of it in concrete terms if it is to be meaningful. This is not to say that abstractions are not necessary. Of course they are but only if brought into the concrete.

I was attempting--in the first part of this chapter-- to ground the body. I attempted to think through a single event. I spun many pages out of one day of my life. This kind of writing requires attention to small spaces, requires attention to particularity. One day in a life can be profound. Many days pass without much notice. I tried to capture one day that turned upside down the taken-for-granted.

The event around which this chapter turned dealt with issues of the head. When something goes wrong in your head it is extremely frightening. The scholar's job is to use the head. When the intellect is at stake, everything else pales. Some suggest that the head is like the stomach. These are two crucial organs of the body. The stomach has a head of its own and the head has its own appetites. Although I speak in abstractions here, I mean what I say in the most concrete sense. Pathography deals with the concrete. But in order to get at the concrete one must think in abstractions. Further, the intellect and emotions are not separate, they are inextricably tied. Talking in abstractions can relieve the heart of its emotional load. But it becomes important to face that emotional load and bring abstractions into the concrete. Writing serves to unburden, to make meaning out of trauma. Yet, sometimes writing re-traumatizes.

What is particularly striking in these two kinds of writings (that of the heartmind and that of the mindheart) is that each suggests a mood. Writing from the heartmind emphasizes feeling-moods while writing from the mindheart emphasizes intellect-moods. The event, around which this chapter turns, was written in a heartmind mode. The chapter is highly emotive, frantic almost. The analysis and post (script) is being written today with the mindheart. Distance allows the mind detachment from the storm. Here, the emotions have faded. Intellect seems to be taking over. Here, I am calmer and my mood is one of steadiness. How can one write about the ill body without being emotional or moody? Anger can be the first stage before grief. But I do not think I was ever angry. I was more depressed than anything. At times, my heart was so heavy I thought I just couldn't go on. How could I get through another day being in so much pain and not being able to eat? What next would go wrong? There were many other manifestations of this illness that were-to-come. Not being able to swallow very well was one of them. Spasms. And then there are the side effects of the various medicines which I've already talked about. But it is to the grief that I would like to turn. When psyche is steady, she forgets the grief. It is easy to forget it. Just put it out of the mind. Years later one cannot capture those grief states. But upon re-reading the text years later, re-imagining that grief takes place. Re-imagining the grief has its own grief. Still, the re-imagining is not the same as the deep grief that was experienced during the initial stages of shock.

Today I am re-experiencing a new grief--as I talked about earlier--with the news that my mother has been diagnosed with a disease called multiple systems atrophy. The grief that I feel now is unutterable. I know that years from now I will forget what this felt like, but that is little consolation for getting through these difficult days-to-come. One grief is layered on top of another it seems. Grief compounds. What to do with this grief over my mother? How to articulate it. How to teach while this dread comes up in the middle of a lecture? I never would have thought that I would have to deal both with my illness and the illness of my mother. I never thought my mother would get sick. Children think that their parents will always be well and will always be there for them. But this just isn't the case. Kierkegaard (1971) speaks to the unutterable. He says

My soul is so heavy that thought can no more sustain it, no wingbeat lift it up into the ether. If it moves, it sweeps along the ground like the low flight of birds when a thunderstorm is approaching. (p. 28)

Under the shadow of the object of my mother, the heaviness suffocates. Once again, everyday life becomes tainted. A student will start talking to me and I will zone out thinking about this tragedy that has struck my mother. It is really unbelievable. And again I have to go through another round of I can't believe that this is happening. Just because you go through a state of denial once, doesn't mean you won't have to go through it again. It is hard to get things done, it is hard to concentrate. Why did my mother get struck down in such a mean and wicked way? I look around at all of my students wondering about their mothers. Are their mothers all fine? In the past five years I have had so many losses. Have they? Teaching is once again made rather difficult because of yet another tragedy in my family.

Adding this layer of the now—in this post (script)-- illustrates the complexity of teaching when time(s), place(s), and relations with primal others pain. Time is not one thing. Time is always multiple. There is the now and the then. Memory and the now mix. It is as if we deal with one pain on top of another one.

We are always writing about our mothers--Mary and I say to one another. Mothers and daughters have strange relations that differ much from mothers and sons. The mother is the most primal figure for both sons and daughters simply because we emerge literally from her body. We do not come from the body of the father. This is a very strange thing to think about. Psyche is built from both mother and father. Sons and daughters struggle with under the shadow of the object of the mother or the father. But for me the mother has always been more troubling. The shadow of the object of the mother colors our entire lives. The mother is in us and we in the mother. She is Other to us. She is a towering figure; the shadow of the object is a heavy shadow, a dark shadow sometimes. When the mother gets sick, the shadow gets heavier and darker even still. I turn again to Kierkegaard (1971), for he articulates this better. He talks about creating "shadowgraphs" (p. 171). And he calls these shadowgraphs kinds of "sketches." Kierkegaard states,

> I call these sketches Shadowgraphs, partly by the designation to remind you at once that they derive from the darker side of life, partly because like other shadowgraphs they are not directly visible. (p. 171)

Following Kierkegaard, these "sketches" that I discuss are just that. Snippets of memories and snippets of the shadow of the now. Snippets are like foxes. Foxes move quickly in and out of place.

This book is like a Fox, not a Hedgehog (Berlin, 1997). The Fox moves around quickly and in jagged paths, shadowy paths. This book is the Fox. The book's motion is fox-like because thinking through the ill body messes up straightforwardness, it messes up time; it messes up memory and place. And it is the shadow under which one must operate. The complexity of memory, identity, relations and time cannot be underestimated. Pathographies deal with all of these things. And pathographies deal with taboo subjects. The shadow of the ill mother is one of them.

Shadowgraphs, Kierkegaard tells us are "not directly visible" (p. 171). Shadowgraphs of the mother are not directly visible or clear either. The messiness of the mother- daughter relationship goes beyond the bounds of this text. I will say, though, that the illness of the mother is enough to shatter worlds. To think of not having a mother troubles deeply. No matter what the relation with the mother, when the mother gets sick and dies, the child changes. When children are children— as against grown up children that is-- the possibility of the mother disappearing (via getting sick and dying) can lead to incredible, irreversible psychological damage. What one does with that damage of course is another question. The question here is what does one do--psychologically-- with the death and illness of a parent? Is there any way to really deal with this? Thomas Moore (2004), in an aptly named chapter titled *The View from the Moon*, states that,

> In your dark night of the soul you need not give up your intelligence, but you may have to change your idea of what it means to be wise in the conduct of your life. You may have to adopt a different kind of knowing, one that is suited to the darkness and not in conflict with it. Nicholas of Cusa, the fifteenth-century theologian, said you need the night-eyes of an owl. (p. 69)

How can one not be in conflict with the dark? How does one not wrestle as Job did? Going into the dark means conflict. And yet, I know what Moore is trying to get at here. One must not repress the dark but welcome it. Welcoming it--however--does not mean being comfortable. Going into the dark, I think, involves many conflicts. Integrating an illness or death into one's life is going to bring up many conflicts of love and hate, regret, resentment and unspeakable loss. Job was highly conflicted in his struggle. When Thomas Moore talks here about getting into a "different kind of knowing," I think I know what he means. For me, a different kind of knowing is a melancholic knowing. Melancholy is grief that is extended over long periods of time; it is an ongoing state of mind that is unrelenting. Waking up with a sense of dread is the way the day begins when one finds out that the primal figure is going down into the underworld and eventually will disappear. It is the disappearance in life of the Other that causes great angst. After my father died, it was hard for me to think that he was never coming back. I am sure that is a common reaction to death. The word 'Never' with a capital 'N' is the word that stuns. To watch a parent suffering goes beyond the bounds of language and thought. There are no words to express this profound melancholic knowledge. Melancholic knowledge is not a singular knowledge, it is always doubled; it is always collective, no matter how private. Melancholy is something that most of us deal with especially with the death of a parent or a child. Melancholy is the psyche's way of coping.

Psyche is not one thing. Psyche is a relation to primal others. Psyche is always already a relation and in relation. When psyche is ill, others are affected. Care givers often suffer psychologically too. These sufferings might be on different registers but no one goes unscathed.

When I wrote the first part of this chapter, although I focused on myself, in the shadows were also other people. Psyche, illness and others are mixed up in a web. Even if primal others are not there when illness strikes, they are still installed in the psyche—as either good or bad objects, or both.

And then there are the rocks. Mary--my partner--has been my rock through it all. I am one of the lucky ones to have such a solid, loving, caring, empathetic partner. Many relationships fall apart when somebody gets sick. The stress and responsibility of the care giver is enormous. Let the care givers not be forgotten but honored.

CHAPTER FOUR

ILLNESS, PEDAGOGY AND MUSIC

Drawing on the work of Eve Kosofsky Sedgwick's (1999) *A Dialogue on Love,* this chapter examines the ways in which illness leaves its traces in and on the lived body and "traps" it. Sedgwick grapples with "the mechanical elegance of the trap this disease has constructed for an anxious and ambivalent psyche. . ." (p. 5). This space-of-the-trap is nearly un-representable and yet demands re-presentation and ex-pression (by ex-pression I mean literally to press-out). One must press-out the illness, in order to get some understanding of it. Intellectual exploration through study, of course, is one avenue toward understanding the ill body. Artistic expression is another way of getting at what illness means to psyche. This chapter turns toward a discussion of the intersections between illness, pedagogy and music.

ILLNESS AS BODILY TEXT

Illness-as-bodily-text is experienced in unique ways. Illness is the Other-of-the-Other as it invades the body, becomes-body with its own "coursings" (Doll, 2000, xi). Mary Aswell Doll (2000) comments that "[t]he work of the curriculum theorist [or depth psychologist] should tap this intense current within, that which courses through the inner person, that which electrifies or gives life to a person's energy source" (xi). Illness "electrifies" but in a negative sense. Michael Eigen (1993) suggests that being unwell emotionally is like walking on an "electrified tightrope." Living with chronic illness is like walking on an electrified tightrope. One minute you feel okay--not really, always buzzing with the sound of sickness-- the next minute you feel awful. Chronic illness is the land of horrible surprises and abrupt disruptions.

The constant disruptions and horrible surprises make for a chaotic life, especially when one is a teacher and scholar. As a teacher I am dependent on being able to talk, to lecture, to stand up. As a scholar I need to be able to think, to work intellectually and to write. These basic tasks become nearly impossible when the stomach is distorted, twisted, tormented and pained. One is always already de-centered when ill. Disruptive episodes of illness de-stabilize thought and literally knock you off of your feet. Getting the wind knocked out of you means getting speech and writing knocked out of you. The inability to speak, that is to lecture, and to write—the task of the scholar—pains. Every time you get the wind knocked out of you, the fall into hell begins all over again. The Fall is not the Fall of Adam and Eve, but the Fall of-the-body into the world of sickness and de-bilitation. And unlike the Biblical narrative, the Fall into illness is repetitive, continual and for some chronic.

Illness has a mind of its own as it destroys what it needs to. As I pointed out earlier, Georg Groddeck (1977) terms the 'IT'-- the mind-- the mystical unconscious, the unconscious that acts as a trickster figure leading one down the road to the surreal. This is the will-to-unconsciousness that tends toward (un)certain (un)paths that makes one sick or well. This is the groundless-ground of Being that drives blindly forward only to go backward and horizontal-ward. Groddeck (1977) comments,

> But the sickness is also a symbol, a representation of something going on within, a drama staged by the IT, by means of which it announces what it could not say with the tongue. (p.101).

What the drama of illness is remains a mystery, but one thing is certain, it is a drama.

The IT decides when psyche steps into the underworld. The drama is a tragedy. At every turn, Oedipus warns. The drama of illness happens within a certain time (chronos) and place (topos). Time and space are out of joint.

I want to explore the particularity of time and place within the drama of chronic illness. In order to re-(script) the narrative that has always already taken place, one must be ever aware of duration, of time. Here I refer to what I term time-against-being which weighs heavily on the heart-of-being. There seems to be no-becoming in the time-of-illness. Illness moves along a dis-continuum of dis-order and dis-location. Illness has a way of undoing-time, where there is no longer any time at all; this is the place where time stops. Clocks stop ticking. This is a (non) Bergman film because there are only silent clocks. In Bergman's films, it is a well known fact that clocks are always ticking. Marking time in very slow film is very different from marking the no-time in the slow life of the sick. Sickness slows and stops time altogether. No ticking at all. Time has gotten thick.

Psyche lives in what one of Thomas Mann's (1996) characters in *The Magic Mountain* calls the "horizontal position" (p. 71). Time stops in the horizontal position, time stops on that lush brown velvety couch, that oh-so velvety couch in the living room where I have spent years in the sickward, in the sick land of the living-dead. "The horizontal position" (Mann, 1996, p.73) becomes my trope of the topos, the topology of pain and dis-ability, of pain and no-movement, of stilted reverie, of a phenomenology of suffering. No servant suffering, no suffering servant, but only Being-against-itself, being-against being. Here, in the world of chronic illness where the chrono-topos of ill-begotten-being is to be for-ever, tormented, soul sinks into an awful alone-ness. Illness over-takes and takes-over, possesses the body, life becomes all body, nothing but body, body dis-torted, twisted and wracked with pain. Body is text.

I take my courage for this con-fession from Eve Sedgwick's (2003) as she dialogues with her therapist on illness, queerness and other assorted topics from her mother to cancer to AIDS. She talks about the horrors of entering into what I call the full-metal-jacket of the medical world. Sedgwick (2003) remarks,

> . . . a person with a grave disease in this particular culture is inducted ever more consciously, ever more needily, yet with ever more profound and transformative revulsion into the manglingly differential world of health care under American capitalism. (p.34)

Manglingly resonates. One feels mangled by the machines of medicine, the full-metal-jacket of the machines that mangle in order to heal. The mangling manometry measures pressure; the snake tube gets shoved down the throat raw; the mangling 18th century torture pipe they stick down your esophagus terrifies. And through its damage it heals. The mangling manometer. My advice to you—don't ever get a manometry. The day I got one was the worst day of my life. You wouldn't believe how barbaric this procedure is. Think of it this way: take a small pipe and shove it down your throat and keep pushing it around while swallowing. There is no anaesthesia. You are totally conscious. You hear the footfalls of the doctor's shoes running through the hospital hallway because something has gone wrong. Of course, the patient is not privy to that. Your hands turn blue. You feel as if you are choking to death. But from the doctor's point of view, the test is nothing. For one thing, he had it five times and it was no problem. Talk about making the patient feel hysterical. What must it be like for medical students to open up a cadaver for the first time? Is it nothing? Been there, done that. No worries. It's really a breeze. So too is the manometry. Not.

Pain persists for duration(s) afterwards. But more, the mangling machines that test, measure, test, measure, test, measure, find little that is measurable. Yet it seems to be all about numbers. If they can't prove it with numbers, it doesn't exist. This is why pain is not often treated. It doesn't exist if it can't be seen. Ah, the simplicity of empiricism!

So why do they do it after all? Manglingly, the micromachines of medicine work to light you up through the barium machine, the CT scanning machine and other various horror devices to see inside your organs. Worse though are the invasion-machines of rods and tubes, needles and poisons. The mangling of being knocked unconscious, the mangling of the after-effect of surgery. And they call this "care"? Must the medical community be so cruel to care? I think Foucault had it right all along. Medicine is a torture chamber. Medicine is sadism. And yet—without doctors and medicines many of us would be dead. A debt is owed.

Once mangled by a machine and the machinery of machines, the body becomes all body, a writ-large body, a body mangled. The heaviness of the organ, the sick organ (s). Being-against-itself; Not Being-for-itself. The body on two sides is stained and mangled with the trauma of medical "care." The doctor pokes and prods and leaves you lying on a metal table without even saying goodbye or hello or even have a nice day. Why do they never say goodbye? The maniacal nurse shoves a tube down your throat without saying hello, goodbye or have a nice day. She just says to you, 'if you have to throw up here's a napkin.' How nice. The micro-machinery of medicine troubles. So much medical care wounds. It isn't as if doctors do not know about the problems of the technical side of medicine, they do. Some doctors are even sort of human. But that is not enough. Moments of humanity. Sometimes doctors are humane. But still the medical community troubles. Critique is needed.

Many experience short bursts of illness during a lifetime. Others suffer from chronic illness. Chronic comes from the word chronos, meaning time. Time is all you have when you are ill. Time becomes the enemy. When in pain, the days are long and dreadful. A character in Thomas Mann's (1996) *The Magic Mountain* remarks,

> Quickly and slowly, just as you like, . . . it doesn't really pass at all, there is no time as such and this is no life--no, that it's not . . . (p. 14)

Time doesn't pass quickly when one is chronically ill. Suffering from debilitating pain slows time. Time stops. The clock stops. The world stops. Time is motionless without rhythm, de-bilitating. Time, as Shakespeare would have it, is out of joint. It's not just out of joint for a moment, or for a week, but for the duration. For all time-- time is out of joint, it is out of joint for the duration, for all time. And yet, there is no time in illness, even the concept of time becomes invalid, in-valid. As Adolf Guggenbuhl-Craig (1980) points out, "[i]nvalidism is a chronic state of being 'out of order'" (p. 17). Being is in a constant state of there-is-no-cure where all time seems to be of two times: one is the-before-the illness and the other is after-the-onset.

The onset was violent and sudden.

The onset of chronic illness knocks any sense of time out of you. When time is out of joint, one seems to float in a no-time hovering over and against Being. At times, this causes what Michael Eigen (1996) calls "psychic death" (p. 4). Eigen notes that "[f]or some people, the sense of deadness is pervasive. They describe themselves as zombies, the walking dead. . ." (p. 4). Without the rhythm of time, one experiences a psychic death. The psyche becomes swollen and mangled alongside sick organs. Somehow the psyche remains in a state of dissociation, floating above and outside of the body. Perhaps this dissociation works to defend psyche against the reality of the illness-at-hand.

Chronos stilted, dead. Dead-time. Dead-time. Here the trees stand still. The rats on the wires never run; they seem to be stuck in place. There is too much time and no time at the same time. Part of the psyche just blanks out, becoming -blank. I suppose this is what Freud meant by de-cathexis; to detach from objects, from life, from the rhythm of life.

Gaston Bachelard (2000) points out that "the concept of rhythm is the fundamental concept of time" (p. 20). Without rhythm-- time seems to stand still. In the stillness is horror. The horror of nothingness; the horror of Being-Against-Itself. This is what Eve Sedgwick (2003) refers to as "the trap." To detach from being-able, from being-able-to-do or to think anything. This is what Guggenbuhl-Craig (1980) terms "Eros on Crutches." When psyche is on crutches, walking falters. Crutches weigh psyche down. Crutches are too heavy and the legs too weak. Eros on crutches suspends all time. Eros on crutches. Being frozen in a timeless hell. Here, there is nothing, there is deadness. Is this what philosophers refer to as nothingness? Nothingness is not some abstract concept; it is real and it is lived in the space of traumatizing illness. Traumatism, as Jacques Derrida (2003) points out, concerns the future. Derrida remarks,

> Traumatism is produced by the future, by the to come, by the threat of the worst to come, rather than by an aggression that is "over and done with." (p. 97)

The to-come of the future perhaps. What is the to-come of the future for the chronically ill? More chronic illness. Naomi Rucker points out that illness manifests itself as variations on a theme (personal communication). Moves are made both lateral and vertical. More of the same-- timelessness and chronicity of pain and medical intervention. And worst case scenario anxiety. Anxiety, anxiety, anxiety. Living in a state of 'what if.' Strictures, rings, webs, spasms. Variations on a theme. Not being able to swallow, migraines, eye strain, early satiety. Variations on a theme.

Well into the third year of my illness, I found out that my best friend had been diagnosed with full blown AIDS. What right do I have to dwell on chronic illness when I do not have a really serious condition like AIDS? I do not have AIDS. What I have can be managed with medicine. He—on the other hand-- will die of an AIDS related complication of some sort. My condition is not as serious. There is a sense of guilt I have when talking to him about my condition. We are both in our early forties and things have gone dreadfully wrong for both of us. It is funny how our lives both went down the tubes at the same time. We are both fighting in our own ways to get by, to deal with these blows.

In his case, things have really gone wrong. When he was diagnosed and I first learned of his T-Cell count at 20, I cried and cried and cried. My whole world with him is coming to a close I thought. At the time, I did not know that the life expectancy for AIDS patients is much longer than it used to be. I had an image of him dying in less than a year. The dying god. We all have our dying gods.

He is a cellist. That whole world I shared with him-- including the world of the cello-- will disappear. My youth was spent with him learning music, learning to love the cello and the world of artistic sensibility. I will always remember my friend walking down campus with the cello slung on his back with cigarette in hand, looking dapper as ever, talking of Pablo Casals and Jacqueline Du Pres. Now, we share the burden of the chronicity of illness. Vivus is the only person I have ever known to truly create his own world. He was always able to fascinate me by pulling me into his unique space. He has the mark of creative genius. But now this creative genius is chronically ill. Again I think of the web of sicknesses that a life brings. Sickness cannot be an alone to an alone, but rather it is an alone with another alone. Connections build that alone to the other alone. Chronicity is never isolated literally.

Talking of the chronicity of illness is the "stuff" that no one wants to hear. As Madeleine Grumet (1995) puts it, when talking of AIDS (and I would add any other chronic illness) this is the "stuff" that nobody wants to think about. Grumet (1995) says,

> And then there's all the stuff nobody says to anybody. The parts of the world that are not spoken do not disappear. They are still there in the streets, on TV, and at home when school is over. . . . (ix)

When school is in session, the teacher teaches through the ill body. And this is the stuff that nobody talks about. But the students know that the teacher is not well. Or maybe they don't. The teacher cannot even stand up in class from pain and weakness. Maybe the students notice. The lectures are shorter, the dialogue less sparky. Clearly there is something wrong. But students probably do not notice and are only worried about getting A's. Missed days, notes on the door, "Dr. Morris will not be in today due to illness." Not that the students really care, they probably delight in days off as I did as a child when snow days were in abundance back in my hometown of Pittsburgh.

Teaching through the ill body exhausts. What lesson is the body teaching? The past and present mangle the ill body. Trying to focus on the lecture of the day, I get side-tracked thinking of my past, my old past of some twenty years before. And then I make the phone call and find out that my oldest and best friend has AIDS. I head out on the first plane to Memphis.

Going to the hospital in Memphis to sit with the cellist, my heart sunk, what heaviness. Time stopped. Our lives have come to a violent halt. All our dreams as young musicians have been shattered by chronic illness. Time is the enemy. For Vivus, time certainly weighs on him. Even though he might live another 20 years with all the new AIDS drugs, his body will weigh him down and he will struggle to make decisions about the end time. When he dies part of my world will die as well. All I will have left will be my memories about those gray days in Pittsburgh, circa 1980. This space--of timeless time-- leaves gaps open for memory. Chronic illness makes you think of your whole life in retrospect. How have I lived? Have I lived the life I really wanted to? Did I really live in those days? Am I living now? Why can't I live now the way I used to live? Levinas (2000) says "Time is reminiscence and reminiscence is time. . ." (p. 29). In the meantime, though, time is dreadful. These sudden turn of events in our lives upset the dreams of our college days. Back then, life seemed care-free, fun. In college we stayed up all night listening to recordings of Palestrina, Bartok and Hindemith. Time is no longer care-free; nothing is care-free now. Time is that nothingness of the trauma-to-come. Bachelard (2000) points out

> the soul does not continue to feel, nor to think, reflect, or wish. It does not continue to be. Why go further in search of nothingness, why go looking for it in things? It is in us, scattered along our duration, at every instant shattering our love, our faith, our will, our thought, our temporal hesitation is ontological. (p. 47)

That nothingness that is within is only made more evident by a negative change of events. Illness opens the space to nothingness. Buddhists say one must welcome it. Dust to dust. Illness absolutely shatters. Temporal hesitation. Slowing down. Seriousness. Blue. Anxious.

I hate to think of what is to come for Vivus. AIDS shatters the entire universe. I remember watching him in orchestra practice thinking he's got it, now there's a talent for you. My illness seems to pale against AIDS. What a heavy heart I have. In the meanwhile, we laugh about our childishness on that campus twenty years ago. I have that memory etched in my mind of him with his cello slung on his side and cigarette-in-hand. OH, but the hospital scene puts it all in perspective. A much ravaged body, sunken cheeks, weakness. It was almost too much to take in. Our youth is over and now the illnesses of middle age take their toll. Nostalgia for better days or days when things seemed to be better. The reality is that friends die from AIDS. Time is now, not then-- and things aren't fun anymore like they were in college. Jonathan Silin (1995) remarks,

> . . . the hospital vigils, times of reassuring connection and painful separation, are not shameful adult secrets that occur in a different world from the one we share with children. Nor are we different people as we move between the sickroom and the classroom. (p. 39)

PEDAGOGY

When I returned from Memphis, I taught Jonathan Silin's (1995) book on AIDS and education in a course on multiculturalism. I told the students my personal reasons for choosing to teach this book. I shared with students that my friend was suffering from AIDS and why teaching and living-- and dying-- are interconnected. I could not Not teach Silin's book at this time in my academic life. Moreover, I simply could not teach Silin's book without being honest with my students. This admission made for a more dignified class, a more dignified way to deal with such troubling subjects. I did not want AIDS to be just another theoretical discussion from the arm chair of the philosopher. I wanted my personal story to be shared with students so they could know of the pain of pedagogy and the pain of watching someone suffer from such a horrible disease. Knowing that he will die. How to teach under the sign of death?

I did not feel ashamed to talk about my friend with AIDS, but I feel ashamed of talking about my own condition. Shame and pedagogy cannot be separated. The shame of being ill and bringing that shame into the academy and into the classroom is taboo. In American culture, illness is not something talked about. Illness is shunned. In the academy it is no different. The teacher is supposed to em-body health and knowledge. Knowledge is supposed to come from a healthy body, not from a sick one. Thus, I feel a sense of shame walking the halls of the academy. I am not the teacher they want. Pedagogy gets heavy when in intense pain.

Trying to play hero-teacher, I lectured to doctoral candidates about Donna Haraway the night before they stuck the torture instrument down my throat to stretch out my esophagus. Luckily that night, much of the time was taken up by watching the film *Gorillas in the Mist*. I could barely swallow. It felt like I had a golf ball in my throat. That is what an esophageal stricture feels like. Yet, my time was spent meaningfully with my students. Students cried after the film. Wow, a real class. Learning should be emotive as well as intellectual. I have always thought that tears are a gift. A moving testimony to a woman--Dian Fossey-- who believed in her work and fought for animal rights. The ethical treatment of animals has been a long-standing issue for me.

I now pick topics to teach--since I've been ill-- that matter most to me. Before I got ill, I do not think I was as careful or impassioned about what I talked about with my students. What I lecture on now-- after the onset of this illness-- matters. My pedagogy has become more and more steeped in social justice. My lectures are impassioned as never before because time weighs on me. The illness has driven home the weight of time. Not that I taught trivial matter before. No. I did not. Here, I mean that now I teach perhaps with more care and deliberation because I know that time has taken on a different meaning for me. There is an urgency like never before. Mine is an urgent pedagogy.

Re-scripting the narrative of this illness is not unlike writing a work of fiction. Life-writing, lifehistory, lifememory, autobiography, confession, pathography are all fictions of sorts because they are meant to be creative acts of ex-pression. Creative acts of expression are not exact representations. Pathographies are creations. But this does not make them any less real or important. Re-writing one's past is re-inventing it.

Ex-press, to press out the illness in order to capture it phenomenologically as metaphor. This is the task here. Illness-as-metaphor and illness-as-real is what narrative is about. But my story is not just my story; it is the story of relations, relations to the past, to reverie, to memory, and to the future, to the end game, to a teleology, to an eschaton, to the traumatism of the end-time and most especially to others. One is ill only in relation to others, even if one feels isolated. The repetition of this relation becomes necessary. This book is not primarily about me. It is about the thickness of relations we share when we get sick. This book is about everybody because we all get sick sometime during our lives.

The narrative of illness sweeps one into the story quickly, with quickening. But the story is slowly unfolding for me, and in fact, it doesn't seem to unfold at all. I feel as if I am stuck in time. Ontological deadness and stillness. Umberto Eco (1994) speaks to these points when writing fiction.

> . . . any narrative fiction is necessarily and fatally swift because, in building a world that comprises myriad events and characters, it cannot say everything about this world. (p. 3)

But later on, when talking of Italo Calvino, Eco states that

> when he praised quickness, [he] continued, "I do not wish to say that quickness is a value in itself. Narrative time can also be delaying, cyclic, or motionless. . . This apologia for quickness does not presume to deny the pleasures of lingering." Unless such pleasures existed, we could not admit Proust into the Pantheon of letters. (p. 49)

Proust's (2003) slowness in *Remembrance of Things Past* could have been due to his experience of chronic illness. Walter Benjamin (1929) comments on Proust's struggles with asthma and the connections with this and his creative outpourings.

> This asthma became part of his art--if indeed his art did not create it. Proust's syntax rhythmically, step by step, enacts his fear of suffocating. And his

ironic philosophical, didactic reflections invariably are the deep breath with which he shakes off the crushing weight of memories. On a larger scale, however, the threatening suffocating crisis was death, which he was constantly aware of, worst of all while he was writing. (p. 246)

Intellectuals and artists write for many reasons. To ward off bad thoughts, or to dwell on them. To explore an idea or feeling. To simply tell a story. Intellectuals and artists write toward-death, or write as an escape-from-death. Perhaps we write out of a sense of shame. There might be a lingering shame in dwelling on gloomy thoughts like these. When experiencing chronic illness, these thoughts occur all the time. One has to find a way to cope psychologically with the heaviness of thoughts like these, or suffocate.

The day I made out my Last Will and Testament, I was convinced that my stomach would be the death of me. That dreadful day, I could hardly digest my food. It just sat there and sat there and sat there. I thought secretly to myself I will die of gastroparesis. I can't go on like this, I thought, thinking of Beckett. I must go on. That broken stomach phase is now "managed" by medicine, but a small amount of food still stays in my stomach for 10 hours or more. Food is my enemy. Food has caused this big mess. This disease encourages one to not eat, to die of starvation. The medicine I take for my condition does nothing to soften the pain. I take courage from Sedgwick (2003) as she says, " I've never known what I was supposed to ask of my pain" (p. 89). I do not know what to ask of my pain either. What does pain teach us? Pain teaches that the body can be cruel. The body can be sadistic. Pain teaches nothing. There is no point to pain. What is it trying to tell me? When in the midst of a bout of pain (a bout that can last 12 hours or more) I wish for a time when time has a rhythm, when time moves quickly, when I have a project, when life takes on meaning. Pain has no meaning. It is just cruel. Illness strikes. It takes you hostage. Illness takes you hostage for life. Illness swallows you up and spits you out, relentlessly. Gloria Anzaluda (2002) speaks of illness as a kind of 'snatching.'

> Every arrebato--A violent attack, rift with a loved one, illness, death in the family, betrayal, systematic racism and marginalization--rips you from your familiar "home," casting you out of your personal queendom. Cada arrebatada (snatching) turns your world upside down and cracks the walls of your reality. . . You are no longer who you used to be. (pp. 546-547).

I have indeed been 'snatched' up by chronic illness and am no longer the care-free person I used to be. Like Chronos, the god of time, I have swallowed a stone and have vomited up my children. The children of which I am speaking are the children within me, the ideas, the pleasures, the care-free, playfulness of youth. I have been snatched up and fooled by my own foolhardiness thinking I could go on and on like I did before I got sick. I must therefore, cast out my children to make room for my new life, cast out my old ideas, my old plans, my old way of living and write the new life, no matter how horrible it is. Ariela Royer (1998) comments that,

> Chronic illness may [lead] to great changes in . . . priorities and to a renewed
> sense of urgency to leave a legacy of accomplishments. (p. 3)

The drive to leave a legacy of accomplishments has grown more intense in the last five years. My priorities have indeed changed. Even when I am sunk in the no-time of the brown couch, listening forever to the *music of old, to the music of my youth*, I am struggling to find the words to capture this experience so that others will have a friend along the way, so that doctors might become just a little more empathetic, so that suffering will not be so lonely for others, so that teachers may become a little more understanding of children with chronic illnesses, and so that students might become a little more sympathetic when teachers teach through the ill body.

Living with chronic illness, is like living on a roller coaster of emotion. Some days you feel somewhat functional, other days you feel just awful. Some days you feel elated at waking up in the morning, the next day you feel totally down in the dumps. Sander Gilman (2003) points out that "[t]oday health is often not the absence of illness but a productive life with illness. Today people with chronic illness or disabilities can be "healthy" (p. 48). A healthy day or what I would consider a good day for me is when I can eat real food and not feel sick from it. A day when I can eat a piece of bread, or a potato. A bad day is when these foods make me feel sick. A bad day is drinking a mocha and suffering 12 hours from the pain of knives in my chest, or being full after eating a grape. A good day is being able to eat a bowl of cereal without feeling sick. To be able to do the most basic things in a life is a good day. A bad day is not to be able to do anything at all. Every day is a surprise, a trauma and a drama.

James Hillman (1985) talks about the meaning of the Latin word power, *Potere*. He tells us that this word means "to be able" (p. 97). 'To be able' to do something is power. Power is to-be-able to period. Dis-abled, means not to be able to do the simplest things in life. To be in any way dis-abled is to be and to feel powerless. There are all kinds of dis-ablements. Gastroparesis can be completely debilitating depending on its ferocity, depending on the day of the week. In the early days of my illness, before I was finally diagnosed, I nearly stopped eating altogether. Everything I ate made me sick. Everything gave me acute chest pains, acute enough to send me to the emergency room. Everything made me full. A grape. Early satiety--the doctors call it.

To-be-able-at-all is something we take for granted. To be able to speak, to be able to swallow, to be able to eat--these are the things we take for granted and these are the things gastroparesis and its related horrors interrupt.

MUSIC

To press-out (to ex-press) illness through musical expression heals. Ex-pressing illness through music allows exploration of Otherness as it gets ex-pressed in sound. Oliver Sacks' (1984) admission, in his book *A Leg to Stand On*, that music led him back to the world of the living and literally taught him how to walk again after taking a terrible fall gave me the courage to take up my musical life once more in order to better cope. Sacks (1984) comments:

> I felt in those first heavenly bars of music, as if the animating and creative principle of the whole world was revealed, that life itself was music, or consubstantial with music; that our living moving flesh, itself, was "solid" music--music made fleshy, substantial, corporeal. In some intense, passionate, almost mystical sense I felt that music, indeed, might be the cure to my problems—or at least, a key of an indispensable sort. (p. 94)

Music is not a cure for my condition, for there is no cure for gastroparesis. But music helps me forget pain and helps me get in tune with deeper aspects of my psychical life. For years my condition has been awful and at times utterly disabling. But through playing music, I have found a soulfulness and peace that I cannot find in anywhere else. In musical expression the Otherness-of-Otherness manifests through sound. The piano has always been my first instrument. Last year I discovered the guitar, this year the cello. Now I own seven guitars. I know that is a bit much. Seven is a Biblical number, a mystical number. I've got two Martins, one Lakewood, one Santa Cruz, and three Taylors. The cello is, hands down, the most expressive of the instruments and the most difficult. It has taken me a year to play a single scale. I have made much improvement over the past year, but I'm no Yo Yo Ma. However, I would love to master the cello during this second half of my life. I would also like to be an accomplished guitarist. I have much to do on this planet. I will NOT let my illness get the better of me. Fighting the good fight.

I had a dream where a voice said to me, "you have unfinished business." My unfinished business is music. This illness has made me re-turn to my music. I would not have done so otherwise. This is the gift and the irony. I performed for the first time in twenty years at a coffee house. I played the guitar in classical fusion style. It felt right and good. It also felt terrible. Just the way I felt when I performed in music school. Music performance for me is a completely conflicted conundrum. But this conflictedness seemed a wonderfully familiar life force. Preparing for piano competitions at the age of 15 damaged my psyche. There is no fun, no point really to competing. I associated performing only with terror. But playing in a coffee house is not like playing on the concert stage, it is not like playing a jury for teachers, for judges, for competitions. Playing the guitar in coffee house is cool and yet extremely nerve wracking. To feel delight and horror while performing was also to re-turn to my deeply conflicted musical psyche. It feels good to be conflicted once again!

Instruments vibrate through the body differently. The cello--especially-- moves through the entire body pressing out the illness (metaphorically) as the vibrations course through the center of one's Being. This Otherness--of resonance--is symbolic of the most basic state of life. No two sounds are the same, nor are two illnesses, even though two diagnoses might be. To (ex-)press these extreme states of Being— this is the task of the musician. The fear of death drives me to dig deep into the madness of illness through the symbols of sound. Music is highly symbolic of unconscious life. Sounds come of their own accord and in their own time. How one can learn the cello at the age of 40? A generational gift of music is at hand. My grandfather and father had native musical talents. Those I inherited from them. Playing music helps to get the rhythm of life back. Playing stops rumination. Playing keeps out the demons. The mad rhythm of life on the other side of health has a sound all its own. The oracle of Delphi is this undercurrent, this inner flow of extreme states. In fact, Bachelard (2000) claims,

> A sick soul--especially one that suffers the pain of time and despair--has to be cured by living and thinking rhythmically, by rhythmic attentiveness and rhythmic repose. (p. 21)

A sick soul suffering from chronic illness does not have the luxury of cure, though. However, being sick allows one the time (chronos) and space (topos) to listen to rhythms of the IT. (Groddeck, 1961/1923). If the IT says rest, then one must rest. If the IT says write, then one must write. If the IT says play then one must play and one must play the right instrument at the right time in the right duration in the right rhythm. That's why I have seven guitars. All of them speak differently and speak to different parts of psyche. Living-in-illness, means living right in the moment of pain, right in the moment, in the moment of Being. The IT demands a complicated living, one that is made up of simultaneous registers and an awareness of that simultaneity. Life can no longer be lived in a one-dimensional way. Even in the "horizontal position," (Mann, 1996), one lives vertically, one moves up to go down, one moves forward to go backward. These embodied positions are wrapped around a rhythm, since psyche is shaped most of all by rhythms. In fact, Bachelard (2000) calls for a "rhythmanalysis" (p. 21). In this kind of analysis one takes apart various rhythms such as the heartbeat or the rhythm of the key stroke, the rhythm of sleep or dreams, in order to synthesize and orchestrate the score, the text of a life. When one lives in the horizontal position one of the most important rhythms becomes sleep. Being ill means sleeping a lot. Intellectual work must obey this new rhythm. Sleep becomes the number one priority when one is ill. Sleep serves to heal and re-generate, at least for a time. I have never felt so weary, psychically and physically. Exhaustion causes psychic breaks. Hallucinations. Flying spiders and tiny flying tomatoes. Giant gingerbread men and floating light bright sets. Such psychic breaks are the stuff of myth and myth is the stuff of life. I try to brush the myth-spiders away because they are coming at me like torpedoes, but the IT--in the symbols of spiders or tomatoes-- is trying to ex-press something to me. Go down, go down, go into that deep place called sleep and the spiders will take you there, they will take you on a journey back to your childhood. Ah, that line between psychic states of awakeness and sleep is not so clear, especially in states of exhaustion. The IT tells one when it is time to shut down for the night and sleep. The tiredness is exhausting to think about because it is exhausting to live in an exhausted state. It is astonishing that I've been able to continue teaching or working at all. It is astonishing that I've been able to produce any scholarship-- living in the land of the sick. But something drives me onward. The IT. IT is unstoppable yet weary. Levinas (2001) comments on weariness, a sort of existential weariness, to which I can certainly attest. He states that

There exists a weariness which is a weariness of everything and everyone, and above all a weariness of oneself. What wearies then is not a particular form of life--our surroundings, because they are dull and ordinary--our circle of friends, because they are vulgar and cruel; the weariness concerns existence itself. (p. 11)

But Levinas says that in this state of weariness there is the "reminder of a commitment to exist. . ." (pp. 11-12). The commitment. Here is the ethical imperative; here is the categorical imperative of the IT. One MUST remain vigilant, one must remain cathected to the very lifeblood of rhythm, otherwise death becomes a less-than-virtuous death. To die the good death, to die a virtuous death, the good fight must be fought till the bitter end. Life must follow the dictates of the It; life must be lived the way the IT wishes it to be lived. To live one's life the way one wants to live, to live the way of the 'this' and 'that', the constant tugging in the muck, to live out childhood dreams. To re-turn to those childhood dreams, not in a naive state of nostalgia but as taken up seriously in the age of sickness, in the being- toward-the-end. Ernst Bloch (1999) comments that

In order to know itself, the bare self must go to others. Intrinsically it is sunk within itself and the inwardness lacks its counterpart. But through the other where a normally clouded inner life comprehends itself, it readily enters foreign realms and travels away from itself again. Only sound, and that which is expressed in sound, is referred back to an "I" or a "we." (p. 195)

The sound of the Other speaking is the connection missed while waiting in the waiting rooms of doctors. The sounds of the other teaching (or the teachings of the Other) ring out. The sound of my dog breathing lets me know I am still alive, his company is my company--he is my world. The sound of reading a text in one's head fills the void; musical sounds fill up what is otherwise empty and vacant. Words, texts, music fill up the sacred space of life. The chronotopos of lived-experience is finally re-cathected--because of playing music. Psyche moves once again in a rhythm that pushes onward; duration becomes adagio or presto.

Music speaks. Richard Strauss's *Metamorphosen* speaks the unspeakable. I am thinking here too of Samuel Barber's *Ballade opus 46.* Listening to music heals. Even if and especially if it is sad. From the alone to the alone.

Object-relations have never felt as important as now, and have never meant as much as now. The world of objects takes on new significance. Without a basic cathexis to the world of objects, time stops, psyche withers. A world cathected to objects oscillates inside of the basic rhythm of life. Here, one finds voice, time, place in relation. Objects like cellos connect back to the ground of life. The sound of a cello string vibrating connects to the sound of the hearbeat beating. Both play in sync. Here I am thinking of the profundity of the Bach *Cello Suites.* Casals played them best, even though his critics accuse him of exaggerated feeling and too much rubato. But this is what I like most about his interpretation. Critics accused Du Pre of too much emotion. How can music contain all that emotion? The cello has a soul. That soul must be interpreted.

When one connects and re-cathects to the IT, communication with the Other and for the Other becomes possible. As Bloch (1985) points out, it is through sound that communicability becomes a potentiality. In potential. To be able, *Potere*. To-be-able means to sing rhythm in time and place (this is a sound connected to a place chronotopos). Connected to one's innermost movement. The cello connects the soul to the ground and to others who can feel or hear the vibrations of the strings. Du Prc expressed the soul of the cello. She could make the cello sing.

Inner movement is song. Levinas (2001) reminds us that "a melody was, in fact the ideal model from which Bergson conceived pure duration" (p. 21). *Duree* is melody. Interesting that a philosopher might talk this way. How is that rational? It is not. When does philosophy become mysticism? I hummed always while standing in line at elementary school waiting for the doors to open to a new school day. Pure duration. Humming kept me. It kept me warm. I kept humming throughout my young adult years. I seriously hummed studying the piano. My first serious teacher played with Stravinsky and Pablo Casals. I grew up listening to recordings of Casals. I still have those recordings in my collection and continue to hum along. Now I am humming on the cello, well-- squeaking-- for now. But in a few years I will be able to hum on the cello as I understand better how to work that sound. The strings of the cello move in a vertical fashion; they resonate up and down the body exactly where the esophagus meets the stomach. This couldn't be a more perfect instrument for me. When I play the cello the strings move through the wood into my body; the vibrations go deep into me, through my organs, into my back, up my spine, into my ears, down deep into my lungs. The cello, my humming instrument warms me, exhilarates me, helps me keep down the chaos by working it. Levinas (1998) comments,

> Possessed, inspired, an artist, we say, hearkens to a muse. An image is musical. Its passivity is directly visible in magic, song, music and poetry. (p.3)

The sound of sickness is the muse that calls. The symbolization of sickness through the sounds of the cello works the damaged organs in some ineffable way making pain tolerable, making the entire bloody condition disappear in the repetition of notes. There is something about repetition that puts one into another state of mind, a deeper state of mind. Altered states of consciousness. Trancelike. Possessed indeed. When I'm playing the cello I'm not in the world, not of the world, not anywhere but everywhere in myself and yet communicating with and through the outer limits of sound. The dogs come and sit by my side moving their heads side to side. I cannot hear phones ringing, or the mowing of lawns. Trivial thoughts abandon me. I am completely focused on the sound, rhythm and movement of my entire body. Perhaps I have found a god or a goddess in the cello, or my own muse, or the IT. Whatever it is I am humming again like I did in elementary school and nobody can tell me to stop humming now. I will never be Pablo Casals but I will get through this illness with the help of my cello. Yes, I play piano and guitar, but it is the cello that I find most satisfying. And the most difficult. How can four strings be so hard? I'm totally amateur. I have no teacher and have never studied cello formally. But all of this is the draw for me. To do it on my own, by my GUT and my 'It.' The cello will get me through this crisis. It is through the cello that I am a child again, learning from scratch, starting all over, "becoming-animal" (Deleuze & Guattari, 2002, p. 232). There is something about the resonance of cello strings that harkens back to animality. The gut. Gut strings. Steel strings are even more powerful.

In an interesting book titled *The healing power of sound: Recovery from life-threatening illnesses using sound, voice and music*, Mitchell L. Gaynor (2002) tells us that he treats cancer patients--partially--by having them play singing bowls. Gaynor argues that,

> If we accept that sound is vibration, and we know that vibration touches every part of our physical being, then we understand that sound is "heard" not only through our ears but through every cell in our body. (p. 17)

The singing bowls doctor is a pretty remarkable fellow considering that he was schooled in Western medicine. I believe that sound does something to our bodies because our bodies are made up of sounds to begin with. Sounds resonate with our deepest energies. Sounds are healing and warming. Sounds move through us as energy fields. But sounds must be interpreted. I am thinking here of the teachings of pianist Aube Tzerko. Now, here was a teacher who understood the art of inter-pretation-the difficulty of interpretation. This was a master teacher who changed my life forever. I am only able to teach myself the cello because of studying piano with Tzerko. Makes no sense. Makes perfect sense. Tzerko had a way about him, an extraordinary way. Although my studies with him were brief, I learned more from him than all of my other teachers. He was a master teacher. He was a lightening rod, a firebrand and a gentle soul. He is with me now, in my head some twenty years later. It is Tzerko who is teaching me how to play the cello! And I will become a virtuoso. I am determined and Tzerko is showing me the way. The dream of virtuosity keeps my illness at bay and keeps me preoccupied. Music heals even as it frustrates. The cello is the hardest instrument for me. Strings are much more difficult than keys. At least for me, the difficulty is the draw. Teaching through the ill body means remembering our teachers and hearing their voices within. I can still hear him and see him, although he has been dead now some ten years or so. The dead live on in the memories of others. He was the most gifted teacher I ever encountered in the music world. His gift still lingers. Teaching is a gift. Tzerko was highly eccentric and offbeat. These are the marks of a great teacher.

Speaking of offbeat. As offbeat as all of this seems for many traditional doctors, medical science is undergoing a radical change in the way it views the importance of sound. In an article titled "Signal Discovery?" Mark Wheeler (2004) reports that chemist Jim Gimzewski recently made some important discoveries about cells, sound and illness. Wheeler (2004) tells us that the upshot of Gimzewski's studies suggests that,

> The research, though still preliminary, is potentially "revolutionary" as one
> scientist puts it, and a possible, admittedly far-off medical application, is
> already being pursued: someday, the thinking goes, listening to the sounds
> your cells make might tell a doctor, before symptoms occur, whether you're
> healthy or about to be ill. (p. 30)

Gimzewski argues that particular cells make sounds. Some, like yeast cells vibrate
at "about a C-sharp to a D" (p. 32). And when "sprinkling alcohol on a yeast cell to
kill it raises the pitch, while dead cells give off a low, rumbling sound. . ." (p. 32).
If doctors could develop fine-tuned instruments to listen to cells, they might be
able to ward off illness; doctors might be able to detect whether cells are getting
ready to die by their pitch. Sounds crazy, but I don't believe it is crazy. Why do
singing bowls work? Why does playing the cello warm? Why did I begin gaining
weight when I re-turned to my humming, to my music, to the piano, to my Pablo
Casals, to the strings that sing? Why did the pain begin to fade? Why did my rest
become more peaceful? Why did my scholarship come back from the psychic
dead? Why did I feel differently? Perhaps the sounds of the cells are in tune with
the sounds of musical instruments. Being at one with the cello is a potentially
profound experience whether you can play masterfully or not. I am not naively
arguing that playing an instrument can cure illness, I am not cured. Though,
something does happen psychically and physically when sound vibrates through
the body.

And then there are machines. The world of medical machinery gives me pause.
This patient has lost patience with the cold steely machine-world of the medical
system. I find little solace in the "care" of the medical machines. My critique here
is mainly against the turn toward the technological and the turn away from what is
human. Of course, without the technological, many diseases would go undiagnosed.
I am not saying we don't benefit from the machine side of medicine. Clearly, we
do. But the human element of medicine needs work. I am not saying anything new
here. There is much in the medical humanities literature to attest to these problems.
Experiencing the technological side of medicine—as I have—drives home the need
for continued work in the field of the medical humanities. How to put the human
back in medicine is a question many doctors are asking as well.

Part of getting well--or at least being able to functioning-- means re-covering
damaged psyche. Here I am concerned about the brutality of medical procedures
and their psychological fallout. Yes, I think medical procedures such as I have
suffered are brutal, violent and revolting. I suppose I ask too much of the medical
world to help me re-cover my psyche through this horrible process of testing,
procedure, testing, re-testing and living as a cyborg citizen on drugs with side-
effects not totally understood by the God's eye view of medical micropowers. I
suppose I ask too much of the health "care" system to care about my psychic well
being. Illness demands some serious soul searching, especially during the process
of diagnosis when the cold machines blink on and off and the needles poke and the
tubes are thrust down the throat. The psyche demands a turn inward. The psyche
makes demands not met by medical machines.

The psyche, when it is suffering, demands spaces of reverie. Here, I am not talking about a soft and mushy reverie, but one that is hard, painful. I am not talking about a sense of reverie in the way that Bachelard does as he points toward the "vertical axis" of being. Reverie must be experienced in what Thomas Mann's (1996) character in *The Magic Mountain* terms the "horizontal position." Joachim, a character in Mann's (1996) novel says "We have to rest, always lying at rest. Settembrini says we live horizontally--we're the horizontals. . ." (p. 71). In the horizontal position, the patient has nothing but time and only time to dwell-in-reverie on childhood and childhood songs. What did I sing as a child? "Puff the Magic Dragon lived by the Sea." The theme song to the TV show *H.R. Puff and Stuff.* The songs my parents used to play on the record player have stayed with me as well. "Bridge over Troubled Water", "Blue Moon", "Moon River". The songs my older sister used to blast on her record player: Cat Stevens' songs from his album *Tea for the Tillerman,* "Stairway to Heaven." Ah, a child of the '70s. The decade that should never have been. I often--without thinking too much about it--start singing H.R. Puff and Stuff. And then I stop. I say to myself, why am I singing that stupid song? Sounds echo. Sounds repeat. Sounds have a memory. Memory is made up of songs. That is kind of strange to think about.

The danger of lapsing into a mushy nostalgia remains. Close attention to memories of that old house, to that elementary school, to those songs sung in the schoolyard help to make better sense of a life. Close attention is work. If memory is worked it does not lapse into nostalgia. This is what William Pinar (2004) calls currere and part of currere is the regressive movement. Regression, in psychoanalytic terms, becomes necessary to progress through the present. The present is not understood unless memory work is part of that present. The present moment is always already historically contextualized. Regression and progression, therefore, are part and parcel of the autobiographic movement. Pinar (2004) states,

> In calling for autobiography in education, I have been asking teachers and students to reconstruct themselves through academic knowledge, knowledge self-reflexively studied and dialogically encountered. The reconstruction of the public sphere cannot proceed without the reconstruction of the private sphere. (p. 21)

I do not see a separation between public and private spheres. My work—which will be made public through publication---is fiercely private. My body demands talk of the body and talk of illness. My body-IT demands that I work through this illness psychologically and intellectually in order to survive and in order to help others. Helping others means living and working in the public sphere.

The public and private are one.

The past and the present are also of a piece.

To look backward in order to look forward. The Biblical myths got it all wrong. One does not turn into a pillar of salt when one looks back. One turns into a pillar of salt if one does not look back. How is it that some of us keep going forward pretending we do not have a memory or a past or that memory does not inform our present and future days-to-come? Memories of childhood come flooding back when traumatic events burst on the scene. Memories, both good and bad, appear on the dream-front. Dream a little dream. The IT demands that one pay attention to these memories as they serve as clues. Memories of that house, that yard, my early childhood friends and my elementary school teachers re-invite me to take part of that world of childhood. The memories come unbidden, sometimes unwanted and mostly through song. A little repetition on a theme.

What is it that drives this memory-of-things-past? The IT, again, is that something that is not a thing, that drives one backward and forward. Groddeck (1961/1923) claims,

> I hold the view that man is animated by the unknown, that there is within him an "Es," an "It," some wondrous force which directs both what he himself does, and what happens to him. The affirmation "I live" is only conditionally correct, it expresses only a small and superficial part of the fundamental principal, "Man is lived by the It." (p. 11)

There are primal forces that guide our lives, primal forces over which we have little control, but to which we must pay homage. Thrown violently forward through the years, one is tossed hither and yon. It is not economics that shapes human lives only, it is rather the It, that ineffable something that drives on. The IT gets ex-pressed, moreover in symbols. Groddeck (1961/1923) points out,

> For the It there exists no watertight ideas, it deals with whole structures of ideas, with complexes, which are formed under the influence of symbolization and association. (p. 49)

The symbols of the IT, I think, are the clues, the symptoms, the illnesses. What does the body try to ex-press vis-à-vis these symbols? What does the body do to cope with illness? Can words fully ex-press illness? Is the condition of illness ineffable? Is it incommunicable? Is illness inexpressible? Is the condition of being sick simply beyond representation? There are many ways to (ex)-press illness. Symbolic ex-pression takes on a variety of forms, and these forms are not just semiotic or linguistic. Symbolic ex-pression may be found in gestures, sighs, states of nothingness, annoyances, sounds and music. The symbolic expression of a beating heart, a heart that is beating too fast tells the bodily-ego that something is out of joint. The symbolic ex-pression of tics tells the bodily-ego that the nerves are wrapped up too tightly, that the neurons are misfiring, that something is wrong. Symbolic ex-pression through rage, tells the bodily-ego that the psyche is agitated. Rage is a symptom. Symbolic expression is the way communication occurs but on a deeper level; expression needs untangling. Symbolic ex-pression vis-à-vis music might suggest a healing through vibrations.

What do we mean when we talk of expression? What is expression, what does it mean to express--philosophically? Is expression purely emotive? Is it intellectual? Is it both? Is it more than these? What does it mean phenomenologically to (ex)-press oneself? What does this mean psychologically? How is this term useful when talking of illness? What forms of (ex)-pression make illness tolerable? I take my lead from Emmanuel Levinas (1998) who speaks philosophically to the issue of expression. He claims that most primordially,

> What is expressed is not just a thought which animates the other; it is also the other present in the thought. Expression renders present what is communicated and the one who is communicating; they are both in the expression. But that does not mean that expression provides us with knowledge about the other. . . . expression invites one to speak to someone. (p. 21)

To express an idea, a thought, or a musical note is, as Levinas points out, an invitation to speak to the Other. One wants to be heard. This is a crucial point in medical care because the patient is often NOT heard. The patient is often a voice in the wilderness. The wilderness is not a place of silence; it is a place where creatures want to be heard. To express an idea or a thought is most fundamentally a call of the wild, a call to be heard.

One speaks and writes scholarly treatises and plays musical instruments to be heard--at last--by the Other. We express ourselves ultimately for the Other. One writes or plays as an ethical obligation to the Other. Expression of pain and illness, whether through the spoken, written or played note, is not solipsistic but communal. Tortured, maybe, but not solipsistic. What is solipsistic is curling up in a ball; curling up and dying without speaking.

So what is this invitation of expression-toward-the-Other? What is the invitation about? What kind of invitation is this speaking and writing and playing? Who shall be invited and for what purpose? My invitation is open to all, especially to educators, therapists, patients and doctors. The goal of writing this testimony is to encourage compassion. This invitation is open to all who want to read a raw, honest phenomenological account of Being-in-sickness. In the tradition of Kierkegaard's Sickness-Toward-Death, I write a Sickness-Toward-Becoming. The rawness of this text might raise eyebrows among our more conservative colleagues in the academy. But getting sick is raw. And there is nothing pretty about rawness. To describe illness in flattened language is to flatten out the truth of the matter. An honest phenomenological account of sickness must be raw. Memory is raw. And being sick forces one to go back in time to those raw states.

Becoming more of who one is demands the regressive movement back to childhood. One must re-member those woods, that house, the fire, the walkway to school, those childhood friends, those third grade teachers, the songs one used to sing as a child. School is so much a part of the re-membering of childhood. School. How school shapes or de-forms humanity.

Standing in line in elementary school my sister used to yell at me to "Stop humming!" I can re-member that to this day. My sister now has my old piano in her house and she says she plays Carly Simon songs and she sings (or hums?) "The Carter Family Lived Next door for almost 15 years...." "My father sits at night with no lights on. . . ." Now, my sister hums. She even bought a guitar.

I still hum at school. At the university, I sing along with my CDS in my office hoping that my colleagues do not hear me. I sing loudly in the car--like Tony

Soprano--on the way to school. A graduate student told me he saw me driving around Savannah singing. BUSTED! Caught humming just like in elementary school!! So childish!

I use the word ex-pression in this chapter to emphasize the pressing out of symbolization. The pressing out releases tensions and yet conceals much that cannot be ex-pressed when talking about illness and pain. The word (Ex-)pression is akin to the word ex-patriate. To be an ex-patriate is to leave one body- of- land for another. To (ex-)press illness is to leave the old healthy body for the new ill body. To be an ex-patriate of the body, one must be willing to give up the old self and begin integrating the new sick self into the body. The work of mourning requires that one give things up, to de-cathect from the old self. (Ex-) pression of illness cannot be tame, or calm, but chaotic, frantic, without pause, without rest. Time is of the essence, since in the land of the ill time no longer works, time is out of joint, time is running out.

Illness, pedagogy and music are three inter-related forms of ex-pression. Music can teach through the ill body what the body needs to ex-press.

POST (SCRIPT)

Looking backwards requires new perspective on old thoughts. The old thoughts reflect another time. Time and memory interweave. Gaston Bachelard (2000) talks of time as a sort of doubling. He states,

> . . . it seems to us impossible not to recognize the need to base complex life on a plurality of durations that have neither the same rhythm nor the same solidity in their sequence, or the same power of continuity. (p. 19)

As scholars know, there is always a lag time between the time of writing a manuscript and the time of the publication of that manuscript. That lag time is one kind of time. Another kind of time is looking back and re-reading and commenting on that old manuscript. Commentary on the old time. A commentary on one's own work. Scholars are taught to comment on others' work, but not on their own. Can you see inside of your own work? Maybe not. And that is the impossible situation here. Can you read what you've written and comment from a different perspective? What would that different perspective be? Could it truly be different from the initial time of writing? Can we really change perspectives at all? We know that the unconscious is rigid. And yet neuroscience teaches that the brain is in a constant state of change. Still, our behaviors—if they are habitual—testify to a certain rigidity in psyche. If writing is driven by the unconscious how to break with that rigidity? The rigidity comes when it is thought that time is nothing more than chronology. To think that life is lived as a single chronology will never yield complex insight. Bachelard (2000) argues that alterity and heterogeneity are at the heart of time(s). He puts it this way: "[d]uration always needs alterity for it to appear continuous. Thus, it appears to be continuous through its heterogeneity. . ." (p. 65). Time and memory, therefore, are aporetic. The illusion of continuum breaks up as difference juts through memory. Memories are revealed piecemeal, out of time. They come up whenever they want to--in their own time. The time of memory has no logic. Time is not pure duration--as Bergson would have it-- Bachelard points out. There is nothing pure about duration. There are many duration(s) that break open or erase a seeming continuum of memory. Time and memory are like labyrinths. Jorge Luis Borges (1964) addresses the notion of the labyrinth. He states,

> A labyrinth is a structure compounded to confuse men; its architecture, rich in symmetrics, is subordinated to that end. . . . dead end corridors, high unattainable windows, portentous doors which led to a cell or pit, incredible inverted stairways whose steps and balustrades hung downwards. . . . (pp. 110-111)

Borges could be talking here also of the complexities of time and memory. The architecture of time and memory confuses. As soon as memory takes hold of an image, it dead ends into forgetting. Images get interrupted by "inverted stairways" of thought that jut through and in some ways destroy those images. Most memories are "unattainable" in fact because the window of thought closes as soon as the event passes. Memories slip through time disappearing forever down into the "pit" of nothingness. How to archive anything at all if memory and time slip out from underneath us? I cannot get the memory back, time vanishes. This is the fear but ironically it may also be the consolation. Some things are better off not remembered. But it is to the things that are better off not remembered that we need to turn. It is to the forgetting that we should turn. But how to remember what is forgotten? Hypnosis. Psychoanalysis. Writing. Working on the texts of Others. Working through the texts of Others. Working on the Other helps one to remember that which is forgotten.

David Jardine (2006) suggests that "[e]ducation must become like textus, like a text, a story whose telling is not yet over" (xii). The aim of education is to educate the self through the other. This is done by storytelling of things past and telling stories of the yet-to-come. Academe, however, does not often validate storytelling. What it validates is the hard cold eye of the scientist. The data. The numbers. Proofs. The only way to prove that you are sick is to be tested objectively by instruments that measure. In one sense we do want our machines to tell us what is wrong. But the machine only tells one version of the story. The story told by the patient is not thought to be valid. The patient is not to be trusted because memory is unreliable. The patient might lie. How to tell if the patient is telling the truth? There are people who go to the doctor and make up illness. Or, some people like to stay sick or even make themselves sick to get attention. This is what psychoanalysts call secondary gain. Doctors must rely on machines at the end of the day because many feel that patients tend to be 'poor historians' (Delese Wear, personal communication). The testimony of the patient therefore is not wholly trusted by the medical community.

In the beginning of my illness I often felt like they did not believe me. What did I have to do to convince them that I couldn't eat? I am clearly not an anorexic. It is not that I didn't want to eat, or thought food made me fat, or had a negative body image. Plain and simple I couldn't eat. Early satiety. The very first day I consulted with the gastroenterologist there was a question raised on one of the forms about meals. I wrote "what meals, who can eat a meal?" I felt like they did not believe me from day one.

It took some three months to get diagnosed. But I am one of the lucky ones as I have stated earlier. Some people are diagnosed when it is too late and they have to be hospitalized. So my diagnosis came--as far as the doctors are concerned--relatively quickly. But for me, the time between the onset of symptoms and diagnosis seemed like years. Three months of pain and torment feels like three hundred years. And this is the strange thing about time. Time feels slow, time feels fast. When illness strikes time stops. Dead time. Again, a little repetition on a theme here. Memory is made from repetition. The present is made up of a repetition of moments.

Music is made in time. Music helps pass the time. Music heals. Developing a more aesthetic sensibility is what I was trying to get at in this chapter. Playing music is playing time and playing with time. Time is the enemy. Music confronts that enemy of dead time and makes time meaningful. Meaning must be made when illness strikes or one might as well die. Illness, music and the drama of living must be played out so as to express the ongoing torment. Expression needs outlets and music is a healing outlet. Writing about the ways in which music can heal the wounded body is in a sense a tragic drama. Georges Bataille (1998) speaks to the issue of drama. He states that

> [i]f we didn't know how to dramatize, we wouldn't be able to leave ourselves. We would live isolated and turned in on ourselves. But a sort of rupture--in anguish-- leaves us at the limit of tears: in such a case we lose ourselves, we forget ourselves and communicate with an elusive beyond. (p. 11)

Playing music is a form of dramatization in sound. The cello is a drama. It is able to imitate the human voice more so than percussive instruments. When one is able to mimic the human voice and connect deeply to the overtones which the cello produces meaningful dramatization of feeling happens. There is no other instrument that can so meaningfully mimic the cries and whispers of the suffering servant. When I am utterly and hopelessly depressed I turn to the cello. Cello catharsis. Catharsis is a healing experience. The cello allows for a deep catharsis like no other instrument. The cello is the most intimate of musical dramas. The cello is drama; it is the theatre of the emotions. To dramatize is to press out, to pull out and to play out what one cannot express silently. Silent meditation helps when turning inward toward the soul, but expression needs to move outward. To get outside the body is what ec-stasy is about. The cello profoundly moves one deeper into the body and simultaneously pushes one outside the body into a state of ec-stasy.

Both inward and outward movements are needed for healing. Writing things out is an outward movement of head, heart and soul. Thought as an invisible--as Merleau Ponty teaches--needs outward expression. Speech and writing are the expressions of thought. Playing music is yet another kind of language that speaks pain and anguish.

As educators know in public schools when budgets shrink music and art are cut from the curriculum. People who cut these subjects believe that the arts are just fluff, extra, superfluous. My argument here has been to the contrary. Music is not some kind of beside, some kind of nothing. It is healing, it is an expression of the soul. Cutting music programs from school is in effect castrating the soul. Public schooling in the United States is hardly soulful.

That which is soulful is also mystical. Music is mystical. Music is the language of the mystics. Mysticism is a turn inward, yes. But music is the expression outward (in sound) of that mystical inward turn. What is highly private is made public through the playing of an instrument. Evelyn Underhill (1911/1990) explains that mystic experience is a story that needs to be told. She states,

> The mystic, too, tries very hard to tell an unwilling world his secret. . . . First, there is the huge disparity between his unspeakable experience and the language which will most nearly suggest it. (p. 76)

Why is the world unwilling to listen to the mystic? Because the world [of machines, nuclear weapons, empire] does not believe that there is such a thing as a mystical experience and even if there were, to what use could it be put? Mystical language has always been thought to be heretical. No dogma needed. No church needed. No appeal needs to be made to authority. No permission needed. And there are no standardized tests for mystical experience.

Can education become more mystical? Is music a language of the mystics? At bottom music is about mathematics, time, rhythm but mostly soul. Can mathematics be thought of as mystical too? Think of Pythagoras. Walter Kaufmann (1968) tells us that Pythagoras started a mystical cult. Kaufmann says that Pythagoras "considered the study of mathematics essential for the conversion of the soul from the world of the senses to the contemplation of the eternal" (p. 10). It is interesting that mathematicians become mystics. We see this in the case of Wittgenstein as he transitioned from his rational-logico days to his mystical-spiritual days toward the end of his life. The mystical, the musical, memory and mathematics are all interrelated. If we cut music from the school curriculum we damage the soul, memory and even the mathematical. Cutting out music is like cutting out the soul. Without music, children will not know how to walk [I am thinking of Oliver Sacks (1998a) in his *A Leg to Stand On*] through the world with elegance and grace.

When we think about pedagogy, rhythm comes to mind. Isn't good teaching about timing and memory? Ex- temporaneous thought is one of time, memory and rhythm. Isn't the best teaching done when one gets distance from the text at hand and makes connections across other texts? The connections make teaching interesting. Pedagogy is inherently musical. It is a sort of musical text. When one teaches through the ill body one teaches through a melancholic musical text. The language of speech slows, the cadences move downward, thought pauses. Memory gets interrupted. Lectures get entangled. The past invades the present. Teaching is made impossible. George Bataille (1998) addresses the impossible here. He states,

To face the impossible--exorbitant, indubitable-- when nothing is possible any longer is in my eyes to have an experience of the Divine; it is analogous to torment. (p. 33)

Teaching as torment. Profound pedagogy is that which pauses before the unutterable. The divine is not the light, but the darkness. Bataille keeps company with Jungians who argue that when we talk of spiritual psychology what we are talking about is turning toward the dark night of the soul. (Moore, 2004). Jungian spirituality is not that of the Enlightenment, for it has little to do with the light. One is not enlightened by the divine, one is endarkened by it. Teaching through the ill body resonates with this endarkened mystical musicality.

THE SPEAKING BODY, TRAUMA AND ARCHETYPAL BODYART

I begin this chapter in the company of Ursula Le Guinn (2001) as she states, "[l]ife is the most incredible mess. . ." (p. 95). The thing about chronic illness is that it is an incredible mess. As soon as you recover, the illness creeps back and once again you are sick. I had just finished paying off my medical bills and took a trip to visit my grandmother in Pittsburgh (believing that finally I was well again), when I started getting that sick feeling in my throat. It all begins in small ways. Sore throat, things getting stuck, can't swallow, strictures. Must submit once again to the physician's magic machines. The machines they use to fix strictures are like the stuff of Sci Fi. Reading Ray Bradbury's (1996a) *Fahrenheit 451*, I came across an interesting metaphorical passage that might aptly describe what I experienced during the medical procedure that undid my strictures. Bradbury's character says,

> They had this machine. They had two machines, really. One of them slid down into your stomach like a black cobra looking for all the old water and the old time gathered there. . . . It drank up all the green matter that flowed to the top in a slow boil. Did it drink of the darkness? Did it suck out all the poisons accumulated over the years? It fed in silence with an occasional sound of inner suffocation. . . . (1996, p. 14)

This is the third time I've had the cobra stuck down my throat to stretch me out, to widen the pathway. Things keep closing up on me. What darkness and poison do I need to get rid of? Of what psychic green matter do I need to expel from that dark place? For the rest of my life I will have to undergo the cobra treatment.

Chronic illness is so unpredictable, it is a postmodern life. Health, illness, health, illness, fine not fine, fine not fine. Strictures, rings, webs, cobras, paresis. Uncertainty. Future or no future. Swallowing or no swallowing. It's one thing to have a cold; it's another thing to continually have your throat stop working.

When you are ill, you enter into a liminal state of Being. It is indeed a lonely place. It's you and your doctor. That is at how it feels. They called my doctor 'Joe-Joe' before they put me under. The anaesthesia felt like a cloud of heaven. Maybe this is what death feels like, a smooth peaceful feeling, a lightness of Being. But the cloud of heaven soon wears off, pain begins again and reality sets in. Here we go again. There is something intimate and disturbing about a doctor shoving a cobra down your throat and surgically modifying your body.

The place of illness is a far away place. It is a dark place, a place of green matter and poison. In Jack London's (2003) novel *White Fang*, the narrator describes wild dogs in the north country. For me, the wildness of the north country is a good metaphor for illness. "The land itself was a desolation, lifeless, without movement, so lone and cold that the spirit of it was not even that of sadness" (p. 91). In another short essay titled "In a far country", London (1994) talks again of landscapes that could serve as metaphors for illness. He states,

> When a man journeys into a far country, he must be prepared to forget many of the things he has learned, and to acquire such customs as are inherent with existence in the new land; he must abandon the old ideals and the old gods. . . . (p. 11)

The northland of illness is a place that is the afterward, the place that freezes out health. Once in the afterward of health there is no turning back, there is always already a chill. One must abandon the idea of the ground of health, for there is no ground on which to stand. Abandon hope all ye who enter here! Everything is a shifting floor; the shifting floor of illness wobbles. Illness is the *House of Usher* (Poe, 1976). Psychic walls collapse.

There is no one there but you. You are alone with your illness. No one can get into that cold place but you. Isolated in the north country, you must find your way as a wild dog in the snow. Unlike London's White Fang--who eventually becomes domesticated-- there is no domesticating illness. It cannot be made fully part of one's domicile. Integrating illness into a life does not mean taming it; it simply means living with it as an intruder in the old dust. Traces of Faulkner. This ongoing trauma, this negative space forces the otherwise of thinking. This is the Otherwise of the northland of dusty Being. Traces of Levinas.

This ongoing trauma has forced my body to speak in ways that have surprised me. The trauma of living in negative space has produced--in most fantasy--like ways--- kaleidoscopic colors that have appeared on my skin as bodyart.

PRIMAL BODYART: A RETURN TO THE ANCESTORS

Bodyart and illness are topics to which I would like to turn. Living more aesthetically has helped me cope with illness. In the last chapter I spoke about music, here I would like to speak about art--in particular-- bodyart.

I would like to show the ways in which decorating the wounded body helps to heal psychically. The speaking body is the decorated body, the body bedecked with artwork.

Bodyart sanctifies illness.

My body is talkin' back to itself in a mysterious dialogue. I feel strangely empowered and perplexed. I have long thought about the possibilities of what the expression of color might mean philosophically and psychoanalytically. Why might color heal? Why is color numinous? Jung (1977) states that "vivid colors seem to attract the unconscious. . ." (p. 294). What does it mean to attract the unconscious? Is the unconscious pulled in the direction of color? I certainly experienced this as I felt compelled to explore bodyart as a way toward healing. I cannot explain why I suddenly became interested in body modification; perhaps my unconscious wants to express itself in technicolor. Angela Carter (2003) speaks of a "polychromatic unfolding" (p.15). What does this polychromatic unfolding signify? Colors unfold as they emerge on text. Interestingly enough, Marion Milner (1957) tells us in her groundbreaking book *On Not Being Able to Paint*, that the more she was able to let go--to free associate--the stranger her paintings became. It was as if the paintings painted themselves. She had no idea what would emerge on the canvas. This is an unfolding of the unconscious as it gets expressed on canvas. Bodyart needs a canvas, that canvas is skin. What emerges on the skin is an expression of the deep unconscious. Images paint themselves it seems. The unconscious speaks and makes strange the flesh. Bodyart becomes flesh.

Both music and art involve color. Different instruments speak different colors. Cellos speak in the deepest purples, guitars in light reds and pianos in "polychromatic unfoldings." But what about colors, what do they speak? If they speak the language of the unconscious perhaps they are trying to send a message? What is the message of the unspoken northland?

THE ARCHETYPE OF THE TIGER

William James (1998) says *in Pragmatism and Common Sense* that "[o]ur minds thus grow in spots; and like grease-spots, the spots spread" (p. 83). Our minds are mostly unconscious. The unconscious, then, grows like spots. Projected onto the canvas of my skin are spots, grease spots of color. What are these spots, the reader must wonder?

Tattoos. *Tattoos are bodyart*. Etchings on skin illustrate (literally and figuratively) the power of animality--the anima-- fighting disease. I began getting Tattoos because I felt that I needed power to fight my illness. So I chose Tigers. My tattooed Tigers scare. They scare away the illness. They also scare away other people! But my students think tattoos are cool. The ultimate in cool, in fact. Students often ask, "Can we see your tattoos Dr. Morris?" I say "Only if you promise not to tell!" And so we share a secret—my students and I.

Emerging from my animal unconscious are archetypal figures. Archetypal figures serve to heal, to fight the beast of illness, to make the body a site of art. Something deeply repressed comes up onto the skin. A sanctification rite. The ritual of color. Color as myth. Traumas, wounds, the deep green slime of illness transmogrifies into multi-colored tigers, archetypal tigers. Tigers. Blues, oranges, reds, blacks, yellows, greens, purples. After being tattooed, I was astonished to learn that Jung had written about the image of the tiger. Jung says that when tigers appear in art they are archetypal. They are part of the anima. It is interesting to note that the root of the word animal is anima. Anima is a key term for Jung. Jung (1977) declares,

The anima is not the soul in the dogmatic sense, not an anima rationale, which is a philosophical concept, but a natural archetype that satisfactorily sums up all the statements of the unconscious, of the primitive mind, of the history of language and religion. It is a "factor" in the proper sense of the word . . . it is always the a priori element in his [her] moods, reactions impulses, and whatever else is spontaneous in psychic life. It is something that lives for itself, that makes us live. . . . (p. 27)

Illness makes you do crazy things, things on the spur of the moment-- like covering your body with tattoos. My decision to tattoo my body was a spontaneous one. As Jung teaches, spontaneity is a mark of the anima.

I began seeing changes in myself. I became obsessed with bodyart. I started buying magazines, reading literature and thinking about my next tattoo. But once again, the next one wasn't my conscious decision, it just seemed to happen. William James (1998) says, "truth happens to an idea" (p. 97). Well, tattoos-- if they are truly archetypal-- happen to the body. The unconscious decides. I allowed 'It' to lead me. Techni-color tattoos are analogous to the basic elements: fire, water, wind and earth, air. Fire is red, blue, water is blue, green, brown, white, wind is white, earth is red, brown and green, air is colorless. Bodyart can be done in all of these primal colors. There is something basic, primal about painting animals on the skin. Perhaps painting is too tame a metaphor. Getting tattooed is akin to blood letting. Release.

Tigers are primal. Black and white tattoos are especially powerful. But mine are not black and white, mine are multi-colored. There is just something about bold colors. And tigers.

When I first started getting tattooed, I felt as if I had crossed a line, I crossed a threshold in my life. This is ritual. Ritual is what the Jungians talk about. Maureen Mercury (2000), archetypal "activist", argues that people perform body modifications such as tattooing, piercing, scarification and even branding because bodily alterations "refer beyond themselves to a field of mythic imagination. By isolating an image and considering it for marking, one enters into mythic unconsciousness, even if one is unaware of it" (p. 45). To the image one must go. Images heal. Tiger images heal. Tigers are symbols of power and healing. Tigers are also symbols of starting over again. 1962 is the year of the Tiger. That is the year I was born. Uncanny.

Images appear in fields. Image-fields. These fields are energy release fields. The energy that is released is the energy of color. Color heals and color transmogrifies. Bodyart is a scandal, no doubt. It is a school for scandal. It is considered repulsive and crude by many. However, body art is old. It is an ancient ancestral tradition. We have forgotten our ancestors. Tattooing is an ancient art form. There is nothing new about Tattoos. In an interesting book titled *Extreme bodies: The Use and Abuse of the Body in Art*, Francesca Alfano Miglietti (2003) declares that,

art bursts into reality and becomes visible through "scandal" almost always a "scandal" that has to do with morality, sexuality, norms, prohibitions, a form of visibility that often succeeds in transcending the artwork itself. . . . it is always the display of the body that provokes indignation, it is always the display of the body that creates irritation, discomfort, reaction. (p. 11)

Tattoos are a school for scandal.

Artwork on the body upsets people. Something about the body. Why are Americans, especially, so uncomfortable with the body? What is it that gets under the skin--as it were--about tattoos? In the Jewish religion this practice is completely anathema, especially since the Holocaust. But some younger Jews are getting tattooed as an act of defiance, as an inverted in your face, as a reaction to the slaughter of millions of European Jews. Younger Jews are saying--with their Tattoos, hey, here we are. Tattoos are in your face. Tattoos are a form of social activism.

There are all sorts of reasons why people get tattooed. The TV show *Miami Inc.* is a good ethnographical exploration of the psychology behind why people do this. The tattoo culture is a fascinating one. Mostly people get tattoos to mark major transitions in their life. Getting tattooed is a ritual.

In American culture we seem to be okay with face lifts. Face lifts are more radical than tattoos because you have to undergo surgery. Getting tattoos--still considered taboo--are not unlike getting face lifts. But no surgery is needed. Changing the body--whether by surgery or with needles and ink--is after all, modification. Why is one kind of modification more acceptable than another? It is interesting how social mores dictate what we should and should not do, what is and is not acceptable. But who is to say which social more is right and which one wrong? I would never get a face lift, but I have no problem with getting tattooed. Many would rather get a face lift than a tattoo. But to me these body modifications are--more or less--the same thing. Changing the body is changing the body.

Like tattoo artists, plastic surgeons, according to Arthur Frank (2004), call themselves "flesh artist [s]" (p.20). Is it okay to use a knife to cut off your nose, change your chin or get rid of crow's feet around the eyes, but not okay to tattoo the body? Is it okay to drink yourself into oblivion (which seems to be acceptable in American society) and not okay to get tattooed? It seems strange to me that drinking is more acceptable than tattooing. Drinking is toxic, drinking is a drug. Why is drinking any different, say, from smoking pot? Smoking pot has beneficial effects, especially for cancer patients. But pot is outlawed in the United States. Interestingly, altering your nose is a way to fit in. Nose jobs signify assimilation into Hollywood mainstream culture. But tattooing is an act of alterity. When you see someone in a coffee house with tattoos crawling up the neck, the usual response is*: oh my god*! Or, *good lord*! Tattoos symbolize difference. Nose jobs are normalizing.

Children stare at tattoos. Adults are horrified. Children seem more open to seeing animals painted on skin than adults. Children are more open to things than adults. Adults are so hardened in their belief systems that anything that threatens them is outlawed. Tattooed people are thought, by many suburbanites, to be dirty, scumbags; just as Jews are thought--by anti-Semites--to be or dirty, subhuman. Jews are certainly not unclean or subhuman and there is nothing dirty or impure about getting tattoos. In fact, in some cultures tattoos are considered sacred.

Tattooing is a ritual. Tattooing is actually a very ancient practice. Some draw the practice back to Neolithic times. Kathryn Gay and Christine Whittington (2002) report that "Animal-style tattoo art is visible on [a] three-thousand-year-old mummy found in Siberia" (p. 16). Gay and Whittington (2002) go on to tell us that "The Pazyrks might have believed that when tattooed with a picture of an animal, a person gained that animal's power" (p. 16). Tigers are power. Tigers, as Jung points, out are archetypal images. These archetypes are about power. When Psyche feels vulncrablc, she needs power, she needs to be empowered. Tiger images serve as symbols of empowerment. Maureen Mercury (2000) argues that "it is important to understand that as with tattooing . . . or reforming the body is not a wounding or a mutilation of the flesh, it is a homeopathic attempt to heal oneself" (p. 54). Most people who get tattoos are trying to heal from a traumatic incident in their life like a death, returning from war, or an illness.

Sociologist Clinton Sanders (1989) has written an important book on tattoos called *Customizing the body: The art and culture of tattooing.* Here he argues that what counts as art is socially constructed. What counts as trash or high art depends on the culture. In some cultures tattooing is considered high art. In American culture tattooing is considered, by most, trashy. But Sanders points out that academe is to blame, in part, for the tattoo-trash-status. Sanders (1989) argues

> The amount of serious typically academic, attention devoted to an activity also affects its chances of artistic certification: Products and production enterprises derive importance from being the focus of abstracted, critical, theoretically oriented legitimization. (p. 152)

Sanders attempts, in his book, to legitimize the tattoo subculture by giving it serious academic attention. His book is interesting and important in the way that it legitimizes an art form that is usually discounted. His point is that tattoo art is "real" art. As a serious topic for sociological study I think we must take Sanders' book seriously. He is one of the few brave academicians to study this subculture. The tattoo culture is like any other subculture with its codes of morality, rules of engagement and codes of behavior. In many tattoo studios today symbols of hatred, like 666 or the swastika or gang symbols, are not allowed. Good tattoo studios do not want to give racists a platform. And this is something that many people do not know. There are high standards among good tattoo artists. In many ways, tattoo artists have higher standards of morality than some academicians.

Part of the appeal of the tattoo subculture turns on issues of gender, sexuality and performance. I recently saw a show on TV about what is termed the "butch mystique" in the African-American community among queer women. Is there something butch about getting tattoos? For men I think the answer is yes. For women, I am not sure. At any rate, there is a real draw to toughness--especially in American culture. Butch is another word for animus is it not? Perhaps many people--both men and women--are trying to get in touch with their animus. Many men, especially, get tattoos to show their friends how macho they are. Ironically, I am told by tattoo artists that the more macho types who get tattoos are the first ones to throw up and pass out! Talk about the crisis of masculinity!!

Clinton Sanders (1989) declares that the power of tattoos, like graffiti, is "primarily derived from its ability to outrage members of conventional society" (p. 162). I do not know if the right phrase here is "outrage" society but rather 'shock'. Some do like to shock others for complex psychological reasons. Shocking someone is a way of saying 'look at me.' Shock is a way of getting attention for sure. Some academics like to shock as well. Here I am thinking of Peter McClaren and bell hooks who both shock readers in different ways. They certainly get your attention.

Maybe some people who get tattoos were ignored as children and are trying to fix psychic invisibility. No longer allowing "civilization" to dictate and command, those who get tattoos become, as Deleuze and Guattari (2002) put it, "animal" (p.232). The more animal we become the more we shock. Becoming animal means re-turning to our roots, returning to our primal selves. Human beings are animals are they not? Most have forgotten this and this is one of the reasons the ecosphere is such a mess. We have managed to separate nature from human nature in order to destroy it. But by destroying nature we are actually destroying ourselves.

ARCHETYPAL BODYART EDUCATES

Jim Garrison (1997), in his interesting book titled *Dewey and Eros*, states

> We become what we love. Our destiny is in our desires, yet what we seek to possess soon comes to possess us in thought, feeling, and action. That is why the ancient Greeks made the education of eros, or passionate desire the supreme aim of education. (xiii)

The archetypal tigers are what I love. I have become Tiger. Their color fascinates, enlivens; they give me energy and light. The tigers sadden too. They remind me that they are here to fight the negative spaces, the wounds, the damage. They are both shadow and light, they are anima and animus. They are my desire. They are my performance.

I have left something of my old self behind. The world of wellness will never be again. Now I am living in an after-place of illness surrounded by tigers. Tigers adorn my body.

It is said of Frida Kahlo--who suffered from a chronic back injury-- that she dressed elaborately as a sort of death ritual. She dressed-over her wounded body to adorn the mess. Carlos Fuentes (2001) remarks that,

> The clothes of Frida Kahlo were, nevertheless, more than a second skin. She said it herself: "They were a manner of dressing for paradise, of preparing for death." (p. 23)

Kahlo's clothes were elaborate, she was always bedecked with jewels and surrounded by animals, monkeys. Kahlo understood what animality was and why it was important for her to be immersed in animality. Her paintings tell the tale, many of them are self portraits with monkeys. Dressing up for death is a very interesting idea. Death is an occasion when one should dress up. Death should be a celebration as it is for the Second Liners in New Orleans. When one celebrates one dresses up. I think Kahlo had it right.

Bodyart is more than a second skin; it too is a death ritual. When one crosses over that psychic threshold, when one gets the first tattoo, the old self is no more. Tattoos go with you to the grave. Clothes do not. Tattoos do not wipe off the skin; they are deeply etched into the skin so when you are buried you are buried with your tattoos. Death and life should be celebrated and tattoos are a way of celebrating both. I do not mean to romanticize death and I certainly do not mean to say that any kind of death should be celebrated. Freud talked about two kinds of death(s). Naturally dying from within is one kind. This kind of death should be celebrated because it is a natural part of the life cycle. The second kind of death about which Freud talked was that of murder or accident (in his case he was particularly afraid of train accidents). Murders and accidental deaths are not celebratory but tragic.

THE ILLUSTRATED LIFE

When I was a child, my favourite book was Ray Bradbury's (2001b) *The Illustrated Man.* I can remember very clearly reading and re-reading this novel about a man covered in tattoos. These tattoos told stories, these tattoos came to life; these tattoos were of animals, people, they were of evil and good, they were scary and the whole thing. As a child, nothing delighted me more than reading *The Illustrated Man.*

The narrator of Bradbury's (2001b) tale says,

> Each illustration is a little story. If you watch them, in a few minutes they tell you a tale. In three hours of looking you could see eighteen or twenty stories acted right there on my body, you could hear voices and think thoughts (p.4).
> . . . . [H]e was a riot of rockets and fountains and people, in such intricate detail and color that you could hear the voices murmuring small and muted, from the words that inhabited his body. When his flesh twitched, the tiny mouths flickered, the tiny green-and-gold eyes winked, the tiny pink hands gestured. (p. 3)

Marvellous prose for a child. What incredible imagination. Bradbury comments in many of his essays that his own stories surprise him. He is often surprised by what he writes, or what writes him. That is what stories should do.

Like good fiction, bodyart surprises and tells stories. Living the illustrated life, the illustrated body, is a way to tell your story. When people ask, why tigers? The narrative begins. Bodyart is deeply psychological. We want our stories told; these stories are driven by the unconscious. The unconscious has some need to tell stories. Children love bedtime stores; adults love stories too but we call adult stories biographies or autobiographies. What is reality TV if not storytelling? Art, says the composer Ned Rorem (2000), "is a retention of childhood not a return to childhood" (p. 280). Storytelling--as an artform--is a "retention" of childhood indeed. In many ways we have never left childhood, it is always there in that archaic sense. Telling stories through pictures, or images, is very popular in youth culture. Today we live in a mostly visual culture, a culture of images. Children spend more time playing video games than reading. Children love to watch cartoons; adults love to watch movies. Films are probably the most popular artform in American culture. What is film if not a turn to images? And the point of film is to tell a story. Good film is an art.

Art (whether defined as fine art or trash) can be experienced mystically. Here I am thinking of Rothko's powerful paintings installed at the Rothko Gallery in Houston. There is something mystical about standing before these giant canvasses of pure color. There is something about color which is numinous. Color draws one in. Perhaps this is because bodily auras are also colorful. We are colorful creatures. Color is part and parcel of who we are. It is no wonder that we are drawn to color because it is part of our animality.

There are exceptions here though. I am thinking of the colorblind. Their world is mostly seen in grey. What must it be like to not see color? This is an impossible thing to imagine for those who do see color. Perhaps the colorblind would be most attracted to black and white tattoos. There is something very profound about black and white.

There are those who are blind. What must that be like? Oliver Sacks (1997; 2000; 2007) deals with many of these difficult ontological questions from a neuroscientific perspective. He suggests that many people who are colorblind or blind turn to the auditory. The auditory becomes more developed—sometimes—in those who are blind or colorblind and that is why many of these people become musicians. Conversely, many musicians who suffer injury and can no longer play become visual artists, painters or poets (Sacks, 1997; 2000). The brain, as Sacks points out, is amazingly plastic. The brain compensates for losses in the most amazing ways. The brain is a site of tremendous mystery and power.

The body is a site of power. The body is both negative and positive power. It is the site of healing, or the site of a refusal to heal; it is the power of pain, the power of feeling, the power of seeing, of hearing, of touching.

The power of the body in pain. When the body pains, it feels heavy. This heaviness forces one to remember that psyche is embodied. Illness forces one to BE in the body, to BE the body, to be educated by the body, to teach through the ill body.

Intellectualization is a defence mechanism that allows one to escape emotions. It seems natural to intellectualize the wounded body as a way to not deal with it psychologically. But if one allows oneself to live in the body, rather than detached from it, the body has things to teach. Pain returns Psyche to her embodied self. Pain forces one to live squarely as body, in the body. Pain allows an exploration of interiority, of inner spaces that are often ignored or explained away. Pain forces one to move inward. The body teaches through pain that the interior life needs tending, attention and tending to. The body teaches through pain that it needs care, as Psyche needs care.

ARCHETYPAL PATTERNS, PAIN AND THE MYSTICAL

Archetypal patterns are found in interiority. When patterns appear on the skin they mirror what is always already in psychic interiority. Many scholars disconnect from their bodies because their scholarly work comes from the intellect only. Of course intellect and emotion cannot be separated out from each other, but still intellectual work is primarily the work of the intellect. Intellectual work is so natural for me because I have always tended to live in my head. But intellectual work must be embodied, emotional, intuitive and grounded in the senses. That is what I am trying to accomplish in this book. For the first time, I am writing a book with my whole body, not just my intellect. To try to capture something phenomenologically and psychically one must think not only with one's head but from one's embodied being. Working from the gut, as it were, is a difficult task. Pain is felt in the gut. Writing pains.

Seeing colors within psychic interiority might seem insane, but I think not. Close your eyes—if you are not colorblind or blind that is-- and you will see colors, not just of black but of flashings. Sometimes fractal-like patterns appear. Fractal-like patterns are not dissimilar to mandalas. Fractal-like patterns are not only found in the larger cosmos, but also in the cosmos of our bodies. Fractals are very colorful and so too are patterns visualized in mystical experience. A natural reaction to pain is to close the eyes. When the eyes are closed, psyche amplifies colors within. Pain lends itself toward the mystical, the spiritual. I do not mean to romanticize pain however. Yet, there is some connection between great discomfort and the mystical. Mystical experiences, although private, can be communicated and shared with others, even if others do not have similar experiences. In Philip Wexler's (1996) interesting book, *Holy Sparks: Social Theory, Education and Religion*, he states that mystical experiences help to move beyond what he calls "socially petrified energies" (pp. 17-18). Wexler states,

> The value of innerworldly mysticism is not in a permanent silence, an anti-educational non transmissibility, but in its recollection and recentering of presently socially petrified energies. (pp. 17-18)

Likewise, recognizing mystical patterns in our everyday world(s), (in the workaday world(s) of scholarship and teaching) moves us beyond what Wexler terms "presently socially petrified energies." Stultified writing and teaching--being stuck, or repressed, or caught up in webs of transference-- kills. The mystical spirit needs to be released. Perhaps this is what Maxine Greene (1995) means when she talks of "releasing the imagination." Releasing energy from within sets free-- not only imagination--- but also *painful* imagination. Experiencing pain allows one to *feel* animality. James Macdonald (1995) talks about the importance of feeling, thought and imagination as avenues to becoming fully human. In *Theory as a Prayerful Act*, Macdonald (1995) states,

> To be open in thought--fluent, flexible and original, and open in affect--experiencing the potential of feelings in an activity; and open in perception--

meeting the potential stimuli in the world: these are the ways to maximize development of human potential. (p. 20)

To be fluid, to be open to affect also means to be open to pain, the pain that illness brings. To be open to experience means feeling it all, going into the pain. Problems begin when one fights the pain. Rather, one must go with it, be with it, experience it. Visualize the pain, see it in *Technicolor*, see it in all its deep reds and blacks, blues and purples. Tattoos write that pain on the skin, they etch pain into skinmemory.

Life is not linear, it is cyclical, there is no progress in illness, only cycles of pain and healing, pain, deterioration and integration, healing and deterioration. Things move laterally, backward, down and up, all over the place, radiating here and there jaggedly. Jim Garrison (1997) tells us that for John Dewey, "all experience . . . displays the rhythm of integration, disintegration, and aesthetic reintegration" (p. 17). These movements could also describe the course of chronic illness. There is no final getting better, the dis-ease is always creeping around inside. It is easy to live in the good times, in the times of no-pain, in the times of relative health, but the real test of character comes in times of pain. How to make something out of one's pain. How to be with the pain, live in the pain. How to make use of the pain. It is what one does with the pain that tells the tale. Pain can be used in generative ways. When one is in pain, artistic expression is ripe. As a matter of fact, without pain-- whether it is physical or psychological--there is little artistic expression. I cannot think of a happy artist. Many suffer from depression. Depression is yet another form of pain. Pain gives us new things to think about. As William James (1998) says, "experience is a process that continually gives us new material to digest" (p. 208).

The road less travelled is the one where we meet unwelcomed guests. Illness is an unwelcomed guest, illness is an intruder. Turning illness into images is the work of creative artists. The more imaginative one is the better one might be able to cope. Turning illness into art is a form of integrating it into psyche. There is a certain madness in embracing pain. Pain is madness. Jack Kerouac (1957) says,

> the only people for me are the mad ones, the ones who are mad to live, mad to talk, mad to be saved, desirous of everything at the same time, the ones who never yawn or say a commonplace thing, but burn, burn, burn like fabulous yellow roman candles exploding like spiders across the stars. . . . (p. 8)

Illness makes you mad, like exploding spiders. Illness makes you "burn, burn, burn" with life. Eros is on fire when thanatos burns. For some, the nearer to death, the more intense eros becomes. A certain urgency is at hand when one walks on the precipice of death. The urgency to write, to teach, to live become heightened under the sign of illness. Life isn't a dead place, but a lively place, yes? When death is integrated into life, life becomes livelier.

Life should be like a carnival. A character in Ray Bradbury's (1997) *Something Wicked This Way Comes*, says

> A carnival should be all growls, roars like timberlands stacked, bundled, rolled and crashed, great explosions of lion dust, men ablaze with working

anger, pop bottles jangling, horse buckles shivering, engines and elephants. . . .
(p. 51)

Life should be all growls, roars, buckles, tigers and elephants. The desiring,
performing, colorful tattooed body is, in a way, a carnival. It is, as Angela Carter
(2003) tells us, a "polychromatic unfolding" (p.15). This polychromatic unfolding
and the carnival of life are not all light however. Under the shadow of the object
are growls and roars. Deborah Britzman (1998) points out in her book, *Lost
Subjects, Contested Objects: Toward a Psychoanalytic Inquiry of Learning*, that
for psychoanalyst D.W. Winnicott, anger and aggression-- animal growls-- are
what we need to be educated about. Britzman (1998) remarks,

> Analyst D. W. Winnicott would continue to explore Freud's insights into the
> importance of the individual's capacity to acknowledge the dynamics of
> internal aggression. The beginning of education, for Winnicott, would reside
> in that strange tension between construction and destruction. . . . Winnicott
> relates that capacity to tolerate the vicissitudes of one's own destructive
> impulses to the question of education. . . . (p. 53)

Psyche is bent on destroying itself; this is the aim of thanatos. The aim of
education should be, at least in part, an attempt to understand the negative as well
as the positive. The aim of a psychoanalytic education should be to grapple with
what we do not want to grapple with--rage, growls, pain. Like stars, we are born;
explosions birth stars. We have potential explosions going on within us all the
time. It is to the explosions that we should turn. One of the interesting things about
body modification is that it can alleviate aggression. Tattooing is like blood letting.
When the needles do their work it hurts. But there is something about the ordeal of
sitting through hours of pain. Needles release bottled up aggression. Cutters often
tell therapists that they feel release when they cut. This is the same theory behind
acupuncture. The talking cure also releases negative energy. There is a sense of
great relief in talking about rage or suicidal ideation. Once talked about those
feelings tend to go away. Hence, the magic of psychoanalysis.

Psychoanalysis is the cutting of words. The first cut is the deepest.

What is that the ill body attempts to teach? Illness is aggressive, it is all growls,
it is insidious, it is sadism. There seems to be no stopping it. It happens, it grows, it
changes, it mutates, it destroys. How to live with illness more philosophically. To
be fully alive, in all the destruction. Illness teaches one to be more attuned to inner
workings. Being a good patient means paying attention to what the body is trying
to teach. Paying attention to pain, sometimes also alleviates it.

Like the good patient, the good scholar--as William F. Pinar (2004) says--

> must listen to one's silences, observe the shadows among which one moves.
> One must identify the ghosts who haunt us now; one must "talk back" to
> oneself as well as to those who will listen. Theory so understood becomes a
> passage out of the knotted present. . . . (pp. 126-127)

Ah yes, theorizing is a passage out of stultification. Theorizing melts frozen repressions. Theorizing the body offers a way out from underneath the shadow of the object, a passage out of the Oedipal drama, a passage out of childhood, a passage out of the tyrannical schoolhouse of the mind, a passage out of the sadistic superego.

Bodyart is a curriculum vita; a lifestory, a herstory. Bodyart is inscribed as aesthetic text. But living aesthetically means living *in* both the ugliness of deterioration as well as living *in* the 'sense of beauty'--as Santayana (2006) might have put it. Here I emphasize the word 'in.' I want to suggest that really living is living inside things. If I say that you are really into your art, I mean that you live inside of it. If I say that you are really into your teaching, I mean that you are living inside of your teaching. Being outside of yourself—metaphorically—might have several meanings. To say, I am beside myself might mean one thing; to say, I am emotionally distanced from my art or from my teaching means something else entirely. The aloof and distant artist or teacher stands apart from her work in a way. Somehow this has a bad ring to it.

Teaching aesthetically means teaching the gamut. Britzman (1998) points out that

> pedagogy might provide the strange study of whose feelings break down, take a detour, reverse their content betray understanding, and hence study whose affective meanings become anxious, ambivalent, and aggressive. (p. 84)

People who do not feel much, people who are dead to life, who are dead to the world, cannot possibly understand what Britzman is talking about. They simply do not live in the chaotic swirl of affect and intellect. Illness can change that. Illness, if one is attuned to it, makes one live in the swirl. I do not mean to romanticize illness, as I've previously stated. Illness doesn't make one a better person. One has got to make serious choices when one is ill-- to either live fully or die while alive. I've chosen to live at the extremes of thanatos and eros. My pedagogy and scholarship reflect this choice. The point is that making choices can change the ways in which one experiences things.

Writing this testimony is an opening to a world; teaching is an opening to a world. James Macdonald (1995) argues "[c]urriculum, it seems to me, is the study of what should constitute a world for learning and how to go about making that world" (p. 137). A world includes: pain, aggression, epiphanal experiences, art, music, noise, rage, color, shapes, forms, stars , tigers, elephants and illustrated men, the books of childhood, the ghosts, bodyart, the music that turns one around, cellos. Red, gray and black, love and hate. The world of affect and intellect, the world of pedagogy and scholarship, the world of text, text as world. A world is a site of deep interpretation and deep interiority. A world is made up of place, space and time. We can choose to translate this world or not. Translating deep interiority is one way out of the stultifying silence of solipsism. Translating interiority is an ethical task when the body has something to teach others. It is an ethical imperative to translate and interpret illness, to tell of it, to allow the body to teach us so that we may teach about illness through the body of illness. What a body of work illness provides. A library of work.

What happens when a teacher or scholar expresses herself? To express well is to become an artist. If scholarship is an art-form, if teaching is an art- form, then both scholar and teacher express themselves well. Composer Ned Rorem (2000) argues that, "an artist, having said something, has really found a form in which to say it. Many great ones spend their lives repeating themselves in different *colors* [emphasis mine]" (p. 95). Musicians, painters, body artists, doctors, therapists, teachers, scholars--if they are any good at their professions--express themselves in good form. Speaking well is speaking in good form. A flatfooted teacher is not teaching well. She has no form around which to shape her words. A flatfooted doctor does not heal well. Something remains unformed in his diagnosis. A body artist who is no good messes up the skin with ink blobs. Let us not teach in ink blobs, let us not write in ink blobs. Let us write a symphony driven by well formed animal spirits.

Animals, like spirits, do not travel single file through life. Animals roam in packs and sometimes digress. When wolves roam looking for prey, sometimes they get off track. Wolves digress. Lived experience is a pack experience--we do live in communities--and communities digress. Lived experience is one huge digression, nothing is straightforward; life is a huge zig zag. Ray Bradbury (1996a) comments:

> For let's face it, digression is the soul of wit. Take philosophic asides away from Dante, Milton or Hamlet's father's ghost and what stays is dry bones. Lawrence Stone said it once: Digressions incontestably are the sunshine, the life, the soul of reading! Take them out and one cold eternal winter would reign in every page. (p. 179)

Illness-- like teaching and scholarship-- is one big digression. From what do we digress? We digress from anger, black holes, spiders in space, psychological vacuums, depressions, angst, ghosts, creeps. We are like the illustrated man who tells millions of stories.

There are millions of stories to tell. And some of these stories aren't very nice. Education should be about the negative stories. Let me list a few not nice stories here.

Little Red Riding Hood. Deconstruct that for a moment.

Or, how about children feeding their parents to lions. Bradbury writes this story in his *Illustrated Man*.

Melanie Klein (1946) tells stories about aggression. These are (psychoanalytic) stories about children who fear that their mothers will kill them. These stories are not very nice.

Or, stories about rocketmen who never come back to earth. (sing along with Elton John and David Bowie). I am thinking of the space shuttle that blew up.

And then there are teaching stories.

Robert Coles (2004) book called *Teaching Stories* deals with mean children. Children can be very mean to each other. When does discourse about education deal with the meanness of children? Maybe we need to have more discussions about third graders—third graders?-- who plot to kill their teacher. This is a true story that happened in Georgia not too long ago.

Mary Aswell Doll (1995) writes about the need to get rid of nice. There is something about nice that is very disturbing.

And then there are stories of illness. Illness is never nice. Illness never makes for a nice story.

The aim of education, I believe, is to de-center the nice story. The aim of education might be about telling stories that aren't very nice. Illness de-centers the story of a life. Here I disagree with James Macdonald (1995) who argues that "the aim of education should be a centering of the person in the world" (p.86). Especially when one is ill, there is no center, the center simply won't hold. The ground shakes, sometimes there is no ground, there is only vertigo.

What kind of pedagogy is groundless and shaking? Pedagogy should un-nerve. Pedagogy should shatter centers. Centering gives one the impression of certainty and clarity. There is no certainty in an uncertain world, in a world that has been torn apart by illness. All there is is raw experience; experience that is hard to digest. Sometimes one can't digest it at all. Ill people stand in the de-centered realm of non-time. This de-centeredness and experience of non-time and extreme visions of color are a result of feeling de-centered in a non-time.

Jim Garrison (1997) argues that a "good education brings out the best in us. It holistically unifies our character in judgment, compassion, and practice." (p.2). Maybe a good education also also brings out *the worst* in us. It brings out anger and resentment; it brings out aggression and hostility.

Being well-rounded means being open to all the colors and shades of lived experience including the mad colors, the messy colors, the colors that cloud vision. Being well-rounded means being open to the color of non-color, being open to see things the way the colorblind might see things. Being well rounded also means being open to the world of the blind and the deaf. To not see and not hear are other ways of being that demand our attention and thought. Too often these are left out of the curriculum. To live in a world without color and without sound is to live otherwise. Our special interest in curriculum studies turns on worlds that are otherwise.

We are falling forever into other worlds we do not understand. And yet we must try to understand. Are we forever disintegrating like falling stars? Are we falling and rising simultaneously? Are we black and blue and pink and yellow and exploding tiger fish? Let us live madly, as Dr. Jeckel and Mr. Hyde, Professor Tar and Dr. Fether. Let us live fully as if we worked for a carnival.

Bodyart should be a carnival of life. Bodyart educates for fullness of Being in the midst of a de-centered existence. Bodyart, like any other kind of art, educates in shadow and light. Maxine Greene (1995) argues that art,

> may radiate [pain can radiate too] through our variously lived worlds, exposing the darks and the lights, the wounds and the scars and the healed places, the empty containers and the overflowing ones, the faces ordinarily lost in the crowd. (pp. 28-29)

When one gets tattooed, pain radiates. Radiating pain is a strange phenomenon. Radiating art is a strange phenomenon. Radiating pedagogy is a strange phenomenon. Drinking a cup of coffee is a strange phenomenon. Looking at colors is a strange phenomenon. And that is the point about bodyart; it is a strange phenomenon. Isn't it strange that people want to paint their bodies and pay for it in pain? The strangeness that is life is not centered anywhere; it is de-centered in radiated Being. Being radiates-out from nowhere, like exploding stars in space. Kenneth Patchen (1941) puts it this way:

> as the emerald thread unwinds from the angry spool of sea, trailing fever-mists above the world, in fog, in night, in death-cries, in velvet moaning of gulls; so do we, in our little place friendless, without faith, companioned by phantoms, go across this dismal frontier, unwound from the secret womb to a damnation profound. . . . (p. 127)

Existence radiates out of the "emerald thread", out of the "angry spool of sea", out of "trailing fever mists." Life is poesis radiated. Life is becoming is radiating. And sometimes radiating means trauma. Radiating pain is traumatic and frightening. Life is trauma. We live trauma.

Bodyart illustrates our deepest psychic burdens spreading like grease-stains over our thin skins, because let's face it we are thin-skinned when it comes to the tough issues of educating young people, to educating ourselves about our fears and revelations. Education--like therapy-- should begin in radiated spaces, in the spaces between the green slime of the stomach and the black haze of cloud mist over head. Being educated and going through psychoanalysis means going back down into interiority, back to those primal spaces, back to the archetypes of the soul, back to childhood, in order to arrive at futurity. James Hillman (2004) argues conversely that depth psychology is about looking at our lives backwards, starting with old age—if we are old. He suggests that we understand our lives better not from childhood on but from old age looking backwards. The aim(s) of education might be to look at life backwards. The pillar of salt story is really a lie. The aim of education concerns also packs of wolves and tigers-for they too walk backwards.

KENNETH PATCHEN, FRIDA KAHLO: ARTISTS AND THEIR PAIN

Thinking about illness has made me curious about how others, especially artists, have lived with their pain. How do artists continue to create when their lives are a complete mess? Here I will briefly look to Kenneth Patchen and return to Frida Kahlo to try to better understand how these artists remained creative while suffering debilitating illnesses. Kenneth Patchen's back was out of whack. To make things worse his doctors carelessly dropped him on the floor. He was virtually crippled for most of his adult life. Patchen (2000) suffered unbearable back pain. He states,

> The pain is almost a natural part of me now--only the fits of depression common to the disease, really sap my energies and distort my native spirit--

[handwritten margin note: ⊛ isn't that when art is powerful?]

The sickness of the world probably didn't cause mine, but it certainly conditions my handling of it. Actually the worst part of it is that I feel that I would be something else if I weren't rigid inside with the constant pressure of illness. . . . I would be purer, less inclined to write. . . . (p. 153)

Patchen remarks on the problem of rigidity here. He suggests that it is rigidity that drives his writing.

Does illness make for rigidity? Does it make one psychologically brittle? It can. When you feel badly anything can make you snap. Tempers are short especially under the sign of exhaustion. Perceptions are out of whack. Everything can seem to be a big deal when it isn't. Illness can make you crabby. Are these symptoms of psychological rigidity? Perhaps.

Patchen's prose poems are painful to read, his characters are nuts, his writing brilliant, poignant and terribly twisted. Patchen's (1941) *The Journal of Albion Moonlight* has been one of my literary companions throughout my illness. This book has kept me company through the dark nights of my soul. The colors evoked by Albion's struggles resonate. Patchen's writing in *Albion* evokes many dark colors such as blacks and grays which are carefully shaded and nuanced. Patchen's (1941) prose poem is an epic drama unmatched. A passage of his book reads as follows:

The evening slowly turns to black stone and the hammer of God chips at the sky making stars. A child stands on the road watching us; upon her forehead the yellow brand of this plague-summer. She waves to us and her hand, like a withered, white claw, falls to the ground. . . . (pp. 1-2)

The withered hand-claw falling to the ground symbolizes illness. The animality -- as the hand turns to claw-- intrudes. The hand falling to the ground is akin to falling in a dream. Forever falling is a symptom of Psyche gone mad, Winnicott teaches. God chips away at the sky, as the yellow-plague of illness daunts. God chips away at your body as you continue to fall to pieces. The plague-- inside the body-- chips away at the organs creating webs and rings, strictures and black holes. The child inside withers, curling up her paws. God chips away at the organs.

Patchen's message is black and gray, finely shaded. He writes his text in pencil, scratching things out as he goes, making huge black marks on the page. He draws black and white pictures all over his text; maybe they are doodles. These pictures look like mandalas, sacred circles, archetypal pictures of pain. The opening paragraph of Patchen's (1941) *Albion* reads as follows:

The angel lay in a little thicket. It had no need of love; there was nothing anywhere in the world could startle it--we can lie here with the angel if we like; it couldn't have hurt much when they slit its throat. (p. 1)

They might as well have slit Patchen's throat when the doctors dropped him on the floor. The angel's throat is slit as the patient's life is dashed. Like a patient etherized. Shades of Eliot. Readers are not ready for this shocking passage. Patchen shocks you into reading. This is exactly how serious illness works: it shocks you into dying. One day you wake up, feel a bump on your arm, in a month you are dead. Life gets dashed just like that.

I am reminded of John Gunther's (2007) *Death Be Not Proud*. This is one of the saddest stories I've ever read. The story of the boy who dies is told from the father's perspective. What is shocking is that it all happened so fast. As a reader, you cannot believe that the boy dies so quickly. Things snowballed down hill very fast, with lightening speed almost. This is part of the reason the book is so sad. The reader just cannot believe how death can steal away a child within months, days, or moments. This angel-boy's throat was metaphorically slit. Few books make me cry, but this one is a real drencher.

Back to Kenneth Patchen. What amazes is that Patchen kept writing; he kept working even while invalided. He worked and he worked; he wrote some 30 plus books. Maybe it was the illness that drove him to write so much. Illness does funny things to you. Are we more productive when our lives are threatened? Maybe. Larry Smith (2000) explains.

> As though Patchen were speaking over the wounded body of his world, his engaged vision and stance echo that of William Blake, Heinrich Heine, of Emerson and Thoreau in its openness to wonder and its brave frankness. (p.175)

I wouldn't exactly compare Patchen to Thoreau and Emerson. They were so tame in comparison.

Indeed, the wounded world of the body. When the body is wounded it becomes the world, the world becomes heavy, prodding, deliberative, chalky, green. Through the green muck, ex-pressing the muck, ex-pressing the pain, ex-pressing the wounds, licking the wounds. Pressing out the wounds. It is as if the wounded body needs to speak, it needs to teach. Teaching through the ill body. The body has something in mind when teaching.

The interesting thing about Patchen's work is that it brings to mind what many of us in the field of curriculum studies do. We work across the disciplines (like education and psychoanalysis) to break down walls and push back boundaries of thought. Likewise, Larry Smith (2000) says of Patchen,

> What he was working on from the 1950's onward was a synthesis of the various arts. Always denying false boundaries between peoples and art forms, he moved from this 1940's experiment at blending prose and poetry, fable and poem, drawing and poetry, into the fuller 1950's synthesis of the prose poem, jazz drama, poetry-jazz, and finally to the picture-poem. (p. 222)

Was it his illness that allowed him to break through boundaries? Or would Patchen have done this anyway? Illness makes one think differently, not better, but differently. Some things take on meaning where other things fade. Things change, things become more pointed and urgent. The child with withered hand-claws writes a painful narrative of illness, of pain unimaginable. Breaking open psychic spaces. One is no longer the professor -- as Jack London (2003) puts it --"broken on the wheel of . . . subservience" (p. 479). One is now the professor, poet, writer, analyst, storyteller. While walking through the valley of near-death, gracious submission will not do. One is called by the wild and to the wild.

Patchen was called by his wild-psychic-energy to mix up genres, mix up what might be thought unacceptable. After reading Patchen, one might begin to wonder what constitutes prose? What constitutes a poem? What constitutes a drawing? What does it mean when these genres are blurred? What does it mean when a man speaks of his pain vis-à-vis violent imagery? Yes, in places Patchen's prose is violent. Angels getting their throats slit? Illness is vile, violent. The northland is a violent country of devouring frostbite, angry tigers, wolves.

Like Patchen, Frida Kahlo suffered a lifetime of illness. She became crippled from a terrible streetcar accident. Kahlo's self portraits depict twisted, manglings. Hearts bleeding and wasting bodies. Always, though, these mangling are monkey-ed up and flower-ed up. I am thinking here of Schreber's (2000) 'miracled up' hallucinations.

Kahlo's art is polychromatic. She, like Patchen, entered the space of the numinous. Like Patchen, Kahlo's art confuses genres. She delves into fantasy, reality, earth, wind and fire; she paints fable, poem, monkey, bleeding hearts, herself. Kahlo's work is the real and the fantastic in one. It is magically real. It is magical realism. Carlos Fuentes (2001) comments that

> A glance at her art tells us the truth: Frida Kahlo was a natural pantheist, a woman and an artist involved in the glory of universal celebration, an explorer of the interrelatedness of all things, a priestess declaring everything created as sacred. Fertility symbols--flowers, fruit, monkeys, parrots--abound in her art, but never in isolation; always intertwined with ribbons, necklaces, vines, veins, and even thorns. (p.21)

Kahlo's vision moves. What I especially love about Kahlo's work is the way she depicts herself always surrounded by animals. I identify with this on many levels.

My dogs are like Kahlo's monkeys. I would have monkeys and tigers and zebras if I could. I would have a Husky farm if I could. Looking into the eyes of my Huskies is like looking into the *anima mundi*, the soul of the world. Jungians speak of anima as animating the world. Deleuze and Guattari (2002) speak of "becoming animal" (p. 239). Becoming animal always "involves "a pack" (p. 239).

"Virginia Woolf experiences herself not as a monkey or a fish but as a troop of monkeys, a school of fish"(Deleuze and Guattari, 2002, p. 289). What could Deleuze and Guattari mean by this? I have no clue! Packs.

Kahlo's paintings are of troops of monkeys. Perhaps Kahlo's psyche is a trope of animals, a trope of *anima mundi*. Perhaps all of our psyches are tropes of troops, of packs.

Illness comes in packs.

CHAPTER 5

THE BODY SPEAKS THROUGH ITS ANIMALITIES

For Jungians, the psyche is multifaceted. The psyche is not only burdened by King Oedipus or Queen Electra. The psyche is a many-faced menagerie. Like the Jungians, novelist Hermann Hesse's (2001) character Steppenwolf says, "this is the doctrine of the thousand souls. Every day new souls keep springing up . . . making clamorous demands and creating confusion" (p. 151). Many souls. Is this not what our dear Dr. Daniel Paul Schreber (2000) describes in *My Nervous Illness*? Psyche is made up of monks, monkeys, angels, demons, daemons, horses, gods and goddesses, minotaurs, monsters. These are our complexes. The body speaks through these animalities. Everything is animal. The human-ness of the body disappears in animal claws, the withering claws of the child. Jung (1977) says, "[t]he anima also has affinities with animals, which symbolize her characteristics. Thus she can appear as a snake or a tiger or a bird." (p. 200). Tigers speak through the ill body, protect the ill body and empower the ill body. The bodysoul speaks in animal voices, animal shapes and animal colors.

Carlos Fuentes (2001) suggests that Frida Kahlo honored her animality. "She would love to see lions come out of bookshelves instead of books" (p. 14). The terrible facts of her suffering forced he to get in touch with the animality of her imaginative soul. Sarah Lowe (2001) reports that,

[A]n awful progression--regression-- is unmistakable, as Kahlo faces the loneliness and terror of her illness. Even as a child, she was familiar with the role of patient. She contracted polio when she was seven years old; eleven years later she had a near fatal accident and suffered a broken spine, collar and pelvic bones, crushed right leg and feet. Kahlo's chronic pain, however, and her encasement and plastic casts for months at a time, the trophic ulcers she suffered on her right foot (which led to its amputation shortly before her death), and roughly 35 operations. . . . [made up the bulk of her existence] (p. 29).

It takes a tremendous amount of animal spirit and strength to work through the wrecked body. Kahlo's work is clearly a testament to greatness. She is one of the most talented painters of our time. She was clearly a genius, as was Patchen. Both artists used their illness as grist for their work. Both crossed thresholds, mixed genres, broke the rules, broke boundaries, broke ground. Both left marks on the art world forever. Both had an animal spirit. Neither of them gave up. Both Patchen and Kahlo taught through their ill bodies.

POST (SCRIPT)

Thinking more about bodyart and art in general, I wonder more about the connection between aesthetics and mysticism. People tend to get tattooed during a crisis in their lives. That crisis--at least for me--was my illness. That crisis also drove me deeper into a strange interiority that I was not able to flesh out at the time that I initially wrote the first part of this chapter. I remember thinking that when I decided to get tattooed I crossed a line. I could not articulate what that line was, but it was some kind of psychic line that I had never crossed before. For me, getting tattoos was a mystical experience. The symbolism of the tattoos gave my illness meaning. These tigers on my arms suggest inner strength and eros, a strong life force. Underneath that life force was a darkness, a spiritual darkness that I could not articulate. So here I would like to try to articulate those connections between art, mysticism and illness in order to get at this third term--the mystical. The third term is missing in the initial writing because it was missing from my conscious mind. Now that much time has passed, I better understand the ways in which aesthetic and mystical experience are linked and the ways in which illness allows one to explore a dark theology, or what is called the *via negativa.*

Art gets enfleshed--tattooed--onto and into the body. What that artform signifies becomes all important when deconstructing meaning. I felt that I needed power and that I needed help from a tiger-like force. So tigers are enfleshed on my arms. Tiger strength is a dark strength, a wrestling with woundedness. Since I had no way of articulating this experience from a theological perspective at the time I was tattooed, I had no way of making connections theoretically between art and mystical experience.

I want here to focus on bodyart as a site of mystical experience. Looking at a painting or reading poetry can also lead to the mystical, but when the artform is put into you and put on you literally the mystical becomes enfleshed. The royal road to the mystical is enfleshed. Crossing into another state of consciousness is an experience of the mystical. The feeling that I had of crossing that line was the feeling of entering into another state of consciousness. Call it madness or call it the divine. Moshe Idel (1988) puts it this way. Mysticism is an experience that "surpasses ordinary consciousness" (p. 35). One need not be a monk, saint, or Bodhisattva to experience the mystical. The mystical experience is there for those who are open to it. The problem of mystical states comes with the translation of them. It is nearly impossible to translate to someone else a mystical experience. Moshe Idel (1988) explains.

> As the components of this experience--the human psyche, the external and inner conditions, and the divine aspects that enter the experience--are either fluid or incomprehensible or both. . . . (p. 36)

Crossing a line into another state of consciousness is indeed a fluid and incomprehensible experience. For me, crossing that line served as a coping mechanism to deal with my illness. Entering into another realm--if even for a few moments-- transformed. But I do not mean this in a way that sounds trite or breezy. The transformation was not one of light but of darkness. Crossing that line enabled me to get at those tigers, to become more open to the terror and isolation that I was struggling with when I was very, very ill. I did not have a vision, I did not see the light, I did not see God, I did not see angels. What I experienced was a feeling, a feeling of Otherness, a feeling of moving deeper into myself and into a tiger state of being. The tiger is that symbol of the theology of the dark. For me the tiger is fierce and unrelenting. So too is a dark theology.

Opening up to that tiger part of psyche allowed me to go deeper into my depression. Depression is part and parcel of most illnesses, especially those of a serious and chronic nature. Depression is a serious problem in and of itself of course. For a comprehensive treatment of depression, I would recommend Andrew Solomon's (2003) *The Noonday Demon: An Atlas of Depression.* A full blown discussion of depression here goes beyond the scope of this book. Still, it is important to at least mention that depression is a related and serious problem for people who suffer illness. When depression is a result of illness it is compounded. This compounding is what mystical experience gets at. Thomas Merton (1981) addresses mysticism here.

> Essentially, mystical experience is a vivid, conscious participation of our soul and of faculties in the life, knowledge and love of God. (p. 16)

What resonates with me here is Merton's suggestion that mystical experience is a "conscious participation." I think work—as a conscious participation with or in something-- is always achieved before a mystical experience occurs. That work is both intellectual and psychological. Soul searching and contemplation is necessary before a mystical experience can occur. Paul was struck down and had his revelation-- but not before he did a lot of soul searching and thinking. Mystical experience requires a lot of work. It does not just come from a sort of hocus pocus magic.

For me—as against Thomas Merton-- the experience of the mystical has nothing to do with love or the idea of God. I have trouble with the idea of God. The idea of God--for me—disturbs. It smacks of fundamentalism and religious wars. The concept of God has caused only torment and suffering throughout the history of humankind. As against this, my thought is that the divine--that which is a mystery—is that which breathes life into us. It is not a thing, an essence or a God. Drawing on Rupert Sheldrake (1996), the divine might be conceptualized better as a mysterious field. For Sheldrake, the soul is a field, not a stand-alone thing. And this field is not anthropocentric, but it is spread throughout all of creation. Matthew Fox (1996), talking to Sheldrake in an interview says,

> You rightly put it [the soul as a field is] in a nonanthropocentric context. Not only does every individual, plant and animal have soul but mountains and places have soul. . . . (p. 83)

Soul, thus, is infused throughout creation. I like to think of soul as energy--this is the way the Greeks thought of it. Edward Casey (1991) tells us that "[s]oul for the Greeks is particularly the source of all animate movement. . ." (p. 277). And it is energy that moves things. Scientists know that energy is highly complex and so that which energies cannot be reduced to one thing. Rather than think of a single field--as does Sheldrake-- I think of soul-as-energy as a complex combination of competing fields. Energy is both chaos and order and these two moving principles of the cosmos and of the soul cannot be reduced to one cause. We live in force field(s) of competing energies.

For me, these complex life giving forces are not supernatural, but natural. I suppose my position is closest to animism or ecospirituality. All of nature is shot through with the divine-as-force--field(s). For me, the divine is a term that lends to horizontal rather than vertical thinking. I think of the the divine as horizontal energy source(s) that move all sentient and even non-sentient things. Terms such as the absolute and the infinite are as problematic as the term God because they suggest that the divine is one thing with an essence. These terms also point upward in a move of verticality toward the transcendent. Transcendence troubles. My image of a transcendent God is the patriarch who gazes from above and protects his children. The idea of the protection of a God-the-father is a deeply disturbing and psychological one. As Freud suggested--for most people-- the belief in God is merely a psychological projection of the father onto an abstraction, i.e. the Godhead. Daddy God is what most people want. Daddy God is nothing more than a wish-fantasy. And as Freud suggested this need for protection from a Daddy God is nothing more than a projection. Transcendence is a theological term loaded with sexist, misogynist and patriarchal implications. The transcendent God is the God of imperialism and conquest. This is the problem with all patriarchal monotheisms. Another problem with thinking that the divine is transcendent is that the everyday or the mundane becomes rather unimportant. The here and now under the sign of the transcendent becomes irrelevant. Martin Buber (1947/ 2002) speaks to this problem. The story goes like this: a young man comes to visit Buber. Buber's got his head in the clouds thinking of more splendid things than the here and now, thinking of the mystical as something transcendent. In Buber's early life he felt that the divine could be found in the heavens, up above the clouds. But then, after this visit by our young man, Buber had second thoughts. This young man, this troubled soul committed suicide. Buber had not paid him enough attention—or so he felt-- because his head was stuck up in the clouds of transcendence. This experience shattered Buber and because of it he re-thought his position on the divine. Buber (1947/2002) states,

> Since then [since the suicide of the young man who came to visit Buber] I have given up the "religious" [by this he means the transcendent idea of God] which is nothing but the exception, exaltation, ecstasy, or it has given me up. I possess nothing but the everyday out of which I am never taken. The mystery is no longer disclosed, it has escaped or it has made its dwelling here where everything happens. . . . (p. 17)

Buber's change in position happened only after a crisis. The misperception about most mystics is that they have their heads up in the clouds, that they do not engage in any social work with people in the here and now. An historical study of Western as well as Eastern theology proves this to be false. Many Christian mystics and ancient Mahayana Buddhists were also social activists. Mysticism does not mean that you have to give up relations with other people in the world. In fact, mystics' engagement with others intensifies because of their mystical experiences. This is certainly true for Martin Buber who believed that the divine relation of the 'I to the Thou' was all. For Buber nothing is more important than that relationship. This I-

Thou relation has many implications relevant to our study here. The teacher-student relation should be one of I-Thou. The doctor-patient relation should also be one of I-Thou. It is in the connection between the I and the Thou that one finds the mystical. Imagine thinking of the doctor-patient relation as a mystical one!

Again, my position on the mystical is that it is connected to complex and competing field of energy(s). Competing and complex forces of energy (s) are of a divine nature because they are life giving. Mystical experience simply taps into these energies. There is nothing supernatural or extraordinary about this. What becomes extraordinary is the recognition of the way in which we are shot through with such energies. Not only that, these energies move throughout all of nature. To be at one with the energies that move through us is a mystical experience. Mystical experiences are probably more common than one might think. The theological literature, however, seems to reserve the mystical for the saint, priest, or Bodhisattva. A mystical consciousness might be experienced all the time, but people fail to recognize it. Or, the fleetingness of these mystical states might be brushed off, ignored, or explained away. When encountering strange feelings, people tend to ignore that which they cannot articulate.

More often than not, people experience the mystical in times of stress. A crisis is at hand and this crisis pushes you over the edge. Falling off the face of the earth is that mystical experience. When one feels pushed over the edge, momentary madness sets in. And that madness is mysticism. Here I am not talking about the madness of psychotics; rather I am talking about the madness everyone experiences at some time in their lives. Death makes us crazy. John Didion (2005) talks about her "year of magical thinking" after her husband and daughter both died. Magical thinking is the equivalent of denial. Too much denial tends toward madness. Didion tells us that she thought her husband would be coming right back, even though he had dropped dead at the dinner table. She waited for him to come back, even though she was there when the medics came. After the autopsy, Didion tells us that she thought that if the doctors could find out what was wrong they could fix it and her husband could come back. That is why she wanted them to do an autopsy—so he could come back. This is madness. We all do this to a certain extent after experiencing trauma.

In this craziness one can become more open to that which is mystical. Death makes us crazy. A death experience opens toward the mystical. The mystical--as I said earlier-- is not light, but dark. Death is dark. Death endarkens consciousness and turns everything upside-down. In that craziness is the mystical. Getting inside of the madness is getting inside of the mystical.

Getting inside of the madness means going deeper into dark waters. The Jungians talk about this all the time. Their main concern is how to get into the dark and not run away from it. If you are going down, you need to really go down. In theology, this is not a new idea. In fact, there is an entire tradition of Christian mysticism that addresses these issues. Thomas Merton (1981) explains.

> There are, in Christian tradition, a theology of light and a theology of darkness. On these two lines travel two mystical trends. There are the great

theologians of light: Origen, Saint Augustine, Saint Bernard, Saint Thomas Aquinas. And there are the great theologians of darkness. Saint Gregory of Nyssa, Pseudo-Dionysius, Saint John of the Cross. (p. 25)

Merton also points out that there are other theologians who straddle between lightness and darkness. Buddhists might call that the middle way. My way is neither the middle way nor the way of lightness. I want to find my way in the dark. Although I am not a Christian, I certainly can relate to the dark theologies of Gregory of Nyssa, Pseudo-Dionysius and Saint John of the Cross. It is in the dark that one experiences the mystical. Crossing the line into madness is going over to a dark place, a place that is utterly terrifying. Death terrifies. Sickness toward death terrifies.

What terrifies is the sublime. That dark place might also be called the sublime. Experiencing the sublime means going deeply into terror. Standing on the edge of Bryce Canyon can be a sublime experience-- especially for those of us who have a fear of heights. I broke down at Bryce Canyon once. I temporarily lost my mind. Now that is a very strange expression. Where does the mind go when it gets lost? I lost control of my emotions and became rather hysterical. For what reason this momentary madness happened I do not know. Bryce is the most beautiful place in the United States, but it is also the most terrifying. And that is the sublime. That is also the mystical. Utterly unglued. We stand before the mystical with fear and trembling. Falling off the edge of the world psychologically is a mystical experience because consciousness shifts. It may shift for only a moment but in that shift is a fleeting feeling of the unknown and that unknown is dark. Thomas Merton (1981) tells us about one theologian of the dark, Saint Gregory of Nyssa and Nyssa's explanation of the mystical. Merton explains that for Nyssa,

> The mind must detach itself [I would call this a shift in consciousness] from sensible appearances and seek God in those invisible realities which the intellect can apprehend. And this is what we have been talking about with theoria --an intellectual form of contemplation. This darkening of the senses is like a cloud in which the soul becomes accustomed to travelling blind. (p. 50)

It is during intellectual work--theoretical work-- that senses darken. Monks call intellectual work contemplation. Scholars call it studying. Many think mysticism flighty. Kooks are spiritual. Of course there are lots of kooks who call themselves mystics. But a careful study of theological traditions--both East and West--show that the mystics who have left their mark historically were also intellectuals. Not to say that some intellectuals are not kooks. At any rate, to understand the mystical one must exercise the intellect. This is the message of many mystics. It is through study and contemplation that one gets at "invisible realities."

Mystical experience happens in psychological blind spots. The natural tendency is to ignore those blind spots and pretend that they are nothing. But the mystic knows better. An intellectual and emotional exploration of those mystical blind spots becomes necessary to unpack their significance and meaning. It is in those moments of existential crisis that one encounters the what-is. And even though study and intellectual work can open the doors of perception, ultimately the what-is cannot be known or understood or even described. The understanding that we do not understand takes intellectual work. Evelyn Underhill (1911/1990) explains that mysticism

> is final and personal. It is not merely a beautiful and suggestive diagram but experience in its most intense form. This experience in the words of Plotinus, is the soul's solitary adventure: "the flight of the Alone to the Alone". (p. 82)

Ultimately we are alone with our mystical experience. We are also alone in death. But somehow we must attempt to build a bridge between one alone and another alone, for as Martin Buber (1947/.2002) puts it "deep calls unto deep." (p. 240). The bridge of the alone to the alone is built mostly on paper. And the word became flesh. And flesh became the word. It is to the word that we turn to build bridges. Mystics who have left texts behind allow us to study and make connections to our own lives and struggles. We understand our own struggles mostly in light of studying the struggles of others. Martin Buber (1947/ 2002) knows that people's interrelations are tenuous and so too are our relations with the texts left by others. Buber says, "on the narrow ridge where the I and thou meet, there is the realm of the "between" (p. 243). The I and the Thou meet on that 'narrow ridge' historically in and through texts. Texts are our "between." Those who have not left texts behind (ironically many founders of the worlds' religions did not write anything down) can still impact generations to come. But that narrow ridge is made even more tenuous when we rely on secondary texts and hearsay to understand. And yet no matter how much study of texts we do, mystical experience eludes. Moshe Idel (1988) puts it this way.

> At its best, the mystic's testimony is a veil covering a psychic process that as such remains beyond the scope of textual studies. (p. 35)

And yet, scholars study on. Intellectual work is always already limited. Ideas, feelings, thoughts, perceptions all elude at the end of the day. Mystical experiences are made up of all these attributes and that is what makes them so complex. Idel's comment that the mystical process is but a "veil' reminds me of Keat's (1959) "vale" of soul making. Recall, he suggests that the world is a "vale of Soul-making" (p. 288). Mysticism and Soul-making are obscure ideas. These ideas are both covered over in darkness. One cannot see what one does not understand. When a veil comes over the eye--as in the case of a detached retina--one goes blind. It is to this blind experience we should turn. Emmanuel Levinas (2000) talks about experiencing the Infinite and the ways in which this experience blinds. He states,

> The Infinite then cannot be tracked down like game by a hunter. The trace left by the Infinite is not the residue of a presence; its very glow is ambiguous. (p. 12)

The idea of the trace is what interests me here. This word is useful when thinking about mystical experiences. In a momentary lapse of reason, it is a trace of "weird abundance", as Paula Salvio (2007) might put it, that is felt. The trace is full and empty simultaneously and it is weird. Shifting consciousness---even if it is for a moment--is weird. It is a weird trace. How quickly the trace disappears. The trace of the mystical vanishes. Because the glow of the trace darkens one's perceptions it terrifies. That moment of the mystical is a moment when the soul loses control. It is as if the bodymind floats, disappears, reappears, flashes, blackens, weakens and undoes. The moment of the mystical is one's undoing. Transforming into an undoing is not something easily translated. Matthew Fox (1988) explains that for Jung, mysticism

> takes us into the darkness of what Jung calls "the lavishing mother"-- the darkness of pain and doubt--and allows us to be there. (p. 61)

The mother who lavishes? Is this not sadistic? Why would a mother want to pain her children? And this is the great mystery of mysticism. It is from dark to dark, not dark to light--even though many theologians want to make this argument too. The mother--or the divine--is felt as a lavishing-- a (s)mothering of dis-content and dis-ease. It is in the break down, the un-meaning, the unmooring where religious feeling is felt. Mysticism is a dialectic that can never be resolved. It is chaotic calm. It is the unmeaning of meaning. It is as the Zen Masters teach, the face before you were born. Mysticism is akin to intuition and yet it is beyond intuition. Mysticism is the joke and it is dead serious. Mysticism is the idea that "[e]very Angel is terrible" (Rilke, 1967 p. 29). How to study these quandaries? How to make use of them? What to think of the unthinkable? I am convinced, however, that scholars must study the dark and study in the dark. As Arthur Rimbaud (1957) says, "I am the scholar of the dark armchair. Branches and rain hurl themselves at the windows of my library" (p. 13). It is to the hurled branches and falling rain that we must turn. We must sink ever deeper into the psychic abyss. As Charles Baudelaire (1982) suggests, "Pascal had his abyss, it followed him" (p. 174). Let our abysses follow us. Let us not run away from our abysses. The problem is, however, that most people are too busy to pay attention to what is going on with them. Or, they ignore symptoms. They go into a state of denial. They engage in a year or more of what Didion (2005) calls magical thinking. Rainer Maria Rilke (1962) addresses this problem. He states that

> . . . the whole so-called "spirit-world," death, all those things that are so closely akin to us, have by daily parrying been so crowded out of life that the senses which we could have grasped them are atrophied. (p. 67)

When intuition is not used, it withers and dies. When perceptions are not sharpened they become dull and useless. When thoughts are not given attention and care, they disappear. What would it be to say 'I have no thoughts?' Many people are indeed without thoughts. What must it be like to be, as T.S. Eliot put it, the hollow man? Rilke suggests that most people are little more than empty shells. Without exploring things that are "so closely akin to us" how can we explore that which is distant? The near and the far get obliterated in mechanized society. And if your soul has been obliterated, what do you do then? Meaningless lives depress. People whose lives become meaningless--more often than not--commit suicide. It is by going into the dark--not running away from it-- and making meaning out of that dark which prevents meaninglessness and suicide. It is when one refuses to go into the dark that one acts out self loathing. And being sick can make you hate yourself. The betrayal of one's body distorts and mangles one's self image. Self blame and suicidal ideation are part and parcel of being ill. What to do with suicidal ideation? Ironically, one must embrace it, allow it to breath, talk about it, think through it so that one does not act it out. This is the talking cure. But sometimes this backfires too. Some people who talk about killing themselves do.

I deliberately quoted poets here (i.e. Rilke, Rimbaud, Baudelaire) because I believe that many poets are also mystics or at least have a mystical sensibility. Poetry comes close to expressing mystical experience. Poetry captures that which is fleeting. Poetry opens small windows that serve to transform psyche. The aesthetic and the mystical--especially on the poetic register--connect. A poetic line can open a world. A single word can be profound. A stanza can yield deep meaning. This leads us to the question of the connection between mystical experience and time. I am interested in fleeting experience, in the momentary, in the line crossed in the instant, in a small move in consciousness. I want to talk about brevity. Joan Didion (2005) says it best. "Life changes fast. Life changes in the instant. You sit down to dinner and life as you know it ends" (p. 3). Didion and her husband sat down to dinner and he dropped dead. These three short lines express a most incredible profundity. Sudden death explodes your sense of certainty and interrupts all of your illusions about security and eternity. Death happens in many moments, but it is experienced as only a moment in time. Done. Death can be a horrible experience. And it certainly was for Didion. That moment of sudden change shifts consciousness. In a single moment your life changes, shifts. The experience of death is akin to the experience of the mystical. Death is what it is, it is final. That which is final is awful. The mystical is the awful.

I want to get back to thinking about the mystical as a moment in time. And this brings up issues around duration. Edward Casey (1991) talks of the connection between the soul and time and the soul in time. We can apply his comments about the soul and time to the mystical experience of the soul in time. Casey says, "time and the soul are profoundly linked, in the depths, in the interiority of each" (p. 279). A soul is a soul only in time. And time means movement as does the soul. The soul in time is always on the move. Time is not one thing for Casey. Time is "polyform" (p. 282) and so too is the soul. This polyformity is not continuous either. As against Bergson--for whom duration is continuous-- Casey says that time is "discontinuous" (p. 282). So too the soul. There are those strange moments when life seems to abruptly stop. Like the moment of another's death, where gaps and ruptures are felt. The fabric of the psyche rips in an instant. These ripped moments are felt to be discontinuities with whatever came before. The before is no longer and the after alters all. And it is in these difficult times that one needs to turn inward. Casey (1991) suggests that "taking time for soul" [allows] . . . time for attention to its afflictions. . ." (p. 279). After the wedge is driven between one time and another, one must settle down into a state of some duration to dwell on what is to come and what has already happened. Dwelling happens in at least two times at once. Duration always already gets doubled by the ghost of the past. To allow the body to speak one must live in many durations. I write this now but am commenting on the past as I write. The now and the past seemed blurred to me. The now and the past are steeped in repetition, re-vision, erasure, repression and sudden memory. Time has passed since the early days of my illness and only now do I realize that the illness made me examine connections to aesthetics and mysticism. If I hadn't gotten ill, I don't know if I could have made these connections.

SOUL-SPEAKING: THE ILL BODY

I begin this chapter in the company of Jack London (2003). He states, "[t]he three great things are: Good health; work; and a philosophy of life" (p. 466).

What if you don't have good health? How to work and how to create a philosophy of life when the body drags you down, down, down into that underworld of heaviness where the organs become larger than life, where the light of day is always under a cloud of pain. How to continue working when in the back of the mind is the reality of the fault line, the irreversibility of chronic illness.

No doubt, it is a great thing to be healthy. It is not a great thing to be ill. In the world of illness one encounters white coats, sterile environments and the constant threat of deterioration. How to work under the cloud of deterioration. Work for me means teaching and writing. Work means teaching and writing while not feeling well. Work is my survival. Without work I would crumble under the weight of my own body. Working, then, means being open to woundedness, to vulnerability. Lisa Delpit (1995) eloquently states,

> [w]e must learn to be vulnerable enough to allow our world to turn upside down in order to allow the realities of others to edge themselves into our consciousness. (p. 47)

When you are sick your world is always already upside down. The danger, however, is becoming sunk in solipsism. It is important to use illness to open out, to find the clearing spaces for conversation. Delpit's point turns on the importance of conversation with others. Entering into conversation with others makes experience social. The body is a social site of course, but when you are ill, you must become even more social via testimony. Testimony is an ethical, philosophical task. Testimony is also psychologically necessary. For without the telling of the tale in a way that speaks to others, falling forever into Hades becomes your fate. But even telling the tell tale heart (Poe, 2006) guarantees little. Sometimes telling the tale works to re-traumatize (Morris, 2001). But what other choice do we have? Say nothing? Telling the tale might be a way to help someone else cope. There is no other choice then but to write and tell the tale.

If curriculum is about educating the public, as William F. Pinar (2004) points out, then one must educate the public about what the ill body has to teach. Every experience teaches, if only one remains open to the teaching. The call to educate, the call to teach the social body beckons. The body is a complicated place to think about, for the body is a fractaled space, a space of luminousness. It sends messages.

And these messages demand interpretation. Let us develop a hermeneutics of the body. Francesca Alfano Miglietti (2003) states,

> It is the body that re-emerges under layers of symbolism and sublimations, to be exhibited, pulsating nervously, participating in a series of uncomfortable references, hidden, secret, which declare the plane of existence, the escape from totalitarianism and anonymous system of the mask, the functional gap of the bureaucracies of socially acceptable behaviors. (p.19)

Illness cuts through the mask of "properness". Pain becoming animal. Animality is not proper. Animality is primal and primal is not proper.

Something strange happens to the body when it is ill; it no longer operates under a 'totalitarian' Oedipal drama. The controls of the Oedipal drama lift. No longer the father's son or daughter; no longer the mother's son or daughter. Illness turns you into an orphan. This orphan-creature invades and in-valids. There is no getting rid of the alien creature. This alien creature torments. The voices of the parents within die because the alien creature of pain overshadows and overwhelms. Illness puts under erasure the law of the father. Every day, piece by piece, the monster of dis-ease grows larger. Is this madness?

A philosophy of life is born unto illness. A philosophy born under the shadow of illness is always already a psychology. Philosophical psychology is built on the bedrock of psyche. One of the few philosophers who believed this was William James (1890/1950a&b; 1998). He was both psychologist and philosopher. He was also deeply spiritual. Let us follow James and suggest that philosophy--if it is grounded in the psychological-- is not built on abstract systems, but on the concrete; it is built on the piecemeal and on what brings chaos. Developing a philosophical psychology springs from deep interiority. A philosophical psychology is built out of the ruins. William Ayers and Therese Quinn (2001) argue that, "[e]ducation is where we ask how we might engage, enlarge, and change our lives, and it is, then, where we confront our dreams. . ." (x). The study of education, psychology and philosophy enlarge and change our lives. A study of the body via a philosophical psychology demands a going under into the unconscious. It is a quest for understanding, a quest for aesthetic living, a quest to live every day, not tomorrow, not in summer, not for the vacation, not on trips abroad, but to live in the everyday, in the now-- making every moment count. A philosophical psychology embodies the body. It honors dreams, the hidden that becomes manifest. Secrets never to be revealed.

Living in the everyday means making meaning out of (un)meaning. Making meaning out of little things. Making meaning out of the sensuousness of teaching, the sensuousness of writing and thinking, the sensuousness of being-with-others. Ned Rorem (2000) captures a small, ordinary moment, an ordinary life-moment that is *made* sensuous by making meaning out of it. Life is made up these small moments. Rorem states (2000),

> The strangest minutes of my life have just gone by. How [to] describe in words that which words can only misshape? Soon the lights in the brownstone

across the street will twinkle through the dawn, the old man there will begin measuring coffee, as he does each morning. . . . (p. 259)

Illness teaches time-passing-- measuring coffee. Measuring coffee is like the Buddhist tea ceremony. Every sip, every pouring, every sound of drinking, every cup hitting the saucer becomes sacred. Drinking coffee is a sacred act. This is especially realized when swallowing becomes a problem. The little things we take for granted every day. Even swallowing. To be able to swallow is a gift.

Living happens in time and time is slowed down during sacred moments because one must attend, tend to psyche. Time-passing. Is the illness working its way toward deterioration? The irreversibility of time-passing. How to think the irreversible? This is the unthinkable. Irreversible moments passing are indeed strange. Because moments--like illness---are also irreversible. Time might be reversible if you have some sort of access to a black hole, then you might be able to go backwards in time. But I have not yet heard of anyone being able to do so. Perhaps in the future we will be able to access these backward time travellings. In the meanwhile, what has been will never be again. And this is strange.

It is in the strangeness that existence becomes a drama. The dog who gazes unexpectedly at you as if to speak, the phone that rings with messages from afar, the wind that blows trees down in the yard, the car that runs out of gas, the student who notices you thinking deep thoughts, the lover who leaves notes on the countertop. These are the flashes of experience. Sickness amplifies flashes. This is life. Life is not elsewhere. Life is not tomorrow. Life is not in heaven. There is no heaven. Life is not in hell. All we have is the now. One makes out of it (the now) heaven or hell. The choice is yours to make. We clearly make our own hells.

What I would like to do in this chapter is flesh out a philosophy of what I call soul speaking. Here, philosophy crosses into the territory of depth psychology. The soul is both a philosophical and psychological concept. It is rare that Freudians talk about the soul. Jungians do. Jung embraces the mystical, Freud does not.

When one is ill the soul speaks and it does so through the mystical. Jung (2002) teaches,

> Natural life is the nourishing soil of the soul. Anyone who fails to go along with life remains suspended, stiff and rigid in midair. That is why so many people get wooden in old age; they look back and cling to the past with a secret fear of death in their hearts. They withdraw from the life process, at least psychologically, and consequently remain like pillars of salt, with vivid recollections of youth but no living relation to the present. (p. 68)

Going along with life--as Jung puts it--means also going along with illness, going into it and down with it. Fighting the illness--by denying its seriousness--does little to help. Psyche weeps. Coping means going along with, not giving in to it. The fate that has been dealt is a blow. What to do with a fate that wounds? Jung points out that the elderly get "wooden" if they haven't been able to accept what is. Young people too can get "wooden." Young people can become hardened especially if illness attacks them at an early age. Becoming wooden also means being defeatist.

CHAPTER 6

Becoming wooden means freezing. Psyche becomes stone. Melancholia. Melancholia is a stony condition because one gets stuck in grief and gets frozen by it.

Jung points out that obsession with memory is also an erasure of the present. However, psyche should not collapse in presentism either. A present without a past is no present at all. It is an illusion. Writing a documentary or auto-ethnography is a good way to trace carefully and historically the stages of illness on life's way (see Kierkegaard, 1845/1972). Writing a pathography documents both present and past. Writing happens in a present even though the tale told might be of things past.

A philosophy of life, as Jack London (2003b) says, is not a system, it is not a whole, it is not a grand metanarrative. Rather, it is a mess, it is crazy, it is wounded. This woundedness demands a psychology, for that is what psychology deals with, our woundedness. Woundedness demands attention and needs to be worked on and worked through. Working through the ill body means working on it by writing about it and telling the tale. Working is what Ray Bradbury (1996) calls listening to 'morning voices.' These voices tell Bradbury to get busy, to get writing, to visit with the ghosts within. This is the task here: to get busy, to get into the everyday, to write it out. Leaving marks, traces, inscriptions, archives. Bradbury (1996b) tells us that writing out lists of words helps him craft his stories. His stories are his philosophy of life. A philosophy of storytelling. Is this not what both philosophers and psychologists do, tell stories? James Hillman (1983) might call this *Healing Fiction*. At any rate, Bradbury (1996b) tells us that he writes out lists of words to help him write. He says that,

> I found that I could provoke memories of odd notions or strange metaphors by listing my favorite nouns, though I didn't know why they were my favorite. Some of my first lists ran like this: THE NIGHT, THE ATTIC, THE RAVINE, DANDELIONS, MIDNIGHT TRAIN WHISTLES, TENNIS SHOES, BASEMENTS FRONT PORCHES, CAROUSELS, DAWN, ARRIVAL OF CIRCUSES. (vi)

Bradbury's words capture seemingly trivial things. The attic. Dandelions. Bradbury captures *trivium* -- the basics. Cracks in the sidewalk, spiders crawling up the walls, newspapers delivered late, the dog who barks at the postman. Amplified. Illness amplifies that which is trivial. There is something profound in the trivial.

Attend to the everyday, to the leaf falling from the tree, to the poem on the refrigerator, to the sideways stare of your cat, to the annoying howl of your dog. The ill body teaches the value of fleeting glances of strangers, thoughts fleeting through the head, the neighbor who pets your dogs, the other neighbor who is mean to your dogs. Making meaning and making sense. Getting into a fight with the neighbour who is mean to your dogs is part of that trivia that needs archiving. Life is made up mostly of little things. How often do we have epiphanies?

Making sense of the terrible. The terrible drags psyche down. The terrible means the negative. The negative means to negate, to negate what is, to negate life. But this negative must be worked on, not ignored or repressed.

Andre Green (1999) calls this the *work of the negative*. When Green uses this phrase, though, he is not speaking about the physical but the psychological. Still, his words apply to the physical as well. He states, "[t]he work of the negative thus comes down to one question: how, faced with the destruction which threatens everything, can a way be found for desire to live and love?" (p. 185). At bottom, the work of the negative has to do with continually finding the desire-to-desire amidst a storm of disease. When desire is gone, life is over. The dis-ease wins out. Desire, work. The desire to teach and do work spring from the desire-to-desire. Desire is both a psychological and philosophical question.

Like Bradbury, I keep lists of words in my head; I keep lists of books I want to write in my minds eye (I). I keep lists of things I want to accomplish on the back burner. I want to spend the rest of my life learning the Bach cello suites. I want my house to become a library. I keep lists of books I want to put in that library. I keep lists of people I want to thank. Gratitude is a lost art. I want to add onto the back burner, burning. Desire is like a flame. The burning is desire.

Burning words are these: CURRERE, PSYCHOANALYTICALLY, PHILOSOPHIC, ANIMAL, COLOR, SOUND, TESTIMONY, TIGER MOUNTAIN, ENO, BODYART, SHADE, STAIRWELL, NEGATIVE, COFFEE, CHOCOLATE, SOUL, BEING, BECOMING, PLACE, SPACE, TIME, EDUCARE, LOVE, EROS, THANTOS, DEATH, THE UNDERWORLD, THE UNIVERSITY, SCHOLARSHIP, PEDAGOGY, IRREVERSIBLE, DETERIORATION, DISEASE, DEPRESSION, HADES, HERMES, JUPITER, ICARUS, ARCHETYPE, NUMINOUS, MATTER-- AND OF COURSE-- SHOPPING. I think on these words, on how I can flesh them out vis-à-vis my work. Word painting. Writing is painting with words. EACH BOOK IS A TWIST ON THESE WORDS. Each paper is a twist on canvas, a twist on parchment, a tiger mountain of words that make meaning in the ill-state-of-the-northland. These words are the *work of the negative.* (Green, 1999). Words are what I love; Words are my rocks, my tiger mountains, my loves, my tools, my way out. Like Kierkegaard, my work is done in multiples. Currently I am writing three books at once. Kierkegaard had different writing tables for different projects. My mystic writing pads--as Freud would call them--are mulling around in my head all the time. It is to these mullings that I turn daily to make sense of the mess of life and the ill body.

Teaching means "soul making.' Soul making gets expressed in many ways. The soul gets expressed in words of course. Maureen Mercury (2000) states that "[d]epth psychology views all phenomena as manifestations of the unconscious levels of the psyche. It advocates that soul-making or soul expression is the primary activity of psychic life" (p. 2). Teaching as soul-making. Studying as soul-making. Educating as soul-making. Therapy as soul-making. *Anima mundi* is the soul of the world and the body is animal. The 'work of the negative' (Green, 1999) is the work of soul-making in the negative spaces of illness. A world continually falling to pieces is a sacred world, a numinous world, a soul-making world. The body falling to pieces is like the shattering of a kaleidoscope or the smashing of an atom. There is no 'sheltering sky'--as Paul Bowles (1998) might put it-- for the ill.

When one falls into a black hole of illness, words come out of the ruins. Words come out of the netherland, words walk down the stairway of mind and into the madhouse of psyche. Words creep out through the voice, through the ink stains of the pen. But one must hurriedly capture the small moments--those small words of sense making-- because time is of the essence, time slips. Words quickly fall away back down into a black hole. One must express time passing in its immediacy, for "[t]he mould in which the human form is cast is exceedingly fragile. Give it the slightest tap with your fingers and it breaks" (Carter, 2003, p. 61). Human fragility becomes more apparent when the body fails. The need to think through this fragility is great. Fragility is something that we do not usually think about because this is a culture of macho. How to write and teach in a fragile state? How to teach when the voice gives way, how to write when pain daunts, how to continue to educate when one worries whether tomorrow will come at all?

Ned Rorem (2000) states that composing music happens when notes take form out of silence. A good composer lets the notes form their own patterns. Notes are self-forming. Notes are driven by an unconscious process that has its own rhythm. Rorem (2000) claims: "I don't believe that composers notate their words, they don't tell the music where to go--it leads them" (p. 133). Like composers, good scholars let words lead them. When the words lead, writing educates. The ill body teaches through words and symbols. Attention to matters of space and time become key if formless thoughts are to turn into words. Thoughts turning into words happen, it seems after much dwelling. The words work their way onto the page themselves. This is a kind of mystic writing. To write as a mystic, psychic retreat beckons. This is why monks retreat; this is why scholars are monkish. It has to be this way. Becoming monkish is the beginning of soul making.

Soul-making needs silence. I am reminded here of Dennis Patrick Slattery's (2004) book titled *Grace in the Desert: Awakening to the Gifts of Monastic Life.* Slattery's book is a beautiful retelling of time spent in monasteries. His is a beautiful testimony of sorting out difficult life issues through retreat--a retreat that is both literal and psychological. Most scholars do not go to monasteries but rather become monk-ish at home. The monastery is the library, the study. And it is necessary to retreat to the study to figure out how to best cope.

THE UNIVERSITY WORKS AGAINST SOUL-MAKING

Retreating into the monk-ish life is often made impossible because university life works against soul-making. Working in a university makes it hard to find the time to actually retreat to one's study. It seems as if the professor needs a sabbatical to get anything done. But who has that luxury, who can afford to take a sabbatical? By the end of the day, the professor cannot profess because she is too bogged down with too many time consuming duties that get in the way of thought. Further, to profess means to profess from the healthy body. Students do not want to study with a sick professor. They want the Adonis-professor. They want Dr. Health. Health is associated with beauty. Sickness is ugliness. No one wants to face ugliness. No one wants to study with Professor Medusa. One must work with one's students to allow them to explore issues around the Medusa complex. This is the work of the negative and the ugly must be faced. Still, students want a healthy professor. But when their professor shows weakness and vulnerability vis-à-vis the fading voice, the grimaced face and even the confession of pain, students squirm. Human weakness is shunned in American culture. The sick are outcasts. A classroom is supposed to be a well-lighted place. But is it?

Deborah Britzman (1998) asks, "[w]hat is actually occurring when education represses uncertainty and trauma. . ." (p.55)? It takes work to repress the trauma of illness. It takes even more work to undo that repression. If we pretend we are fine when we are not we only mis-educate students through dishonesty. Britzman (1998) asks whether education can be "something that is capable of surprising itself. . ." (p. 58). A genuine teacher is one who is real to her students; she is the teacher who surprises, even when she introduces the negative.

The longer I am sick, the more honest I become with my students about my condition. This was not the case at first. It took me a long time to come out to my students (coming out is both problematic for queers as it is for those who are ill). They know. Some of them are appreciative that I am out front with them about my condition. Others, I would guess, are threatened by my honesty. Confession is un-nerving to some. This is the land of Miss America contests and hunky football players, *Bay Watch* babes. When the teacher doesn't match up to these pop culture images, what are students to think?

James Macdonald (1995) points out that "the teacher stands, in many ways, at the crossroads of meaning in the life of the pupil" (p. 28). If this is the case, if we really do stand at the crossroads of meaning, what kind of meaning are we making with our students? Are we making dis-embodied dis-honest mis- meanings? Or are we making embodied genuine ones? A choice must be made at this crossroad. Illness is a crossroad for every-body. Everyone gets ill. Everyone suffers from something--eventually. Shouldn't these issues be part of an education? If not, what are we teaching ? Are we teaching that the world is all light, all happiness, all joy? Without the shadow, Jung taught, the light becomes a menace. One must never repress the shadow side of life in the classroom. Young people have a right to know what life is-- what the crossroads of illness are. Being ill presents an opportunity to explore with young people the problems of the shadow. If we try to protect them from the negative we only do them harm in the long run. Sheltering people from life's difficulties does not help them face what is out there. No one can be sheltered from the gathering storm. Parents may try to shelter their children from the horrors of 9-11, but children have already heard about it and have probably already seen the images on TV.

What kind of teaching speaks through the ill body? College is a good place for students to explore intellectually what disability might mean, what chronic illness might mean. College is a place that we can be real with each other. College might be the place where we *really* talk to one another, where we get into discussions that matter.

College is the place where people can change or become eccentric. Colleges too often, however, are places of normalization. They are places of normalization because people do not know how to be honest with one another; people have forgotten how to be genuine. People have forgotten how to be human. Perhaps I am speaking mostly to myself here. I have had a difficult time being real with my students. Yet, now I suggest we challenge our young people to think differently by teaching genuinely and honestly. Many colleges, however, are merely sites of non-talk. Jack Kerouac (1976) complained about this years ago. He states,

> colleges being nothing but grooming schools for the middle class non-identity which usually finds expression on the outskirts of the campus in rows of well-to do-houses with lawns and television sets in each living room with everybody looking at the same thing and thinking the same thing. . . .(p. 39)

College professors are not doing their job if they model conformity. Kerouac--to escape the horrors of suburban boredom-- dropped out of society, as did many Beat poets of his generation. But dropping out doesn't change oppressive structures of society. One must drop back in and become part of the system in order to fix it. Dropping out does not help.

We live in a post-9-11 era where Columbines and Virginia-Techs happen more and more frequently. We live in mad society, a hurting society that has lost its soul. People have lost touch with the possibility of soul-making. It seems that guns are winning out; it seems that the death drive is driving the soul of this country. Again we are at war, but for what? We train our young people to kill in unjust wars and then expect them to be okay when they come home. Now, thanks to George W. Bush, we can expect another generation to be soul dead when they come home. War kills the soul. The soul of America is at stake and frankly I don't know if it can be fixed.

We want our young people to change things for the better; we want to give them the tools to begin thinking otherwise so that our country will become more democratic--not less. But we live in times where democracy is threatened by The Patriot Act. Democracy-in-public-life seems-no-longer in these post-9-11 times. Democracy begins in honesty and genuine expression, not in conformity and sameness. Working freely as a teacher and intellectual is the beginning of Democracy. What will become of American democracy in years ahead? Big Brother checks out the movies you buy, the books you read, how much money you have in the bank, your medical records, credit card activity. What is next, banning books, how about burning books?

Do teachers have academic freedom? In public school, teachers have to bite their tongues or risk getting fired. Working for the state is working for an autocracy. There are many ways to kill the soul. Not allowing people to say what they think is one way to kill the soul. Public institutions of learning--both American public schools and institutions of higher education-- are a mess.

Like Kerouac, William Burroughs (2003) was fed up with institutions of higher education, as he stated,

> I went to one of the Big Three universities, where I majored in English literature for lack of interest in any other subject. I hated the University. I hated the town it was in. Everything about the place was dead. The university was a fake English set-up taken over by the graduates of fake English public schools. (xxxvii)

I can understand why someone like Burroughs might hate the university. There is much to hate about university life. The university seems distant from the real world, the university is inhabited by scholars who do not pay any attention to student life; the university is filled with people who are not committed to changing the world, but are rather committed to keeping the world as it is. The University, after all, is a place where TRADITION is taught. To break with tradition threatens. Universities are filled with the ranks of the mediocre. University life is akin to military life. Climbing the ranks means being obedient to one's superiors.

Many professors engage in "fake" teaching as Burroughs points out-- in a teaching that is not real, in a teaching that only encourages conformity. A fake education is taught by fake people. Burroughs was real, too real for many. The university -- filled with ranks of the mediocre-- was no place for the likes of Kerouac and Burroughs. They were real writers, real people, they were people who led dangerous, on-the-edge -lives. College professors are, for the most part, sterile, staid, bored and boring. Many become dead because of their dead lessons. William F. Pinar (1994) talks about this phenomenon in one of his early pieces titled "Death in a Tenured Position." Let us not teach through dead bodies. Corpse-teaching. Let us be alive with whatever we teach, even if our lives hang in the balance. Let us teach through soul-making bodies--even if those bodies are ill.

SOUL-SPEAKING

The teacher who is nothing but a walking corpse is "dead in a tenured position" (Pinar, 1994). If the teacher loses her soul, Jung (2005) teaches, "nothing is holy any longer" (p. 97). The Soul Makes the world holy. Holy, Holy, Holy be her name. The Soul animates all things. The world is animated by soul. Soul is the driving energy behind eros. The soul speaks on-and-in the skin of the body. The soul speaks in dream, fantasy and reverie. If we are alive with whatever we teach and write, the soul speaks through us. Aesthetic sensibility soul-speaks. Energy is soul, soul is energy. Wounded souls need to listen closely to soul-speaking energy. Soul-speaking energy heals. Soul-speaking cuts through dimness and dullness. Soul-speaking releases energy. Energy is the driving principle that moves through objects and animals. Soul-speaking stories the animal spirit. Soul-speaking howls, cries, whispers, whimpers. Soul-speaking sounds of lonely electric guitars, or double bass beats. Soul-speaking colors the world, shades it in darkness and light. Soul-speaking signifies sacredness; it is the mystical element of all sentient and non-sentient things-creatures. Soul-speaking happens in colors and sounds. Whirling motions, private moments. Soul-speaking is the heart of illness. In illness the soul speaks, yet this speech is coded, vague. There is no breaking the code of soul-speech, it is always already a mystery, it is always already numinous.

Performing music or altering one's body through bodyart bespeaks soul-speaking. Images, sound, color and movement prepare for mythic passages into nextness. Here, the soul does not literally speak --no-- the soul symbolically manifests as aesthetic experience. Aesthetic experiences are soul-speaking sparks moving through place and space. The chrono-topos of soul-speaking matter. Soul-speaking happens in particular places and times, in particular spaces of mind. One is more open to soul-speaking in moments of reverie, as Gaston Bachelard (1988a; 1988b; 1990; 1994) has pointed out over and over again. Soul-speaking is a kind of attunement to BEING. BEING is not some abstract concept. BEING signifies life in its nakedness. BEING impassions when it is attentive to soul-speaking.

We never know precisely what the soul is speaking, for it speaks through the unconscious. The unconscious is vague, overdetermined. Dense with symbolism. SOUND COLOR and WORDS are kin. A family resemblance. They are basic elements of soul-speaking. Soul-speaking through symbols of sound, color and words provide a kind of connective tissue between dreaming states, reverie and consciousness. The rational part of EGO is that part that prevents us from getting at soul-speaking because it cuts things up, it separates and divides thinking. Intellectualization is soul-speaking's blockage. Understanding the principle of soul-speaking might break this blockage.

Soul-speaking is most evident in the production of colors or sounds. Blues, greens and the rest. Subwoofers bounce sound into the heart of things. Energy drives both color and sound. Energy is motion in space. Energy is not stultification. Energy is the principle that moves the soul. Energy is movement, energy is CURRERE. Energy is electric; it is the body-electric. We are electric-animal-souls.

Soul-speaking happens in the most common places. On stairwells. In elevators. While sweeping the floor. Talking on the phone. Going to the zoo. Flying. Dreaming. Soul-speaking is the experience of eating chocolate.

Soul-speaking is *EDUCARE*. *Educare* means to lead out, to move out, to motion, to cathect, to drive. To truly educate is to soul-speak. Soul- speaking is deeply philosophical and psychological. Soul-speaking is a philosophical psychology.

Soul-speaking also points toward death. Life energy is always already driven by the death drive, repetition compulsion and destruction. Soul-speaking is both light and dark. It is both today and yesterday, it is both backwards and forwards. It is both the death and life principles. Soul-speaking is a sad muted trumpet in the city, it is the primal sound of drum--beat drum-- it is the color of blue and yellow simultaneously. The soul speaks in the most basic element.

THE APORIA OF SOUL-SPEAKING.

The soul speaks without actually speaking. Soul-speaking is a feeling, a sensation. Animals do not speak with words, they speak with their souls. Do human beings really speak only with words? Do we really understand each other through words only, or do we understand one another on a deeper level? The animals can teach us. Do we understand one another through gesture, motion, blank stares, voids, long looks, short glances, sighs? The soul speaks most deeply before language. These are all symbols of soul-speaking, reflections of the soul. It is, however, impossible to look into your own reflection. If you do, like Thales or Narcissus, you drown. It is through the Other that soul-speaking teaches.

Soul-speaking happens in colors, sounds and words; it is energy and repetition. Negative energy is repetition compulsion. Positive energy is repetition. Repetition in sound, repetition in colors and words create ancestral feelings, archaic feelings, primal bonds with animals. Archetypes-to-come.

There are many who talk of the soul, there are many who deny the existence of the soul. The concept of the soul is not postmodern. It is pre-modern. Did Jung teach that we actually have multiple souls? Is *this* not postmodern? Sounds postmodern to me! Multiple souls are de-centered. There is no central command center for the soul. There is no homunculus of the soul.

Human creatures can choose to be either soulful or not. This choice is clearly an ethical one. Being soulful means being open to BEING, being open to color and sound as manifestations of BEING. Being open to small moments on the stairwell, eating chocolate, dwelling in the place of one's deepest felt interiority--these windows are openings to soul-speaking.

Soul-speaking, however, is not a call to solipsism. Soul-speaking is a call to the Other, a speaking to the Other in gut-tones, in guttural language. Colors, sounds and words are the most guttural primal patterns connecting one soul to another.

Speaking designates a speaking-to. Speaking-to means speaking to someone else. Soul-speaking, thus, is intentional. Soul speaking intends an Other. And It is OTHER by its very nature. This Otherness is a form of animation. This animation is both negative and positive, both light and dark. Attempting to define soul-speaking or to articulate what it is is quite difficult because the moment one tries to say what soul-speaking might mean, meaning slips beyond one's grasp. Gilles Deleuze and Felix Guattari (1994) report,

> Nothing is more distressing than a thought that escapes itself, than ideas that fly off, that disappear hardly formed, already eroded by forgetfulness or precipitated into others that we no longer master. These are infinite variabilities, the appearing and disappearing of which coincide. (p. 201)

Soul-speaking escapes representation. Articulation of the very edges, the outer edges of soul-speaking puzzles. Soul-speaking is rhythm, pattern, sound, color, vibration, sensation, thought.

When one experiences illness, colors and sounds and smells intensify. The body seems more sensitive to its surroundings. Smells overwhelm. Sensations break open. as it were. James Hillman's (1975) well known book *Re-Visioning Psychology* teaches that the term 'soul-making' is actually found in the work of the Romantic poets such as Keats and Blake. Hillman (1975) talks of 'soul' in the following passage:

> First, "soul" refers to the deepening of events in experience, second, the significance soul makes possible . . . derives its special relation with death. And third, by "soul" I mean the imaginative possibilities in our natures; the experiencing through speculation, dreams, images and fantasy. . . .(x)

The notion of soulfulness immediately brings to mind depth. Moving down, getting deeper into interiority. Interiority. Dreams. Unlike my work here, Hillman does not address sound and color in relation to soul-making. Artists work in colors, sounds, words, patterns. Soulful artistic creation edges toward the ineffable. Thomas Moore (1992) talks of "care of the soul." He argues that when you do not care for your

soul, it comes back to haunt you. Repression returns. Moore (1992) suggests that
"[w]hen soul is neglected it doesn't just go away; it appears symptomatically in
obsessions, addictions, violence, and loss of meaning. . ." (xi). Caring for the soul
means listening to dreams and fantasies. If one doesn't pay attention to the inner
life, ghosts haunt. Either you deal with your ghosts or they will deal with you.

The soul is the moon of the body. Soul is a vague principle of motion and
energy. It is not knowledge; it is not an epistemological concept. It is the
numinous. The numinous shines like the moon.

Gaston Bachelard (1988a; 1988b; 1990; 1994) addresses the soul throughout his
work He speaks of the soul in terms of a flame, for example. The flame burns
through soul; it is the root of desire and energy. The flame of the soul is the life
principle. Bachelard (1988a) states, "[t]he verb to inflame must enter into the
psychologist's vocabulary. It governs an entire realm of the experiential world.
Images of inflamed language inflame the psyche. . ." (p. 1). To burn with ideas is
to burn with soul-speaking. When one is ill, one often speaks of something being
inflamed, something on fire, something burning. When things burn too high, the
body becomes ill. Flames attract objects; objects turn into fantastic colors and produce
sonic sound. Crackling reds, blues, greens. When we say 'her eyes lit up' or she's
got 'light in her eyes' --these are instances of soul-speaking. It is the flame that
gives energy to the soul; it is the flame that allows psyche to speak in the first
place.

An aesthetic sensibility makes that which is primal, primary. Illness heightens
primary experience. For Freud, primary thought is dream thought. Secondary
thought is rational thought. Aesthetics spring from the primality of dream space.
Dreaming in technicolor, soul speaks. Relations with objects become more inflamed.
Soul-speaking symbolizes attunement to what Dewey (1981) calls aesthetics in its
"raw" form. (p. 527). What "arouses [one's] interest" (p. 527) moves the soul to
speak. A "raw" soul tells the tale through primary thought processes. Let dreams
guide thought. A world becomes aesthetic through raw colors and raw sounds.
Dewey (1981) puts it this way,

> the fire engine rushing by; the machines excavating enormous holes in the
> earth; the human fly climbing the steeple-side; the men perched high in air on
> girders, throwing and catching red-hot bolts. (p. 527)

Fire energizes the soul. Throwing and catching RED bolts. Soul-speaking is
throwing and catching red bolts. Soul-speaking is a more aesthetic way of living.
Dewey argues, "esthetic [sic] understanding . . . must start with the soil, air, and
light out of which things esthetically [sic]admirable arise" (p. 534). The soil, air
and light are primal like color and sound. Dewey's point is that we must look to
what it is that-- in rawness-- gets soul-speaking, moving. The basic elements like
earth, fire, air and water are good places to start. The soul embeds in primal
elements, since bodies are nothing more than fire, air, earth and water.

If the soul ANIMATES all things, it animates them in health and in illness.
Illness is an animated state of psyche. Here, everything is bigger, heavier, more
colorful, more dramatic, more intense, more frightening. An animated soul is not

all light, it is also darkness. An ill body cannot get outside of itself; the ill body cannot get away from the illness. Illness is a presence that cannot be ignored. Illness speaks loudly like men on a rooftop pounding nails. To live in a state of animation is exhausting, no doubt. Because the volume of the nervous system is turned up, exhaustion abounds. Illness animates a sense of the mystical, a sense of the sacred. Illness is the call of death. The fear of death changes dream thoughts.

EDUCARE means to draw out, to pull out, yes? EDUCARE-- means to draw out dream thoughts in times of illness. Drawing out from interiority--the meaning which we teach through our wounded body--is an ethical imperative. Educating through the body is soul-speaking. Educating through the wounded body is soul-speaking through colors and sounds. To educate the public means to educate in both health and illness. To educate means to draw out in an embodied way, in a colorful, soundful way.

What do we wish to tell our children about hard times, about the soul-speaking in agony? What do we wish to tell our children about esoteric subject matter that is ignored in public school curriculum? What is educating about at the most basic level? EDUCARE means drawing out our most meaningful thoughts and sharing them with young people. Education should have deep and lasting meaning. Education should help young people live deeply, fully and wisely. Education should help young people soul-speak. Soul-speaking demands articulation. Soul-speaking is like Keats's "soul-making." The phrase 'soul making' can be found in a letter that John Keats wrote to George and Georgiana Keats in 1819. Keats (1819/1959) is quoted below.

> Call the world if you please "The vale of Soul-Making." Then you will find out the use of the world. . . . I say 'Soul making' Soul as distinguished from an intelligence--There may be intelligences or sparks of divinity in millions-- but they are not souls till they acquire identities. . . . (p. 288)

The world is the place where souls are made. One must make a soul. A soul is not a soul until it is made. What does it mean to make a soul? Souls are made by study, by looking inward and by developing a sense of compassion for the Other. To educate means that we teach compassion for the Other. The aim of education should be compassion. Perhaps compassion is the most important virtue. Soul-making is the making of a compassionate one. To speak of the soul means to extend that soul outward toward the Other. It is not enough to look inward. Keats talks of identity as singularity. I think of identity in relation. As Josiah Royce (1988) puts it, the self is a social self. Royce (1988) states, "[n]obody amongst us men [sic] comes to self-consciousness , so far as I know, except under the persistent influence of his social fellows" (p. 112). The soul is primarily a social soul, a soul-in-relation. Soul-speaking is not an encapsulation but a movement outward. To soul-speak is to express dream thoughts to the Other. Speaking by its very nature involves at least two people. Soul-speaking is primarily compassion. But when we think about our soulless world, compassion is hard to find. Teaching through the ill body means first and foremost teaching compassion.

POST (SCRIPT) : RE-TURNING TO RELATION AND TO THE WISDOM
TRADITIONS

Deepening this chapter, I have re-turned to the Wisdom Traditions. In a while I will address these traditions, but for now I must address a pressing issue about relation. As I talked about above, soul-making is primarily about relation. What is missing in the first part of this chapter is a discussion on a particular relation. I spoke mostly in the abstract. But now, since my life has taken a dramatic turn with the illness of my mother, the idea of the importance of relation and compassion become real, concrete, particular and enfleshed

My mother's struggle with Parkinson's Plus or multiple systems atrophy has profoundly changed me. When I first wrote this book I concentrated on my illness, as is clear from the text. Working through my own illness has helped me to work through my mother's illness. Still, I feel an incredible sense of dread every day. Waking up I struggle to remember what has happened. It is as if upon awakening I have forgotten already and must force myself to remember. Teaching through the ill body means compassion for the Other, for the mother. Relations with the mother are always already fraught. I find helpful the study of wisdom traditions to learn how to be more compassionate. Compassion must be learned and practiced. It does not come naturally.

My focus on the soul in this chapter has been rather narrow. But with my mother's illness I have realized that I must broaden my study and broaden my understanding of the soul. The soul is in relation always. I think I understood this on a certain intellectual level when I wrote the earlier parts of this book. But when you are sick, the world tends to shrink. The soul seems singular, enclosed. Illness can make you feel enclosed upon yourself. You can easily collapse into an unhealthy solipsism. Part of the reason for this is that the pained body occupies all of your thought. It is nearly impossible to think beyond the bounds of the singular body. But when someone else suffers from illness, that singularity and insularity changes. Thoughts shift and move outside the body toward the Other.

I have come back, therefore, to my study of the Buddhist notion of the Bodhisattva. I have always been fascinated by Buddhism but for years dropped my study of it to turn to the study of other things. I have always had a very strong sense of ethicality and have written out of a sense of that ethicality. The notion of the Bodhisattva most fully captures that sense of ethicality for me. "The nectar of compassion is seen on the willow branch held by the Bodhisattva" (Hanh, 2007, p. 56). The Bodhisattva is the one who puts off nirvana--or extinguishment into the flame of nothingness--in order to help others. The Bodhisattva is the one who understands the notion of relation in a deep and spiritual sense. It is one thing to be in relation to the Other--on an intellectual level--but to be in a relation-in-compassion to the Other—on an emotional level-- is something different. This is what Martin Buber called the I-Thou relation. The Bodhisattva is one who realizes in the depth of the heart that all life is sacred and that in dark times compassion beckons. Compassion differs from caring in that compassion is spiritual. Caring is not. To care is to be with the other in the secular world. Compassion is to be with the Other in the sacred world. Compassion is the emotional and intuitive understanding that the sacred is the profane and in the everyday world one can be compassionate if one is mindful--to use the Buddhist phrase--of that compassion. It is mindfulness--or being aware of what one is doing and thinking--of compassion that makes the relation with the Other sacred. "May the Bodhisattva of Deep Listening embrace us all with Great Compassion" (Hanh, 2007, p. 56). In Buddhism there are at least two kinds of Bodhisattvas. There are supernatural Bodhisattvas--like saints in heaven--and then there are those people on earth who are also Bodhisattvas. How to be an earthbound Bodhisattva is the problem at hand. Sometimes experience of great suffering allows one to become more compassionate toward the Other because of the intimate understanding of that suffering. And here I am speaking of illness. Not that experiencing illness makes you a better person, it does not. Yet, experiencing illness can allow you to open up to the Other in a way that someone who has not experienced illness cannot. To the meanest, most viscous, most cruel person, the Bodhisattva opens her heart to engage in "deep listening." It is easy to be compassionate toward the Other whom one already loves. It is difficult and the mark of the true Bodhisattva to listen to the one who is cruel and mean. This is the message of most wisdom traditions. Spirituality is not light; it is tough and troubles our hatreds. To be compassionate toward the hateful one is the mark of the Bodhisattva. I am not claiming to be a Bodhisattva but I am learning about the way of the Bodhisattva. For me, engaging in deep listening with vicious people is somehow not possible. And yet this is my challenge. I must learn to listen to that viciousness. I do not have to accept it, but I have to listen to it. There comes a point at which listening ends. But in the Buddhist tradition, the Bodhisattva listens to all and is compassionate toward all. I certainly cannot be compassionate for all. People who abuse and torture animals do not have my ear, nor do they have my compassion. I only have contempt for these people. I cannot get beyond that contempt. So you see I am no Bodhisattva. The Bodhisattva knows no contempt. Yet, I try to learn from studying the Bodhisattva.

The Bodhisattva--the earthly version--lives among the suffering. And this is the hard part. Living among the suffering means literally being there for them and being with them in the flesh. Pema Chodron (2005) explains.

Bodhisattvas practice "in the middle of fire." This means they enter into the suffering of the world; it also means they stay steady with the fire of their own painful emotions. They neither act them out nor repress them. (p. 11)

When I read this passage I think of the psychoanalyst. She enters into the world of the suffering never acting out her transference, even if she feels it. She remains calm in the midst of her patients' emotional turmoil. She does not repress her own feelings but uses those feelings to help the patient explore the suffering that causes great pain. Teachers also enter into the world of suffering. Social justice is our passion. This means we fight for the rights and dignity of those who are subjugated. We teach and honor subjugated knowledges. This always involves entering into the wounds of the world. Teaching is a helping profession. The highest teaching is that of compassion. But there is always something that gets in the way of our teaching.

This is what the Buddhists call the "monkey mind." Pema Chodron (2005) points out that,

> In Buddhist literature there are many animal analogies for the wildness of mind: monkey mind, for example, or the out-of-control nature of an untamed horse. Here Shantideva magnifies the image by choosing the most powerful of all tamable beasts: an elephant. If a wild horse or monkey can wreak havoc, imagine the destruction that could result from a crazed elephant! (p. 104)

The monkey mind is one of impulse, repetition compulsion. This is the crazed way of walking through the world whereby the unconscious impels one to do insane things. Not being the master of one's emotional house troubles. But there are parts of us that are always already monkey minds. In a sense, we cannot get rid of the monkeys in our minds. They are always there. The question is whether or not we have the freedom to choose whether they control us or we control them. Mad grief is a monkey mind. It overwhelms, it torments, it makes one feel insane. Grief cannot be controlled. It is what it is. And I think the message of the Buddhists-- as well as the psychoanalysts-- is to be with that grief, feel it, get into it. Maybe we should let the monkeys out of their cages and that way they can jump around until they run out of energy. Monkeys can never be controlled, but they can be allowed to run their course. If the monkeys are not allowed to run their course, they will make of the mind a jumping, crazy, schizoid, split off wreck. Thich Nhat Hanh (2006) says that "[t]he [Buddhist] practice is not to get rid of our afflictions. . . . We have to accept them and touch them with the light of mindfulness. This touching will bring about their transformation" (p. 217). Psychoanalysts suggest also that transference can never really be gotten rid of, but we can at least recognize what it means and get distance from it. Transference is the monkey mind. One never gets rid of childhood wounds, one accepts them and makes the best of them. Most importantly one acknowledges these wounds. The same with illness. Acknowledging that one is ill, accepting it is key to getting some semblance of sanity. Moreover, one must be mindful of the way illness alters relations with others. Thich Nhat Hanh (2006) takes this one step further and suggests that not only must we acknowledge suffering, but we must "invite" it "into our mind consciousness" (p. 220). Hanh says,

> We invite sadness, despair, regrets, and longings that in the past have been difficult for us to touch, and we sit down and talk with them, like old friends. But before we invite them up, we must be sure that the lamp of our mindfulness is lit and that its light is steady and strong. (p. 220)

This passage reminds me of the Jungians who suggest that we should have it out with tormenting mythic images. Yet, the most natural response to grief and illness is to push away and deny what pains. Denial can be overwhelming and can last for quite a long time. But we must get beyond the stage of denial otherwise monkey mind will devour Psyche. And if the illness is terminal, one must not only accept that, but in a sense invite it. If one does not fear death--and that is what is meant by inviting it--life in the end stages will be made much more peaceful. If one fears death, the monkey mind will make life miserable right up until the end. Death comes in its own time; some people know when they are going to die. Some sick animals drag themselves off to a remote place to die and leave their human companions. Some animals sense when humans will die. Cats have been known to sit with the terminally ill as they enter into the late stages of illness toward death. Dreams can tell of an impending death. In *The Tibetan Book of the Dead* (2005) we read of some very strange death images in dreams.

> But if one dreams between dawn and daybreak that: One is riding a cat or a white monkey with a red face, While moving further and further towards the east, It is said that this is a sign of death caused by king spirits. If one dreams of riding a tiger, fox, or corpse, Or of riding a buffalo, pig, camel, or donkey, While moving further and further toward the south, This is a sign of death. . . . (pp. 160-161)

Soul-speaking is the speaking of end things. Soul-speaking is allowing dreams to give clues to-the-future-to-come. Soul-speaking is *anima mundi*. These ancient Buddhist symbols may seem antiquated and even silly, but perhaps we should engage in deep listening. Neither Freud not Jung ruled out the fact that dreams can predict. I think that soul-speaking is the speaking of the profound. The profound confounds. The problem is that our minds are so jumbled up with monkey noise that we cannot hear our own inner wisdom speak.

One begins to think on these grave issues especially if a child or parent suffers from an incurable disease. There is no way around thinking these things. The inability to deal with tragic illness can wreck a life. Many fear illness and run away from it because they cannot deal with it. The thought that things like this only happen to other people's parents or other people's children eventually catches up. Things like this happen to your own family and things like this can happen to you. And when tragic illness strikes, questions of where to turn and what to do beckon. For me, I have re-turned to these ancient wisdom texts not in order to explain things away but to get at them on a deeper, more spiritual level. Building a more compassionate relation with the Other is key. Matthew Fox (1997) states that

> We don't have soul until we become a field through which compassion is working. This is not just [Meister] Eckhart. This is the richest mystical tradition East and West, that soul is compassion, the work of compassion. Compassion is work; it's not just being there. (p. 87)

The key for Fox is the idea the compassion is work. To simply say 'I feel your pain' is not enough. In fact, it is ridiculous. I cannot feel your pain. Pain is intensely private. To utter trite statements does little for the Other. It only trivializes the horror of the dis-ease. The work of compassion is the work of soul-making. Compassion is the hardest work of all. Compassion is tough not soft. Spirituality is tough not soft. Compassion is not light, it is dealing with the dark, it is being in the dark and being with the Other in the dark. In the shadow of death is where compassion is found. Compassion is a mystical act. As Matthew Fox (1997) puts it, "[m]ystics may be the people who have seen and understood that reality as we

experience it rests upon darkness" (p. 147). But compassion has its limits. Pain is
intensely private. To assume that one can feel the Other's pain is simply arrogant
and patronizing. Thomas Merton (1983) speaks to this issue.

> What, after all, is more personal than suffering? The awful futility of our
> attempts to convey the reality of our sufferings to other people, and the tragic
> inadequacy of human sympathy, both prove how incommunicable a thing
> suffering really is. (p. 80)

At the limits of language one attempts to show compassion, to work at compassion.
But at the end of the day even compassion comes up short. It too is limited, as
Merton points out. It is important to understand the limits of compassion so as to
not become arrogant.

BERGMAN'S AUTUMN SONATA

Stress, rage and monkey mind are symptomatic. Dysfunction. A dysfunctional
family deals with illness with monkey mind. Nobody does a better job of
portraying the dysfunctional monkey-minded family than Ingmar Berman. It is to
this awful truth that Ingmar Bergman (1978) speaks in his masterfully crafted film
Autumn Sonata. Bergman understands how families are wrecked by illness and
disability, how relations can turn sour, how old resentments and hostilities tend to
surface in the worst of times. Bergman understands how the old wounds of the
mother-daughter relationship are made more intense with the denial of illness. All
the old wounds surface as mother and daughter have unresolved painful issues with
which to deal. The two women in the film (the daughter, played by Liv Ullman and
the mother, played by Ingrid Bergman) do not reconcile and do not forgive one
another. The mother's disavowal of illness in the family makes for strained
relations to say the least. The mother turns her back on her disabled daughter and
abandons her family. When she visits years later, she only comes home to the same
old resentment, anger, rage, tears and hatred. These emotions come to life as the
two characters in the film express—violently-- long buried issues. Bringing these
old issues up when the mother returns to see her daughters after years of absence
does not help resolve anything. Bergman suggests in this film that compassion is
not possible between mother and daughter—if this relation is dysfunctional from
the start. In fact, in most of his films he shows that people are generally isolated
from one another and that hatred wins out over love. Bergman understands that
people generally do not communicate with one another, rather they have dual
monologues. So one wonders whether all of this talk of compassion is realistic. For
Bergman, it seems that there is little compassion in the world. Simply put,
Bergman might say that compassion is not realistic. He was like Freud on this
count. Thanatos is stronger than eros. And families are nothing more than
cesspools of resentments and hatred. True enough. Freud believed that people are
mostly hateful and awful. He had little faith in the human race. Freud suggested
that mental illness makes people less kind. People are generally intolerant of any
kind of dis-ease. Ah, and this is the rub!

So where is our Bodhisattva in all of this? For Bergman and for Freud there is no Bodhisattva. And perhaps--at bottom--they are right. The problem with getting sick is that people do tend to turn away from you. They tend to act out their own fears around you and avoid you. People run away from the sick. Or, they just pretend that it is not happening or that it does not matter. Illness can bring out the worst in families. Illness can kill the Bodhisattva in all of us. The most devastating thing about devastating illness is that people turn their heads and walk away from it. The sick are shunned. The mother in Bergman's (1978) *Autumn Sonata*, shuns her own child because she is ill. How can a mother shun her own child? And this is the question at hand. How can primal figures turn on their children? How can children turn on their ailing parents? It happens more often than not. It is naive to think that compassion is possible in all situations because it is not. Most people have little compassion. And this is why we need to return to the ancient wisdom traditions so that we can learn how to be more compassionate, even if we cannot reconcile old hatreds and old resentments. Can one be compassionate in the absence of reconciliation? Perhaps. Compassion is never pure, no one has a pure heart. Hearts are conflicted. Love and hate go hand in hand. Hearts can both love and hate primal figures. And when illness strikes, all of this comes up. The confusion, the anger, the old wounds seem only to be intensified. At the end of *Autumn Sonata*, the mother abandons her children once again. There was never any warmth between mother and children. Only lies and only the play-acting of warmth. The daughter told her mother that her words never matched her actions. To say 'I feel compassionate' toward you does not mean that true compassion exists. One must speak one's actions, but most often people do not. This is what makes spirituality so hard. Sometimes people are not good and do not have good hearts. And then they get sick. Enter the Bodhisattva. This is the time the Bodhisattva is most needed. It is easy to feel compassion for a good person. But Eva, in Bergman's film, did not feel compassion for her mother because her mother did not love her and her mother only cared about herself and her career. I suppose Bergman's message is that the last song you sing or play-- your autumn sonata-- is how you will be remembered. James Hillman (2004) suggests that what we need to examine is the now to make sense of the then. It is how we behave now that turns a life into something meaningful or hateful. Soul-speaking is made most difficult because of these difficult situations. What song will the soul speak when one loves the unlovable or has compassion for the one who has no compassion? Bergman explores the toughest issues. That is why his films are difficult to watch. *Autumn Sonata* left me cold because everyone in the film was cold. Can a Bodhisattva warm a cold heart? Probably not. But a Bodhisattva loves anyway and has compassion anyway.

CURRERE, COLOR, REVERIE: ARCHETYPAL SOUL-MAKING

CURRERE. Currere is the Latin root of the word curriculum. It means the running of the course. For curriculum theorists, the *movement* of the course is what is at hand. Movement in the context of curriculum is a trope for lived experience. A Curriculum vita is a life story. The life story is movement through time, space and place. Thus, currere is symbolic movement. It is movement backwards, forwards, up and down. Teaching is movement that happens through time, through space and place.

CURRERE is color. An educational landscape is one of color. The educational landscape should be colorful as is the earthy landscape. We must bring earth back into the space of the classroom. The earth is made of many colors and so too should be teaching. Teaching should not be colorless, lifeless. If teaching is lifeless it does not mirror the earthy landscape Colorful movement is the earth's rotation. We too are that rotation, thus movement, color and currere are not just abstract concepts, they belong to the very ecosphere to which we belong. The question is what does color do? What does it mean to be a colorful teacher? What does it mean to have a colorful classroom? What does it mean to have a colorful psyche? The psyche is not a dead thing. It too is colorful. Dreams happen in color. Color happens. Color is everywhere. Eyes are the color-windows of the soul.

Gaston Bachelard (1988b)--Dean of color-- suggests that color is a seminal force.

Knowing that color works on matter, that it is a veritable activity of matter, that color lives from a constant interchange of force between matter and light, the painter [or body artist], with the fatality of primitive fancies renews the great cosmic dreams that bind [humankind] to the elements--to fire, water, the air of the heavens, and the prodigious materiality of the substances of the earth. (p. 26)

Following Bachelard, I suggest that because color is strewn throughout every-dayness, through the hard and soft qualities of the earth, it is not merely an ephemeral something or substance, color is the very grist and fabric of lived experience.

The educational landscape colors. The scholarly life can be quite colorful. William James was certainly a colorful character, a one of a kind. Studying is a colorful endeavor. Studying texts illuminates color. Some texts evoke blues or reds or blacks or yellows. Some texts are written in black and white. These are the most powerful colors. Text is literally black and white. Reading text means negotiating negative spaces. It is in the negative spaces that meaning is made. Scholars must read in the in-between of the negative spaces to generate meaning. If the scholarly life is not color-filled something is wrong at a deep soul level. The scholarly life is one of vibrancy, illumination. Most often scholars work in grays. Grays are the most profound colors.

Scholarship is not built on consensus (which might be represented in bold colors). Rather, scholarship is built on dissensus. Dissensus might be symbolized by a myriad of colors. So too is the psyche. The psyche is built on difference. Difference colors. If symbols are not perceived as being different from each other psychosis sets in. Symbolization separates. For psychotics the concrete is the symbolic. Non-psychosis separates the concrete from the symbolic . And it is this basic difference--between the concrete and the symbolic-- that makes a difference between being psychotic and non-psychotic. Both the concrete and the symbolic are shot through with color. Unless, of course, one is color-blind. Or blind. Do blind people see darkness, and if so is that darkness a color? Jacques Derrida (1990) addresses similar issues in *Memoirs of the blind.* He asks,

> What happens when one writes without seeing? A hand of the blind ventures forth alone or disconnected, in a poorly delimited space; it feels its way, it gropes, it caresses as much as it inscribes, trusting to the memory of signs and supplementing sight. (p. 3)

When one writes without seeing, one writes in the dark. But can the blind see darkness? How to express darkness if one has never seen color?

Writing blind is exactly what psyche does. She writes blindly. She moves through the world blindly. The unconscious blinds. The 'dark night of the soul'--a phrase coined by Saint John of the Cross and made popular for our generation by Thomas Moore--colors soul-making darkly. Through a looking glass darkly. Soul-making happens in the dark. And darkness is a color, although those with sight might be blind to it. Moving blindly, psyche dives down deeply. The deeper psyche goes, the darker it gets.

Bachelard (1988b) suggests that "consequently color. . . possesses depth, it has a thickness, it unfolds simultaneously in a dimension of intimacy and in a dimension of exuberance" (p. 26). Can one argue that color is ecstasy? Can one argue that color, in its depth and exuberance is ecstatic expression, ecstatic BEING? Color is the world. The world is color. Color may seem to be an ephemeral topic, but it is not. Oliver Sacks (1995) points out that

> Color is not a trivial subject but one that has compelled, for hundreds of years, a passionate curiosity in the greatest artists, philosophers, and natural scientists. The young Spinoza wrote his first treatise on the rainbow; the young Newton's most joyous discovery was the composition of white lights, Goethe's great color work, like Newton's started with a prism; Schopenhauer, Young, Helmholtz, and Maxwell, in the last century, were all tantalized by

the problem of color; and Wittgenstein's last work was his Remarks on Color. And yet most of us, most of the time, overlook its great mystery. (p. 4)

As Sacks points out color is not a subject that we should overlook. It demands interrogation especially in its relation to the psyche. Colors become more pronounced because of Illness. Darkness is perhaps the color of illness. Illness endarkens the senses. What was dim in health becomes illuminated darkly in illness. Death might be our darkest hour. Or is it? Does death have a color? Deepak Chopra (2001) argues that death's first color is white. Death is met by a white light. What does this white light signify? A shutting down of neurons perhaps. But for those of us with a mystical bent, perhaps the white light signifies an entrance into another form of being.

Scientists tell us that energy never dies. What is the color of energy? If we are made of energy, and that energy never dies, something about us continues on. Does psyche continue on in a new form? And what is the color of that new form? Color-as-energy moves through the body, does something through the body, to the soul.

What I am interested in exploring here are the ways in which color informs the psychic landscape and the ways in which the ill body compensates for its losses.

REVERIE, REMEMBERING AND COLOR

Currere--as a colorful soul-scape--makes community possible by bringing warmth into the educating body. Currere, if it is colorful, allows dwelling in reverie. A curriculum vita, a life story, might be about a tale of reverie. Many do not experience reverie. We might open our hearts to it. Reverie happens in color. Reverie floats. Reverie ties back. Reverie grounds. Here I am thinking of the Latin root of the word religion, *Religio* which means to tie back. Reverie ties back to an ontological groundedness. Reverie is of the earth because it comes from the earth. And yet, when in a state of reverie, one floats.

Reverie leads to remembering. As analysts know, re-membering always already points back to childhood. Falling into states of reverie deepens memory. Reverie undoes repression. Memory work needs to be done especially through the ill body. Being ill, often, affords the time to re-member. This is a necessary psychoanalytic movement of regression.

Currere demands that we look back, examine the past, not in a romantic way, not in nostalgic way, but in a way that helps us understand why are doing what we are doing in the present so as to better understand how we might proceed in the future (Pinar, 1994). Currere, the running of the course, is the existential and symbolic running of a life. Life runs, it never stands still, although it might feel still when illness strikes. Life is always running. Ongoing inner commentary runs through psyche. Buddhists try to empty ego and stop that running commentary. Instead of trying to stop it, I suggest that one focus on it. Currere suggests focus. Focusing on the lived curriculum. The lived curriculum streams like consciousness. Free association powers psyche. Psyche, under the shadow of free association, courses.

Reverie happens in a psychic nowhere and somewhere. Reverie happens when all is still and moving at once. Reverie reminds one of childhood and grounds in the now. Bachelard (1988b) argues,

> Dreaming of childhood, we go back to the den of reveries to the reveries which opened up the world for us. It is reverie which makes us the first inhabitants of the world of solitude. (p. 96)

Reverie and solitude go hand in hand. And yet, this solitude is not altogether peaceful. When one is ill there is much solitude to be had--and ruminating on memories can disturb. Some people cannot stand to be alone because they have to confront psyche. Solitude is both poison and cure. Traces of Plato's pharmacy. Solitude heals damaged psyche. Or, solitude torments. The soul demands solitude. Psyche breaks down memory. Psyche deconstructs memory. Solitude, reverie and memory break down the past together. Getting sick means confronting memory. Sitting around in hospital waiting rooms forces one into the whirlpool of the past. And this can either be good or not so good.

The solitary child, the withdrawn child, the child who plays alone, the child who suffers from abuse, feels broken. Sitting in hospital waiting rooms brings up old wounds. Everything seems to happen in slow motion.

Being withdrawn, taking refuge in interiority has its good side too. Withdrawn children tend to become good scholars. Scholars must be, in a sense, withdrawn; scholars must go deep inside themselves in order to resonate with texts, with words. Words are formed from deep imaginal places. Introversion helps to form relations with words. Words live inside psyche. Language and psyche are inextricably tied. Scholars do something with that language, make use of language, work through words.

Withdrawn children play secret games. Secret games may serve as defence mechanisms. Reverie can be used by children as a defence mechanism. When environments are toxic, when children are abused, or witness alcoholism, reverie serves as escape and protection. All children have make-believe worlds, but children who are subject to abuse, live intensely in these make-believe worlds in order to protect themselves against abuse. These fantasy worlds become necessary for survival. Children who cannot carve out spaces for reverie become troubled. A childhood that is overly planned by parents can damage. A psyche overfull damages. Psyche needs empty spaces. Reverie emerges in empty psychic space. Reverie is soul work. Those who have little time for soul work, little space for reverie, suffer from ego blocks.

School days are filled with too many busybody activities; there is little time for dreaming in school. No space for reverie in public school. Public schools are factories that pollute. What children need is reverie, space. Dream. Education needs to become more impressionistic. Reverie is like impressionism. Impressionistic paintings are blurred and vague. Reverie embraces the vague. Reverie is not an escape from reality always, it is the very stuff out of which reality is made. The vague is reality. The most primal state of awareness is vague. Ego's false divisions make reality neat and tidy. Without ego, though, life would be mixed up and crazy.

We need ego. But not too much ego. The ego needs to separate things for us to clarify, but regression-to-the-vague is also necessary. Without spaces to dwell in reverie, we would go mad.

Imagination is the stuff of childhood and adulthood, although most adults seem to be lacking in imagination. Think on images for a moment. Most images are vague. The vague is not colorless however. The vague might be mist, but that mist can reflect the colors of the rainbow, or the color of darkness. Darkness is a color. Bachelard (1988b) says of imagination that it

> invents more than things and actions, it invents new life, new spirit; it opens eyes to new types of vision. The imagination will see only if it has visions. And it will have visions if it is educated through reveries before being educated by experience. . . . (p. 16)

For Bachelard, reveries are primal. Reverie--like dreams happen out of time. One might fall into a state of reverie and feel as if psyche floats in a timeless space. The imagination is the site/cite/sight of visions. Visions strike. Visions are of darkness and light.

The imaginal is reverie, reverie is in the imaginal zone and here endarkened visions happen. The imaginal demands regression to get at reverie. The state of reverie is a regressed state. It is in a state of regression that artistic expression is born. Artistic expression is not born of ego, but id. Painting, poetry, music and writing spring from psychological regression. Artists work in a space unlike that of people driven too much by ego. In fact, James Hillman (1985) suggests that "[t]he source of images, dream--images, fantasy images, poetic images--is the self generative activity of the soul itself" (p. 6). Soul-making, then, is imagistic, reverential, id-driven. Children work soul, make soul from play. Artists are like children. Making art is play.

Without the mystical, without mystery, without art, without color and without sound, what would life be like? Depressing. Children should not be depressed. They are naturally drawn to art and happiness. But if they are depressed, something has gone wrong. Childhood can be violent. Alice Miller (2005) has devoted her lifework to untangling the after-effects of violent childhoods. Her books shock. Child abuse is more common than we would like to think. Childhood can be a nightmare. Even Freud was in denial about the horrors of childhood as he reversed his position on the incest theory.

A childlike state of mind is one that floats toward the mystical. And yet, psyche is profoundly earthbound. C. J. Jung (1958) states,

> nobody can deny that without the psyche there would be no world at all, and still less, a human world. Virtually everything depends on the human soul and its functions. (p. 84)

The human world is the world that is grounded. The soul is not floating in space, but grounded in embodiment. Soul-making, therefore, is an embodied happening. And these soul-making events occur in circular fashion. The psyche operates in circles, not lines. There is nothing linear about psyche. She is a shaped like a mandala. The psyche swirls in color, sound, reverie, space.

Soul-making is sometimes fleeting. Images come and go. The fleetingness of soul-making might be captured when watching clouds. Psyche might be structured like clouds. Clouds are a major metaphor of the imaginal, of reverie, of soul-making. Bachelard (2003) suggests,

> The dreamer always has a cloud to transform. The clouds help us dream of transformation. . . . But with clouds the task is grandiose and easy at the same time. In this globular mass, everything rolls on just as you please. Mountains glide, avalanches fall, then regain their composure; monsters swell up and devour each other; the whole universe is governed by the will and by the imagination of the dreamer. (pp. 185-186)

When I was an elementary school student, I can remember watching the blackened clouds hanging over the gloomy steel city sky. These clouds of soot from the steel mills formed thick shapes that looked like dead bodies. These weren't just ordinary clouds, they were toxic. Sometimes I would see elephants or tigers in the clouds but most often I would see dead bodies. At the turn of the century, Pittsburgh was dark at noon from soot. What kind of imagination is formed in a darkened city? Pittsburgh is still a darkened city today. The skies in Pittsburgh darken at mid afternoon in the winter time. Gray and gloomy skies inform psyche. Psyche born to gloom becomes gloom. Perhaps the prophet Amos was born under gloomy skies.

Childhood is both ugliness and beauty, just like the rest of life. As Jung (1963) says, "[t]he world into which we are born is brutal and cruel, and at the same time of divine beauty" (p. 358). Clouds can form shapes of both dead bodies and cotton candy. Clouds are psychic projection pads. Clouds are mystic writing pads indeed.

One must return to the clouds of an imaginal realm to live a full life. Good teaching is primarily imaginal. Teaching without imagination deadens. Let us teach our students to dream on clouds.

Teaching through the ill body demands working through imaginal spaces. In *The Notebooks of Malte Laurids Brigge*, Rainer Maria Rilke's (1985) narrator says,

> And now this illness again, which has always affected me so strangely. I'm sure it is underestimated. Just as the importance of other illnesses is exaggerated. This illness doesn't have any particular characteristics; it takes on the characteristics of the people it attacks. With the confidence of a sleepwalker, it pulls out their deepest danger, which seemed passed, and places it before them again, very near, imminent. (p. 63)

The way one imagines one's illness has a great effect on coping with it. The way one imagines the illness also has great effect on others. Being ill, means being ill in the context of the social. Illness happens in social webs. Illness brings out different things in different people, as Rilke suggests. Illness can bring out hostility; illness can make one severely depressed and anxious. If anything, illness makes one think more profoundly. Illness heightens danger. Illness forces one to think of death. Illness encourages dangerous behavior. Illness forces one to think deeply. When one engages in deep thought, one is taken to other worlds, to other places, to fantasyscapes. But fantasy is not always like cotton candy clouds. Fantasy images dead bodies. And when the body is ill, fantasies disturb.

CURRERE IS DIALECTIC

Currere--or the lived curriculum-- symbolizes a dialectic. The movements of currere are backward and forward, upward and downward. Currere is a dialogue with the soul. Currere is soul-making as a dialectic. Gaston Bachelard (2000) suggests that the soul is always already dialectical. Bachelard claims that the soul moves both in ascent and descent, a continual up and down. There is no steady state of the soul, it is always in motion. Neuroscientists might not talk of soul, but they would agree that the brain is always in motion, it is always changing. This is why the brain cannot be considered a kind of computer. It is far more complex and more mysterious—it will always outsmart us and outfox us. We always outfox computers and outsmart them.

The soul is this and that, it is dialectical, it is not one sided or one dimensional. The soul is multi-dimensional. A soul stuck in one dimension like depression pains. Move into that pain in order to get out of it. A person must not stay in the dark night of the soul too long--as Thomas Moore (2004) suggests-- or depression turns into petrification. Bachelard tells us that one must work toward embracing what he calls an "ascensional psychology." Bachelard (2002) states,

> We take part in imaginary ascension because of a vital need, a vital conquest as it were, of the void. Our whole being is now involved in the dialectics of abyss and heights. The abyss is a monster, a tiger, jaws open, intent on its prey. It seems, Balzac tells us, "to grind up its prey in advance." Ascensional psychology, which is essentially an education in the art of ascending, must struggle against this polymorphic monster. (p. 59)

Throughout Bachelard's work, the dialectic movement of soul disturbs--especially if one is not used to exploring the shadow side of the dialectic. Some are uncomfortable with dialectical thinking because it is too difficult. It is much easier to think in one dimension. It is easier to think that things are either this or that. But life is not an either/or, it is a this and that. And it is to the this and that, that Bachelard turns. The this and that is both darkness and light. All light endangers. All light represses darkness only to have the darkness return as a monster. The return of the repressed wounds. The dialectic feels chaotic because it is chaos.

Especially when one is ill-- when the soul has been wounded-- chaotic states overwhelm continually. Movements of ascent are rare in states of chronic illness. Mostly, illness is dark. And sometimes illness leads to psychic breakdown. Evans Lansing Smith (1990) points out that those suffering from breakdown might seek out a mythology of the underworld. Smith (1990) says that

> The descent to the underworld (nekyia) is the single most important myth for modernist authors who wrote during C.G. Jung's lifetime. . . .the composition

of these works tend to coincide with a psychological or physical crisis in the writers' lives. . . . Jung's breakdown of 1912-1911 which he regarded as a descent to the underworld illustrates this pattern. . . . (p. 251)

The underworld is that place where--at every turn-- you might be devoured. The underworld is polymorphic, it is variegated, it is thickness itself, it is the thickness of death and dying. The underworld is felt as a weight on one's chest, the feeling of endings, the feeling of terror, the feeling of chaos, the feeling of end-things, the eschaton. The underworld is the dead end, the nowhere place. The underworld is not one-dimensional, it is not only hellfire. The underworld signifies that which one cannot fathom, that which is beyond words, the unspeakable, the unthinkable, the great and final un-doing. The underworld depresses. Depression forces one to move downward, to move deeper and deeper into psychic woods. As psyche moves down, she becomes also immobile, stuck in mud, frozen in time, dead. But in death there is life. Energy never dies.

States of depression and breakdown are thick in color. Black is a color. In a piece titled "Mind and Matter in Myth," Eileen Preston (1990) suggests that,

> The dark colors (red and blue and their compound violet) signify the more unconscious zones of the personal psychic sphere. The light colors (yellow and compounds orange and green) signify the more conscious zones. (p. 15)

The underworld of depression is black but it is also thick with blues, reds and violets. Illness and depression go hand in hand. It is impossible to be sick without being depressed. To de-press, is to press down the psyche, to press it down into blue water, into red suns and violet flowers. To de-press is to be both mobile and immobile. Going down means going somewhere. To sing the blues is to be down, but singing is movement in sound. Sound swings. The blues are not static. Depression is part of the dialectic of soul-making. Illness pushes the de-press button way down, down down, down into the unconscious. Here the tigers are waiting, claws out. WATCH OUT! Snakes attacking, creatures eating their own tales, spiders crawling, rivers overflowing. Hades is on the move.

Teaching through a de-pressed body, means teaching slowly, teaching in slow motion. Time seems to stand still and yet it slowly moves along. The body teaches through de-pression, through illness, through being wounded. The body teaches though images, colors, and with the help of creatures of the underworld. James Hillman (1979c) suggests that creatures are, in fact, soul-helpers. He claims,

> To look at them [animals that appear in dreams] from an underworld perspective means to regard them as carriers of the soul, perhaps totem carriers of our own free-soul or death-soul, there to help us see in the dark. (p. 148)

Contrary to thinking that dream-animals are devourers, Hillman points out that unconscious animal-symbols appear in dreams to help us. Hillman (1979c) suggests that when animal images occur in dreams we need to pay attention. He states:

> The main point there is that there are many animal ways into the underworld. We may be led or chased down by dogs [or spiders] and meet the dog of fear

[or the spider of fear] who leads the way to going deeper. We may be driven down by the energetic rapture of hard-riding horsepower; go down through the air like a bird. . . . (p.150)

Going down into the underworld signifies rapture for Hillman. What is the rapture? Is it the end time? Going down into the underworld is an adventure. A rapturous adventure. Hillman suggests that the unconscious means to teach something, to lead one out of horror. *Educare* means to lead one out, to heal. The unconscious is that place of *educare*. Caring for the soul means going into the dark. And animal spirits can help us care for the soul.

The connection between animals, the soul and healing is made by Mircea Eliade. In a piece titled "Culture and the Animal Soul," Hillman (1997) states that

Mircea Eliade, in his complete, pioneering, and extraordinary study of shamanism, observed that the shaman has a special relation with the animal kingdom. He [or she] heals by means of animal potencies, speaks directly with animals, masters them, takes on animal forms, and often bears an animal name. (p.31)

When a person takes on the form of the spider this symbolizes an introjection of spider-wisdom. Spider-wisdom in the Native American tradition means strength. Spider women warriors signify power. Snakes eating their own tails are symbols of eros; they symbolize life giving forces and wholeness. Tigers are symbols of symmetry. Symmetry harkens back to the mandala. The mandala is the circle of the soul. June Singer (1990) comments that William Blake's famous poem, "The Tyger",

is surely the perfect image for symmetry. The Tyger is "fearful." How awesome is the balance of beauty and grace the marvellous lithesome walk and the fierceness in the tyger's eye. (p. 164)

Symbols of tigers-- archetypal tigers-- heal. Tigers help the powerless against the powerful. Fighting illness is a battle of the powerless body against a powerful disease. Tyger, tyger burning bright, must I remain ill throughout the night?
What has happened to our imaginal tigers as we become adults? Schooling squashes our tiger-imaginations. Schooling prevents us from recognizing primal symbols. Schooling de-stroys imaginal flights and descents. Schooling undoes the capacity to understand dream life. June Singer (1990) warns,

Sometime between childhood and what is called maturity, most of us lost sight of the visionary world of childhood. We become involved with learning all we need to know to get on in the world, take our place among our peers. We are educated, trained, formalized, conditioned. Our minds become cluttered with rote learning. We forget to remember our Tygers. (p. 165)

Schooling kills. We are schooled out of imaginal powers. We are schooled out of the most primal powers of the unconscious, the anima, our animal lives. Schooling de-presses and distances us from our primal selves and the primal world around us. The Tiger leads out, *Educare*. The Tiger is ferocious; the tiger represents our

145

dis-content with civilization. Civilization is dis-contentment as Freud teaches. Civilization kills tiger spirit, tames the tiger within, normalizes the tiger. Dream tigers care not for civilization. Dream tigers honor the eccentric.

Schooling puts out our inner fires. Fire, fire burning bright who put out our Tiger in the night?

THE BODY ELECTRIC: HONORING WALT WHITMAN

The body is electricity. Let us honor Walt Whitman and his body electric.

Philip Wexler (2000) reminds us that we are "[a]n energy body (Whitman's body electric). . ." (p. 70). Electrical charges run through us. The body runs on electricity and when the battery is low it needs to be recharged. That is why we sleep. Electric-Energy is Eros; it is the life-force. John P. Miller (2000) puts it this way: "[t]he soul [is] not localized but [is] an energy field. . ." (p. 37). Soul is energy fields plural—in my estimation. These fields are competing, highly charged and highly complex. Electricity and energy seep outside psyche into the ecosphere. The mind/soul leaks. Where the mind and the world intersect puzzles. Mind leaks into world; world leaks into mind. Bad energy is given off by people who are all shadow or all light. Energy must be balanced between the darkness and the light. The soul demands balance. The soul needs to be in a constant dialectical state. Shadow needs light and light needs shadow. Shadow and light are generated by energy fields that leak outside the body. Norman O. Brown (1966) states that,

> The "postural model" of the body consists of "lines of energy," "psychic streams," "Freud's libidinal cathexes," which are electricity, action at a distance, flux, influx, reflux. . . . (p. 156)

To cathect to an object is to be on fire with electric-desire. To attach oneself to something or someone energizes as a magnet. Magnets, the ancients believed, had souls because they move things. To cathect to something is to be an electric magnetic. To say someone has a magnetic personality suggests movement. Magnetic people are movers and shakers. Conversely, de-cathexsis is the state of de-pression and de-spair. De-cathexsis signifies petrification and death. De-cathecting stultifies. Life is a cycle of cathecting and de-cathecting ; life is never wholly one or the other. Energized and enervated. Upward and downward, shadow and light. Is bi-polar dis-ease a natural state after all?

Extreme states of energy and enervation are experienced in illness. A healing might be followed by a wounding. Good days, bad days. Lisa bright, Lisa dark. On a cloud one moment, into the gates of hell the next. This is what it feels like to be chronically ill. Good days, bad days.

Teaching through these chaotic cycles is no easy task. But working with students gives solace, being-in-connection with students helps. Solace is often found in company. It is just that simple. And yet it is also complicated. Company can also crowd. Manic speech crowds out unthinkable thoughts. Psyche must think the unthinkable. Crowding out what is unthought damages.

Speaking to others heals. The word made flesh. The word made flesh is sacred, mystical. How is it possible that the word is made flesh? Words are miracles. Words are not floating signifiers but are enfleshed. Words have a way of clearing out cobwebs. Words can also imprison. What do we use words to do? Words can be used to evacuate the self or heal the self.

Hermeneutics is a healing art. Let us develop a hermeneutic of the ill body. Interestingly enough, Hermes-- which is the root of the word Hermeneutics-- is the trickster who is also called Mercurius. Mercurius is a healer. Jane Cicchetti (2003) points out,

> Mercurius [also known as Hermes] as the archetype of the healer in general and more specifically as the alchemical water of the philosophers, the force that transmutes and transforms in the healing process. As a god who moves from heaven to earth and down into the underworld, Mercurius is not only heaven but also Hell. (p. 16)

Interpreting texts heals. Texts trigger. The act of interpretation can pain too. Texts bring back painful memories. Memory floods. Healing turns again into spider-pain. There is no permanent healing, but only a re-turn to the underworld and the realm of the chaotic.

To write through illness helps articulate pain and suffering. Writing doesn't cure but it can offer temporary healing. Wexler (2000) claims,

> Criticism subverts alienated life when it reclaims the petrified body and enlivens and revitalizes being through intellectual work. (p. 13)

Intellectual work works through the body electric. Intellectual work fosters soul-travel. Intellectual work is mystical. Intellectual work allows one to better understand the soul. Intellectual work sometimes heals and pains the soul. Adolf Guggenbuhl-Craig (2003) says,

> The healer and the patient are two aspects of the same. When a person becomes sick, the healer-patient archetype is constellated. The sick man seeks an external healer, but at the same time the intra-psychic healer is activated. . . . It is the physician within the patient himself and its healing action that is as great as that of the doctor who appears on the scene externally. Neither wounds nor diseases can heal without the curative action of the inner healer. (cited in Cicchetti, p. 17)

The will-to-Eros-- the will to heal-- must overpower to will-to-thanatos. The death instinct must never win out. And yet, the healer within might not be able to alter the deterioration of the body. The body has its own destiny and we are slaves to that destiny no matter how much of a healing heart we might have.

Teaching is eros; it is-healing. The purpose of education, says Wexler (2000), is ultimately to heal. He states,

> The topical move is to the reinterpretation of education as a process of being and meaning, for which healing may be the ideal, paradigmatic type. Its

topics are consciousness, embodiment, emotions, and transcendence as altered states, the sense, energy, and complex transformations. . . . (p.107)

What a refreshing way of thinking about education. Mostly, we are mis-educated. Public schools in the United States are dreadful; they are governed by the death principle. For me, education is not a transcendent art. Rather, it is a descent. Education, for me, means to lead down into and under that de-centered soul toward that which is the not known and not yet felt. Moreover, education—for me—is hardly conscious. Educating the soul is mostly unconscious as we are driven by forces that we do not understand. Education, for me, is following the heart and riding the wave of unconscious desire.

Teaching through the ill body is a tiger burning bright. Teaching through the ill body is beyond school lessons. Teaching through the ill body is being-toward-death. Teaching through the ill body is electric and Electra-like. Education is a way that we work through our psychic conflicts. Or not.

MOVEMENT AND THE NEGATIVE

Thinking through the energetic forces of negativity and positivity. A certain appreciation that these forces are the stuff of the psyche becomes key. To be chronically ill means living mostly in a negative space, however. The baseline is always negative. Being chronically ill means to live in a crumbling zone, a space that always slips into the underworld. Dreams point downward to this underworld even as cycles of health come back. One of the things about living with chronic illness is that one constantly worries about long term problems. Worse case scenario speculations are not uncommon. Living with anxiety and fear can be debilitating. Negative thoughts can overwhelm psyche. Yet Andre Green (1999) states,

> We shall see how the work of the negative seeks accomplishment by expressing itself in different ways depending on the circumstances: as a passage, a procession, a figure, a moment of transformation, the significance and extent of which will only become clear retrospectively, a moment in the process or, conversely, as obstruction, rigidity, blockage. . . . (p.11)

Working through negative spaces is what living with chronic illness is about. Happy days are few and far between. Healing times, times of remission, are not to be taken for granted. Life seems all the more tenuous, time is the enemy. Rigidity and flux and depression enervate. 'Working the negative' is what Green calls for. Working it. This means that one must psychologically work on being in the negative. One must find ways to use the negative, to make use of the negative rather than allowing it to kill.

Phenomenological descriptions of illness trouble the notion of 'understanding,' because illness-- in many ways-- is beyond understanding. And the experience of illness is so private as to be nearly impossible to explain. But illnesses--no matter how obscure-- must be topics of serious discussion so as to help others who also suffer. Deeply negative emotions associated with illness need to be worked on, worked through. Working through something releases soul. Gaston Bachelard (2002) writes of soul-mobility. Is soul-mobility a form of release? Bachelard states, "[i]n a general way, a soul must be mobilized, if it is to receive the visions of any invitation to travel. . ." (p. 99). The soul travels when worked on. Soul travel--after a bout of deep depression--might feel like ecstasy. Michael Eigen (2001), in his interesting book titled *Ecstasy*, writes that he was driven to write about ecstatic states because of pain. He says,

> I wrote this book in response to an inner pressure to express the ecstasy underlying psychoanalytic work, as well as life more generally--an ecstasy coming through, often wedded with, the most excruciating states. (vii).

Illness, in its most negative phases, is often accompanied by ecstatic states. It is living crazy. One day you feel great, the next day you feel awful. Total negative spaces bog, bog, bog down and kill. Michael Eigen (2001) writes,

> One person's ecstasy may be another person's horror. There are creative as well as destructive ecstasies, ecstasies of war and injury, brutal ecstasies. (viii)

Ecstasy, then, is highly perspectival. My wounds are not your wounds. Sadism, for some, is felt as ecstasy. For others, sadism seems rather perverse. Polymorphous perversity, Freud teaches, is the key to ecstasy. What disturbs might also delight.

How long can the body hold out against chronic illness? Icarus crashes. The body can only take so much. Flying into the sun is the aerial dream of which Bachelard speaks. One must fly high in the midst of darkness. The soul demands flight. The soul wants release from constant anxiety and suffering. The soul wants freedom. Freedom from illness. There is no real freedom from illness, but there can be imagined freedom. Imaginal freedom may sustain one through tough times. Robert Avens (1980) states,

> The importance of archetypal psychology is that it has chosen the path of watchful attention to the imaginal realm, giving, in Hillman's words, "the psyche a chance to move out of the consulting room"-- a chance, that is to say, to be yoked (in the Yogic sense of union) to its archaic, emotional and creative core. (p. 41)

An archetypal study of illness helps foster an understanding of psychic pushes and pulls beyond the rational. Illness has a mind of its own and makes archaic demands on the psyche. Paying attention to psyche's demands means honoring impulses and listening to dreams, living fiercely as a tiger.

The sun is light, its rays can feel good; yet it can also cause death. To be badly burned by the sun is to die. The sun can be cancerous.

In Jung's (1974) book on dreams, he says of the symbol of the sun that it is often paired with the moon and that it is often "represented [in mythology] with wings . . . , denoting intuition or spiritual (winged) potentiality" (p. 276). Illness might make one more spiritual; it certainly has made me more aware of the potential of spirituality. Illness makes you more present to yourself. Illness makes you more present to the divine within yourself. And yet it can also make you more absent psychically.

What illness teaches is that teaching—while ill—can become more and more direct, immediate and fluid. Scholarly work, while ill, might take a turn toward the immediate, the at- hand.

I appreciate the company of my students; my relations with my students are what I would consider the at-hand. Our discussions and our community of struggle reward. Sharing the life of the intellect with students is an ecstasy. Ah, but sometimes it is also an agony!! I have been called to teach. I am a teacher. And I have been called to teach through the ill body. I share my intellectual struggles with my students as I share my illness with them. The private is made public in the space of the classroom. Maurice Merleau-Ponty (1964b) in *Signs,* speaks to these issues.

> As my body (which nevertheless is only a bit of matter) is gathered up into gestures which aim beyond it, so the words of language (which considered singly are only inert signs that only a vague or banal idea corresponds to) suddenly swell with a meaning which overflows into the other person when the act of speaking binds them up into a single whole. Mind is no longer set apart but springs up beside gestures and words as if spontaneous generation. (p. 235)

Teaching through the ill body gestures toward gestures. Words made flesh flow out of the daily scholarly work into the site of the classroom. There is an intense urgency in the teaching body. The teaching body speaks out--as Merleau-Ponty puts it-- to pull together more deeply into the community that is the student body. We become one community of difference in the classroom. Conversations become flows of energy between souls, flows that tend toward the unthinkable. The teacher leads the student out, through daring to teach that which is ignored.

The teacher is Icarus. She crashes on days when teaching agonizes. She soars on good days. Working the teaching body means working through the agony and the ecstasy. Classroom life is dialectical, or so it should be. They listen, they speak. I listen, I speak. I say yes. They say no. I say no, they say yes. On the wings of a dove and through the gates of hell. That is what the ill body teaches; that is what teaching through the ill body means. Thinking-together in community is the work of CURRERE. Merleau-Ponty (1964b) comments, "[t]hinking is man's [sic] business, if thinking always means coming back to ourselves and inserting between two distractions the thin empty space by which we see something" (p. 241).

Thinking-together is thinking-through the "thin empty space" that puts distance between one soul and another. Thinking-through the "thin empty space" together opens up possibilities for soul-mobility and soul-making.

Many scholars think of the teacherly life as a burden. But I think of the teacherly life as a gift. Teaching is not all light, of course. Teaching means exploring the work of the negative and the crashing of Icarus.

The scholar must be in touch with her inner workings and dreams, her feelings and experiences. In fact, scholarly and teacherly life must be a constant struggle to understand the self. Jung (1974) states that,

> Every advance, every conceptual achievement of mankind, has been connected with an advance in self-awareness: man [sic] differentiated himself from the object and faced Nature as something distinct from her. Any reorientation of psychological attitude will have to follow the same road. . . . (p. 61)

Teaching and scholarly life are about making conceptual advances, and one can only do this if one is in touch with the self. This means being in tune with gestures, smells, colors, reveries, urges, impulses, wishes, desires, dreams and insanity. Teaching through the *via negativa* is as important as teaching in the light of day. Teaching through the ill body is an attempt to find ways out of the constant dread, gloom and anxiety of an unknown future.

POST (SCRIPT)

Looking back again. As I struggled through those early days of illness I began to think about healing psychically. And I began a discussion of the *via negativa* but did not really develop it. It seems that I wavered between the light of healing and the darkness of dis-ease. Color heals because it gives a sense of peace. Standing before a painting, getting lost in the swirls of color can serve as a curative--if only for a moment. Dwelling in color leads to reverie, I suggested here. As my illness progressed and I settled into it, I began to think about how to pull my psyche out of the mud. Is this not a sign of psychic health? I never wanted to be defeated in my dis-ease.

Last night I taught again Jonathan Silin's (1995) book on AIDS. I owe much to Silin as he was one of the first in the field of education to open a space to talk about illness in the context of teaching. His painfully honest autobiographical work left my students stunned. Class discussion turned on remembering others who suffer from AIDS. One student even cried. The book allowed students to uncover their own fears and sadness. They talked of the ways in which AIDS patients are shunned still. This is my third reading of Silin's book and I think about what courage it took for him to write such a painfully honest narrative. In many ways, my own work is much indebted to his. His courage gave me the courage to speak. What most struck my students was how these taboo topics get ignored, even in graduate education. It is as if the body and its dis-eases are irrelevant to education. What struck me most, however, was that the students opened up to each other and talked in more heartfelt ways than in the past. Students who were usually shy in class, spoke. What is education for if not for speaking? Why do we continue to silence these topics and also silence our students? If education deals with life and death, why is it that still hardly anybody treats these issues? I grow so tired of the ongoing rants about standardized testing and No Child Left Behind. I get so tired of beating a dead horse. I get tired of fighting the right wing. I tire easily these days. The tiredness is not just an intellectual one but it is also a spiritual, physical and psychic one. I don't know if the tiredness is due to age or due to the illness wearing me down. I get tired of all the academic game playing and the trivial pursuit of academic politics. I turn ever inward and away from the academy. My energies are limited and so I direct them to only two places: my writing and my teaching. The rest of it makes me too tired. What I do not need is for the academy to add to my sickness. So I try very hard to find shelter from the storm of academic trivia. Some days I am successful, other days I am not. I felt a great sense of companionship with my students last night and I felt a great sense of gratitude toward Jonathan Silin. A particular passage struck me in Silin's text and allowed me to think again about the connections between aesthetics, mysticism and illness. Silin (1995) states toward the end of the book that he has

> given up rational argument. We declare ourselves in poetry and song, elegy and lyric. By chanting the names of those I have lost, invoking the lives of children who are deprived of their childhoods, publicly mourning the legions of unrealized lives, I turn toward the world and ask how we can make it a better place? What does our work mean? Does it have value? . . . . I turn toward spiritual sources to accomplish this work. . . . (p. 211)

Two words that struck me here are poetry and spirituality. As Silin works through his own struggle with AIDS and thinks about others' struggles, he also invokes the muse and the spirit. His musing has allowed me to think more deeply about my own struggles and my own turnings toward aesthetics and spirituality. When I initially wrote this chapter I focused on the ideas of color and reverie. Looking back now I feel that there is much room to think through these ideas more deeply as they relate to illness. When I think about the idea of color today, I do not think of it literally, but metaphorically as it relates to language, to words and especially to poetry. I have been giving thought to the idea that there is some connection between poetry and mysticism. I began this discussion earlier in the book but did not flesh it out. Here I would like to explore these thoughts. I would like to deepen the discussion I started earlier. My idea is this: that reading poetry can open one up toward mystical states of being. The poet induces mysticism because she cracks open a fleeting shift in consciousness. Reading poetry also induces states of reverie. And I do feel that reverie is akin to mystical experience.

This post (script), then, will explore these poetic, mysticisms as they relate to dis-ease and psychic turbulence. The title of this chapter includes the phrase 'soul-making.' Because the idea of the soul eludes my grasp, I take my lead from Meister Eckhart (1941) who addresses this issue. He states that

> Whatever the soul does, it does through agents. It understands by means of intelligence. If it remembers, it does so by means of memory. If it is to love, the will must be used. . . . The power of sight can be effectuated only through the eyes, for otherwise the soul has no means of vision. (p. 96)

The soul is not a stand alone concept. To talk of soul, one must also talk of all the other mental faculties we possess. Perception, time, space, love, hate, suffering, seeing, blindness, memory are all part and parcel of the soul's work. This I learned from Meister Eckhart. Perhaps I intuited this already. Plato says we already know things; we just have to recollect them. Eckhart helped me to recollect and articulate these complexities. The idea of the soul is an old-fashioned one I admit, but still I am drawn to it because it allows me to go deeper into myself and find a bit of peace in the madness. Eckhart suggests that when one goes to the deepest, most inward regions of the soul, one finds there only silence. And in that silence is the divine. Yet to get to the silence, one must work on all the related workings of soul. Intellectual work, for Eckhart, is one path on the way toward the soul. Again, the connection between scholar and monk. But this is not an isolated monk, but as the Buddhists say, an "engaged monk" or what I would call an engaged scholar. Thich Nhat Hanh (1998) says of the engaged monk,

> But the Buddha does not want to be isolated amidst offerings of rice, bananas, and flowers. How can a Buddha or a bodhisattva stay indoors? (p. 196)

The engaged monk is the bodhisattva who goes outside the doors of perception and opens the doors of the soul to the world, and especially to those who suffer in the world. The work of the soul--or soul making--is profoundly communal. The soul stands not alone but in relation to all suffering servants.

The soul best speaks, I believe, in poetry. Poetry reveals linguistic color. Poetry allows one to dwell in reverie. Poetry brings the soul back home only to go out into the world toward the other. When one is seriously ill, I think the soul looks for ways to find meaning in woundedness. It is through the wounds that the mystic-poet heals. But this healing--again--is not one of light but of darkness.

[margin note: poetry - tying up the themes in the book]

After teaching my doctoral seminar and coming home late at night, I often feel depressed. Depression is an isolating feeling. My depression has deepened since working on these post (scripts) because of my mother's Parkinson's disease--as I have mentioned earlier. The grief hovers over me especially when I am driving home late at night. After leaving the companionship of my students, my thoughts wander through dark terrain. Grief comes up during times of stillness and especially when one is alone.

So, of late I have turned to the poets and mystics to help me cope. Poets are mystics--at least the good ones are. They break through those silent hells that drag one down. Poetry and profundity go hand in hand. Mystical poetry asks questions related to ontological and existential dis-location. Adrienne Rich (1989) is on old poet friend. She is a readerly friend that is. I spent much time reading Rich during my early twenties. Then I put her down to take that academic turn. Years have gone by since I read Rich. But now, during my mid-life, I return to Rich to find much solace in her healing words. She says, "[m]y hands are knotted in the rope and I cannot sound the bell" (1989, p. 95). My heart is knotted as I think about my mother's deterioration. The psychic toll the mother-- in her deterioration--takes on a child is beyond words. The sound of the bell of my grief cannot be told. Such a heavy heart I have in moments when I am alone. I stand helpless in the face of debilitating dis-ease. A Bodhisattva is supposed to take on the suffering of others, not push it away. But what does that mean? Taking on the suffering of others knots me up; my hands are tied in helplessness. My throat tightens. Such anguish I have never known. Witnessing illness depresses. The bell no longer tolls. The sound of the bell becomes more and more distant as the disease progresses. And the witness stands helpless. The only thing the witness can do is be there and work at being there. But is that ever enough? My stomach knots up, I am in knots over this tragedy. When one is deeply dwelling in the dark waters of depression, the world loses its enchantment. I know that that enchantment of the world waits for me but right now I cannot see it. A character in E.M. Forster's (1920) novel *Where Angels Fear to Tread* speaks about enchantment.

> For there was enchantment, he was sure of that; solid enchantment, which lay behind the porters and the screaming and the dust. He could see it in the terrific blue sky beneath which they travelled. (p. 96)

I too am sure that the world enchants; I am sure of it. But I cannot see it and I cannot feel it. I only feel dark to dark and alone to alone. My world closes in on me as the family becomes smaller and smaller. They are almost all gone--that generation and the generation before that. One by one lights go out in the world. I see the blue sky. I too travel under that blue sky. But the blue sky pales amidst the dark night of the soul as St. John of the Cross (2003) put it. He says, "I went forth without being observed, My house being now at rest. . . . In darkness and concealment, My house now being at rest" (p. 1). But my house is not at rest, it is turbulent. The darkness and concealment has shattered my house of soul. Such a shattering. And here is the rub: I teach under the shadow of all these complex emotions. I teach without enchantment. I teach with much concealed even as I try to reveal the truth. There is so much the teacher cannot and perhaps must not tell. And yet the teacher must be authentically present to her students.

Teaching through the ill body ruins. It is to the ruins of the body we should turn. It is one thing to be sick; it is another thing entirely to be witness to a mother who is terminally ill. At this point, I do not know which is worse. Witnessing feels awful. Every day the dis-ease worsens. Multiple systems atrophy progressively gets worse. There is no cure. At the last stages of this disease a number of terrible things can happen. Dementia is one of them. This is the thing I most fear for my mother. Children of parents with Alzheimer's must know this suffering all too well. Time moves on relentlessly and pulls my mother toward a certain awful death. Not a peaceful death, but an awful one. At this point, she can barely stand up; she can barely walk or use her arms. Her speech has slowed. W. B. Yeats (1989) says, "[t]ime drops in decay, like a candle burnt out. . . ." (p. 56). Dropped time. Dementia is just that, dropped time. Forgetting days, forgetting faces and forgetting in and of itself is time dropped. Will my mother forget me? Will she forget my face? Will she forget who her children are? Will she become bed ridden? Parkinson's plus is a serious disease. It's the kind of disease other peoples' parents get. Not this time. "Time drops in decay" (Yeats, 1989, p. 56). My sisters and I know that this is really happening to us, this is happening to our mother but what can we do? Being there is never enough. I want my mother to fight the disease as I have fought mine. But my disease is not like hers. Multiple systems atrophy completely and utterly destroys the body and the mind. And still I want my mother to fight. Dylan Thomas (2003) eloquently says "[t]hough wise men know at their end dark is right, Because their words forked no lightning they do not go gentle into that good night" (p. 122). Even if one's words did "fork lightning", still one does not go gentle into that good night. To me gently going means giving up. And yet, it will get to a point where one must "go [gently] into that good night." At the very end of breath, when consciousness finally slips away, then one goes gently into that good night. Does there come a point when it is right to stop fighting? To allow dying. To die gently. To open one's heart into the peace of rest? These questions are no simple matter. To think of an impending death shocks. In that stopping that is death the mind no longer meanders along woven knotted-up paths. The anticipation of the end remains. Wallace Stevens (1972) says, "[h]is apprehension, made him intricate" (p. 61). Impending death makes one 'intricate'. These stoppings make us "intricate." The intricacies of facing the death of another astound. Moving deeply inside of sadness opens up toward these intricacies of the soul. Soul-making in its most intricate is in its relation to the Other. Relations to the Other are never pure, never clean and never clear-cut. Sometimes that Other is not there for us. But must we be there for the Other who has not been there for us? This speaks to some of the intricacies of relation or non-relation. Years of non-relation complicate. And yet, we are called toward the Other and in relation to the Other to be for the Other. The Other calls. H.D. says "[i]t was enough--a thought called them from the sharp edges of the earth" (p. 119). At the 'sharp edges of the earth', that thought calls especially when one witnesses the deterioration of the Other. That thought is embodied in the silence in the deepest part of the soul. And it is to that silence we must turn. Because as Levinas (2000) teaches, in the face of the Other is the divine. Levinas states,

> The animation, the very pneuma of the psyche, alterity in identity, is the identity of a body exposed to the other, becoming "for the other", the possibility of giving. (p. 69)

To give to the Other who does not accept that giving is grace. I understand better now than ever what Derrida means by 'the gift of death." Not that death is a good thing--as in a good gift--but that in the *via negativa*, in the impending loss, re-conciliations become possible through giving. Or maybe there are no reconciliations. What is the gift of death then? I am not sure. Lessons taught through the ill body are grave and profound.

The death of the mother is grave and profound. The thought of this impending death makes me feel like I am forever falling. Kenneth Rexroth (1954) says, "[p]lunging through the night on a chilling planet. It is warm and busy in this vegetable darkness where invisible deer feed quietly" (P. 31). Psyche embraces those invisible deer because there is nothing else. *Anima mundi* means the deer of the soul made visible.

Plunging into depression and into that dark night of the soul humbles. There is nothing else but love. That is it. All the mystical traditions teach this lesson. Teaching is love. If it is not, it is not teaching. But it is hard to think of love when one "plunges" into a "chilling planet." Teaching while plunging down darkly is no easy task. Those soul-deer graze in the green grass of eros, the life-soul. And yet that green grass is perpetually turning ever browner. Rilke (1995) says, "[s]uddenly, from all the green around you, something---you don't know what ---has disappeared" (p. 41). Those deer are disappearing as the life force of the Other slowly fades. As the Other fades, so too does the self--at some psychic level. When the mother dies, so too dies a part of the child. And all we ever have left is memory. And that too fades. The voice of the mother fades. And then the memory of the mother fades too. And there is nothing we can do about it. Time marches on pulling us all into the future whether we like that future or not. Rilke (1995) says, "[b]ehind the innocent trees old Destiny is slowly forming her mute expressionless face" (p. 121). Destiny seems cruel especially when illness makes one suffer so. Indeed there is a facelessness in the way things get played out. The cards are dealt and you play the hand you were dealt. That is all you can do.

In the meanwhile, I wake up most days with debilitating headaches. Today was one of those days. A headache is nothing in the face of all else that is going on. I get on with the day. W.H. Auden (1958) speaks to this as he says, "[i]n headaches and in worry vaguely life leaks away" (p. 25). Little by little family members die, life leaks away. Life passes ever so slowly and yet how quickly the hours seem to go by. Soon I will be fifty years old. How did it all pass so slowly and yet so quickly? What have I done with my life? Where has it gone? T.S. Eliot (1962) famously says "I have measured out my life with coffee spoons" (p. 5). What a profound statement. That is life. Coffee spoons. Everyday. The everyday coffee. And the spoons in the sink. In the meanwhile, life passes and people die. In the meanwhile, my mother gets worse and worse as her disease progresses. I keep making that early morning coffee and putting those spoons in the sink. That is life. It all seems so absurd, so pointless.

BLACK HOLES, WOUNDED ARCHETYPES
AND HOMECOMING

The Teaching life goes on even when one cannot go on. Teaching through the ill body means going on when one cannot go on. Here I am reminded of the Beckettian (1958) condition. But the teaching continues even when Ill body fights but continues its deleterious turns. When it all comes down to it, the institution of higher education does not want ill bodies inhabiting it. Institutions want health and youth. This is a reflection of the larger culture of American society. The ill are shunned. America is a culture of health and youth. We are a culture of botox. Illness teaches what the academy is really about. The academy is for the strong, vibrant and healthy. It is no place for the sick. In fact, it can make you sick! The academy pushes you into a black hole.

At any rate, illness is not something one chooses. Kat Duff (1993) states,

> Illness chooses us . . . for its own inscrutable reasons, just as surely as the clouds catch up with the sun to cast a net of darkness upon the land. We are caught unsuspecting by the onset of symptoms, and often feel attacked or persecuted, even slain, by this stealthy burglar, this hungry hunter, who has made us its prey. . . . We've already been taken, abducted like Persephone into the underworld of sickness. (pp. 4-5)

Being sick is like living in another world; it is like living in the underworld. The workaday world is one culture; the world of the sick is the underworld. Many who inhabit the workaday world of the academy have not integrated their shadow so they project negativity onto the sick. Being sick makes one feels Othered. The academy--a mirror of the larger culture-- is a site of Othering. The judges of the academy would like nothing better than to be rid of us.

The ill are led by Persephone into the underworld, the underworld of medical technology, the underworld of doctor's offices and hospitals, the underworld of one's own body, the underworld of pain. BLACK HOLES suck in the ill. A phenomenology of illness is a phenomenology of black holes. Whirling in a void, whirling in the face of death, whirling completely and utterly.

Periods of remission from the illness allow one to think and reflect on the big questions of life. Illness can be tied to vision. Jung (1963), after experiencing a heart attack writes,

> After my illness a fruitful period of work began for me. A good many of my principle works were written only then. The insight I had had, or the vision of the end of all things, gave me the courage to undertake new formulations. I

no longer attempted to put across my own opinions, but surrendered myself to the current of my thoughts. Thus one problem after the other revealed itself to me and took shape. (p. 297)

What does it mean to surrender to the current of thoughts? Is this possible? Jung suggests that there is something almost non-human about a current of thoughts. Is this what he means by the collective unconscious? There is something about the mind that is bigger and older than we are. Regression taps into that more archaic thought pattern. Regression holds captive that flow, that current of thoughts. The ego gets in the way. The ego shuts down imagination and intuition. Imagination and intuition are of the Id. The ego must get out of its own way. Thought currents take flight in ariel travel once the ego backs off. A letting go is in order. Free writing is a result of freely associated thoughts.

Teaching through the ill body means capturing freely associated thoughts, sharing them with students. Opening the doors of perception. Teaching through the ill body means paying attention to dreams and to the underworld, because messages are sent and need to be addressed. The importance of listening to our dreams has been commented upon by many in the curriculum studies field (Pinar, 1994; Doll, 1995; 2000, Miller, 1990; Morris, 2001). When one is sick, dreams take on special importance. I had dream where the word 'C A N C E R' was written in capital letters in the sand. My condition makes me more prone to developing esophageal cancer. Perhaps the dream is telling me that my environment—which might be built on sand--is cancerous. The academy is a sand-sinking environment. I always get that sinking feeling when I approach campus. It is true that a large number of my colleagues have cancer. It is true that the building in which I work is filled with toxic mold. It is true that the Savannah River is polluted with nuclear waste. That's got to be cancerous. At any rate, the dream of C A N C E R stays with me as a warning. Murray Stein (1983) remarks,

Dreams can strike like thunderbolt and leave you shaken to the core. It is in the night that Hermes comes forth and does his work. His myth speaks of the soul's awakening and emergence. (p. 4)

Hermes wishes to speak through dreams. Hermes, though, is a trickster. Because the dream is a trick, it becomes hard to interpret it, to untangle it. What codes need cracking? There are multitudinous meanings to dreams. The literal story of the dream is not what is important. It is what the dreamer does with the dream that matters. As I try to make sense of my place in the world, my place in the deep South, in an institution that does not welcome the likes of me (for it has shown itself to be anti-intellectual, anti-Semitic and homophobic), perhaps the illness has helped me to understand just how cancerous a place it is. I have dealt with some of these issues in my last book (Morris, 2006). Is Hermes trying to tell me that being Othered made me ill? Maybe. Maybe not. My illness, more than likely was caused by a virus. But still, one's surroundings can hasten an illness or make it worse. Did the university make me worse or hasten the onset of my illness? Who knows. The university is a place of the great demon Mother, split off from her child, Puer. The university is SENEX, the Old Queen, split from her Puer child. SENEX does not play with her child, she crushes her. The university crushes the vulnerable. James Hillman (1979a) comments:

> So the senex [when split off from the Puer] represents just this force of death that is carried by the glittering hardness of our own ego-certainty, the ego-centricity that can say 'I know".... It is also dry and cold and its boundaries are set as if by its own precision instruments. (p. 19)

SENEX University is no place for sick people. We are Othered; we are the Face of ugliness, the Face of the weak. We are trampled on by the SENEX University, we are discarded and disgraced. Tenure clocks tick away. Who cares if you are sick? They certainly do not care. Those judges who determine whether you stay or whether you go do not give a tinker's damn if you've been sick during your untenured years.

The Senex-puer constellation is the integration of the inner child into the adult. When the inner child is split off from the adult (as in the case of the university where the professor—child is split off and mistreated by the senex-university) trouble looms. When the inner child is not split off from the adult, maturity abounds. A mature university is where professors are respected and the line between administrators and professors is not neatly drawn. Or perhaps a mature university is one where there are no administrators. The French university system is not unfamiliar with this.

Illness can make you both child or elder, or both simultaneously. Illness can make you regress and become infantile. The child split off from the adult, however, is in grave danger. Infantilization dehumanizes. Or, the illness can make you literally older. Parkinson's patients are said to age rather quickly. More metaphorically, illness can make you just feel old and tired. The point is that a balance between the senex and puer is needed to best cope with illness. The archetypal constellation senex-puer is the integration that is needed during times of illness. Hillman (1979a) suggests,

> The archetype per se is ambivalent and paradoxical, embracing spirit and nature, psyche and matter, consciousness and unconsciousness; in it the yea and nay are one. There is neither day nor night, but rather a continual dawning. The inherent opposition within the archetype splits into poles when it enters ego-consciousness. (p. 12)

The university is all ego, all light, all Old King and Chrone. The university runs on a clock, the chronos of tenure. Sickness has no clock, sickness knows no time, for time has stopped. In my case, sickness did not slow down my production but in fact sped it up. But for many, sickness slows down productiveness. In my case, the death call was too loud. I feel as if I am fighting for my life—as irrational as that may be because I do not have a terminal illness like my mother. She is literally fighting for her life. And yet, I feel my internal clock ticking.

My books pour out of my head from I don't know where, from the underworld, from Hermes, from the child, from the Puer. I can't stop writing. I have a terrible sense of urgency which increases over time. I have a great sense of hurry-up, hurry-up and get finished already. Write the next one. Then the next one.

And yet the place in which I work mitigates against this mad productivity. The university is a black hole. The university is a destructive place. To live inside of destruction is to live inside of a Beckettian (1958) universe where one cannot go on but must go on. Beckett's character in *The Unnamable* says,

> before the door that opens on my story, that would surprise me, if it opens, it will be I, it will be the silence, where I am I don't know, I'll never know, in the silence you don't know, you must go on, I can't go on, I'll go on. (p. 414)

I can't go on, I'll go on. The Medusa-mother-university chills. The message of the university is that it doesn't care if you are sick and doesn't care if you do or do not go on. The university is the clock ticking, that is all. It is a Bergman film. Clocks ticking. The university is Chronos.

WOUNDED ARCHETYPES AND HOMECOMING

Archetypal images related to woundedness are these: PAN and ASKLEPIOS. I turn to these archetypes to raise questions about healing and psychological identification. Psychological identification with archetypal symbols might amplify one's condition and help one cope. In an interesting book titled *Pan and the Nightmare*, James Hillman (2000) argues that Pan (which interestingly enough is the root of the word 'panic') teaches about fear. If one pushes away fears (fears of deteriorating for example) things are only made worse because the repressed returns tenfold. To get in touch with fears, is --in a sense-- to heal. Hillman (2000) suggests, "Pan would rule at the deepest level of our frenzy and our fears. At the same time pan heals at this level" (p. 78). Facing my fear of developing esophageal cancer leads me to re-think my life. Hillman (2000) goes on to say,

> If Pan brings the madness, then he is the healer. Like cures like. He belongs in the education of the citizen [emphasis mine]. As master of instinctual soul, he has something to teach about rhythms and range. Pan was a music man and called a great dancer. He made his appearance felt in choral gatherings . . . . Music carries the body out of its separated loneliness. It educates (lit. "leads out") the soul driven into itself by fear. (p. 81)

Pan is a special god to me because I am first and foremost a musician. Playing music heals. Music has been a great consolation throughout this ordeal. Music has been my sanctuary. Pan and I get along well. Pan is the musical spirit, the spirit of the Id, the IT, the unconscious.

Fear can be associated with depression. I have never read such a startling admission of fear as in Andrew Solomon's (2001) *Noonday Demon*. He talks in his book of his frightening descent into depression and breakdown. During this descent, he tells his readers that he fears almost everything. What makes someone so intensely fearful? His fears are clearly irrational, but that does not make them any less real. The fear of getting up, of taking a shower, of walking down the street, of making a phone call, of living. Solomon's (2001) testimony is a real eye opener to the ways in which fear can paralyse. I have never experienced fear in such an intense way as has Solomon. My fears are pretty common. I am afraid of heights. I am afraid of deterioration. I am afraid for my mother because of her terrible illness. Fears and depression that lead to breakdown, are ironically, psyche's way of healing. Getting depressed is a way to protect psyche from some worse fate.

Pan heals via the madness of illness, as Hillman points out. When one is ill one is always already mad. Pan amplifies the madness of teaching in this condition. Without Pan, teaching dies. Neither teaching nor writing can sing without Pan's guidance. To lead out means stepping out on a precipice. Teaching means stepping out. When you are ill, you step closer to the edge. Teaching madly.

Hillman (2000) points out that Pan is closely tied to the god Asklepios. Michael Kearney (2000) remarks that Asklepios

is to be found within the patient's subjective experiences of inner trans-formation and healing, and in the compassionate and caring attitude of those who attend them and stay with them in their suffering. (xxi)

Askelpios is the god of incurable, chronic illness (Kearney, 2000). Askelpios is my god and guide. Asklepios becomes a compassionate questioner. Askelpios is a metaphorical, mythological psychoanalyst who asks questions but gives no answers. He leads psyche out into the murky world of associative thought. Kearney (2000) points out that "[d]reamwork, which is taken here to mean attending to and being animated by a dream, was central to the ancient rite of Asklepian healing" (p. 111). Dreams teach through the ill body. Asklepios amplifies the problems at hand through the dreams. Asklepios spends time with mortals, with mortal woundedness in order to heal. He is there to lead, to lead out of the black holes of illness.

Akslepios was one of the most beloved of the Greek gods because he spent time with suffering mortals (Kearney, 2000). He spent time with the chronically ill. He has spent time with me ---- especially in the worst days-- sending fearful messages, but messages that have been necessary to inner transformation. Asklepios has helped me get at some sort of understanding. Jung (cited in Hillman, 1979b, p. 71) suggests that the organs of the body send messages from the underworld. Jung states that

The divine thing in us functions as neuroses of the stomach, or the colon, or the bladder, simply disturbances of the underworld, our Gods have gone to sleep and they only stir in the bowels of the earth.

During the worst phases of my illness when I could not get up off the couch and could barely swallow or eat, my gods had gone to sleep. I had been abandoned. Now the gods have been awakened by a period of remission and are helping me understand what I must do to heal, what I must do to move on with my life, what I must do to teach through the ill body. The gods are not asleep now; they are wide awake, as Maxine Green (1995) might put it. Being wide awake means digging deeply. Psyche must dig into disturbance. One must be disturbed before one can heal.

HOMECOMING

In the meantime, homecoming is at hand. I must return home, home to my body, home to my illness, home to the home of my heart. I must return not only symbolically to my spiritual home-- to my gods and goddesses who have helped me through this terrible ordeal-- but I must return home to the northland. I am not literally going home, but I am going home to the symbolism of the northland of illness. Integrating the illness into one's life becomes an important step toward healing and coping. Homecoming means integrating.

Re-turning home means re-turning to fantasy images, to dreams, to inner thoughts and feelings. Illness forces one to re-examine life. To ask the large questions. Do I belong here? What would I do if my illness took a turn for the worse? If I had five years left what would I do? What friends would I like to spend time with? What about the animals? Would I start a Husky farm? Would I quit academe? Would I write my magnum opus? Would I record music? What rituals would I engage in to keep me sane? What do my dreams tell me? Am I dreaming? Or am I the walking-dead?

These sorts of questions should always be on the front burner. But when life has become normalized and routinized, questions such as these are kept on the back burner. Getting caught up in what doesn't matter is a commonplace of health and well-being. Illness demands that one make major changes.

Dreams point to broken-ness and shifts in awareness. I had a dream that my bicycle chain was broken and it devastated me. I had a dream that I had a breakdown and was laughing. The broken bicycle chain and the breakdown point to breaks in awareness. Are nervous breakdowns funny? Why would I be laughing? Perhaps this is what Freud would call reaction formation. The broken chain of the bicycle tells me that it's time to break the chain of subservience to mother-imago, to father-imago, to the imago of the university. I am broken in illness but not broken in spirit. In fact, my spirit has never been more alive, more vibrant, more glowing. But the black holes will come-again. There will be days when I cannot get out of bed, when illness overwhelms, when life choices seem narrow, when futurity seems cut off.

I cherish time spent with my graduate students, for they give me sustenance, they are the chorus in a Greek Tragedy. We share ideas and I grow from their insights. I have never loved teaching more than now. But I live in a world where the future forecloses on itself. It is a matter of time before the doctors have to do more work on me, like a broken bicycle. Every set back is a stab at the heart.

I am listening closely to my fantasy-images, for they tell me about my interiority. Interiority is not light, it is thick and dense and webbed with spiders and monsters. Jungians have a specific thought in mind when speaking of fantasy-images. Patricia Berry (1982) teaches that

Following Jung, by image we ". . . do not mean the psychic reflection of an external object, but a concept derived from poetic usage, namely, a figure of fancy or fantasy-image". . . . (CWGp. 743)" (p. 57)

Fantasy-images come from dreams. Dreams shape conscious life; they shade the day. Dreaming darkly. Dreams alter emotional states. Dreams, more often than not, disturb. I have continual dreams about packing up, moving, moving back home, moving to Pittsburgh. I even have my apartment picked out in the dream. I have a place for the piano. I dream often of moving to Shady Side. Significant name. Shady signifies the shadow. I must move closer to my own shadow. I must work always to integrate more deeply my shadow side. I must work to allow the shadow to do its work. James Hillman (1975) points out that,

> Images are the only reality we apprehend directly; they are the primary expression of mind and its energy which we cannot know except through the images it presents. (p. 174)

Packing and unpacking are common images around which I dream. To unpack the psyche is to deconstruct the images, to freely associate around the images. This is the lesson of psychoanalysis, whether of Freudian or Jungian bent.

Teachers who do not unpack their psyches end up unwittingly projecting their garbage onto students. Teachers project their shadows unwittingly and consequently do damage to the student body.

If CURRERE symbolizes lived experience, it means most importantly an investigation of inner dream-images, imaginal-fantasy. CURRERE means first and foremost unpacking the curriculum VITA. It means unpacking one's lifestory, lifehistory, lifememory, in order to better relate to the Other. One cannot relate to the Other if one has not looked deeply within. Robert Johnson (1986) teaches that we must dialogue with our images--talk to our shadows--in order to make sense of our lives. Johnson (1986) states that we must engage in "active imagination" by

> going to the images that rise up in one's imagination and making a dialogue with them. It involves an encounter with the images. . . . This often means a spoken conversation with the figures who present themselves, but it also involves entering into the action, the adventure or conflict that is spinning its story out in one's imagination. (pp. 24-25)

Entering into a dialogue with one's dreams is a difficult undertaking. One must speak to the Self and learn to listen deeply. Moreover, one must be involved with the psyche and move along in the "adventure" of the imaginal, as Johnson suggests.

But what is this adventure? The adventure of the shadow-image shocks, saddens and wounds. Shocking fantasy-images, depressing fantasy-images must be embraced, not pushed away. Wounded Puer cries, wounded Puer curls up in the fetal position because the interior world, the hermetic world is sending messages that are not comforting. In fact, the messages emanating from interiority overwhelm. As the Jungians teach, messages that speak to us must be spoken back to. Jung (1976) suggests that especially if a dream is shocking, one must pay attention to it. Ignoring messages may lead to psychic dissociation. Jung (1976) states,

> Sometimes a dream is of such vital importance that its message reaches consciousness no matter how uncomfortable or shocking it may be. From the standpoint of mental equilibrium and physiological health in general, it is much better for the conscious and the unconscious to be connected and to move on parallel lines then for them to be dissociated. (p. 209)

Dissociation splits the self. A split off self is not healthy. In extreme cases, psychotics completely split off parts of themselves and deposit these parts into objects. This is termed projective-identification. Sometimes parts of psyche get deposited in objects and cannot get re-introjected back into the self. This is why psychotics lose touch with reality. Split off parts of the self get lost and the self has difficulty regaining connection to self and the world.

When the psyche shocks itself, as Jung points out, it may be trying to send a "vital" message. Vital signs are sent in shock-waves. In order to retain vitality one needs to be shocked back into reality. This is the theory behind shock treatment, a literalization and brutalization of psychology. One must never literalize. Shock therapy is cruel. It Is not therapy at all, it is torture. Sadism. The psyche can shock itself symbolically.

The symbols of shock need to be interpreted vis-à-vis free association. Shocking dream symbols repeat. Repetitive dreams are vital and significant. Here the psyche demands an EAR. As I stated earlier, I often dream of packing, moving. Moving is problematic for me. I do not like to move. As a child, we moved around all the time. The geographic cure? Moving symbolizes instability and chaos. Moving symbolizes, for me, the chaos that was my childhood. Dreams might be telling me to move into my depressions. To move intellectually. To put these depressions to work intellectually. My dream-fantasy is to move to the Shady-side, to move deeper into negative imagos. James Hillman (1975) argues that

> Because fantasy is never merely a wisp of unreality, because it expresses personality's archaic, emotional and creative aspect and is a person's primary reality, by focusing on fantasy we touch what is really at work in the soul. The qualitative transformations in fantasy such as [those that] go on in a long dream series represent transformations of the archetypes that rule personality and are its basic nature. (p. 175)

Repetitive dreams teach the unteachable and point to the unspeakable. I have had a repeating dream for most of my adult life. This is a dream of taking stuff out of my mouth, pulling it, pulling it, pulling it. I can never seem to get the stuff out of my mouth. This dream never leaves me; it keeps coming up from below. The stuff I pull out of my mouth in the dream is long like gum and has a sour taste and chokes me, it keeps coming and I cannot speak, I can't get it out of my mouth. The dream has continued in various ways over the past twenty years. No amount of analysis has been able to get rid of it. It just keeps coming year after year. Everything seems to move the wrong way within. Everything goes backwards. In order to understand this backward movement, I must go down into the underworld, the bowels of the earth, the underworld, to the shadow of my psyche.

I have what is termed a motility disorder. Things do not move along as they should. Things do actually move backwards. My dream has been trying to tell me something for a long time. The dreams psychically push backward and downward into the underworld. Jung (1976) suggests that dreams,

> prepare, announce, or warn about certain situations, often long before they actually happen. Most crises or dangerous situations have a long incubation, only the conscious mind is not aware of it. (p. 208)

I suppose these dreams--of stuff coming out of my mouth-- have been warning me for twenty years. These dreams have tried to warn me of the illness-to-come.

Dream images are meaningful, they teach about what is going on within. Dream images speak the unspeakable and are full of deep and rich symbolism. Dreams are mythological and fantastical. Dreams are life, life is a dream and the dream is real. Perchance to dream. But what does that really mean?

CHILDREN AND DREAMS

As teachers, we must allow children to dream, to talk to their dreams, to explore their dreams. Perhaps schools could start dream workshops where children explore dreams with teachers. Children could draw or paint dream-images. Children would live richer lives if teachers allowed them to explore the adventure of dream. Certainly, children's' fantasy lives would be enriched by allowing such activities. Children might be able to grow up to be whole individuals if they learn that dreams are important, that dreams are the stuff of life. Curriculum as dreaming-text. The dreaming curriculum might be an exciting way to engage children with their imaginal lives.

Dreaming could be captured through rituals like story telling, painting, playing music, writing poetry. Acts of creativity are ritual acts. These kinds of creative activities should be more integrated into the curriculum. But as educators know, the first things to go in the schools are the arts and the art of dreaming has never been part of the curriculum---and the way things are going in American public schooling children will never be able to dream their dreams.

Thomas Moore (1983), like many Jungians, comments on the importance of ritual. Moore (1983) states

> To be in ritual is to be like Tristan, rudderless without a steering ego, but equipped with a musical instrument, an imagining ego. Tristan is clever. He knows many languages. He uses his musical talent to arrive, that is, to stream, to high places. To be in ritual is not simply to be adrift, but to be adrift with an instrument that is not a rudder. A ritual sense gives life to the ten thousand things, to multiplicity unimaginable. (p. 3)

It is ritual that allows the imagination to work its magic. The rituals of story telling, playing music or writing poetry might allow children to explore the adventure of fantasy life. Rituals help to ingather, to dwell, to think and feel more deeply. Ritual gives a shape to life, gives a shape to sound and color. Writing is a form of ritual that guides dream-images onto paper. Writing turns fantasy into form.

The ritual of playing instruments helps me cope with illness. Playing the piano, guitar and cello have helped me cope with what is unthinkable. Listening to vibrating strings and allowing these vibrations to move through me has helped heal my broken spirit. The ritual of writing-- the ritual of putting into words the images and fantasies of my dreamlife-- is a release, a spiritual renewal, a spark re-ignited. Writing sets me aflame. Writing is my lifeblood. Writing is dialogue with interiority. The ritual of teaching has helped me stay in touch with others, to BE-in-touch. Teaching through the ill body is a ritual of giving. To teach is to give the gift of knowledge through words, gestures and emotions. To set aflame Others through words. Words are my craft, words are my life, words are not separate from images, for images are always already in words. Writing is painting in word-images. Word-images heal.

Thomas Moore (1983) points out the difference between rituals and ritualism. Schizophrenics engaged in ritualism. Ritualism consists of meaningless repetitive acts. Ritualism is not ritual. Ritualism has no meaning. Rituals, on the other hand, are meaningful, full of meaning and full of awe. Without rituals, life is chaotic. Rituals help to channel anxiety. Anxiety that is channelled can fuel writing or musical expression.

An anxious text is one that simply must speak, that has no time to waste; it is a text that must be written. This is an anxious text, it must speak and it must be written. In fact, this text is writing itself. The unconscious moves the image-thoughts out of psyche and onto paper. Thomas Moore (1983) says that "words can be ritualized acts, if they are put in the river, in the stream of imagination" (p. 7). Words cannot travel in the stream of imagination unless the psyche is open to the imagination. The psyche must be broken open, as it were, to get inside the stream of the imaginal.

To be broken open is to be open to the spiritual-within-the-imaginal. The imaginal and the spiritual go hand in hand. Ann Belford Ulanov (1995) states that Jung

> builds into his picture of the psyche the religious instinct and our experience of the numinous; he sees archetypes as having a spiritual as well as an instinctual pole; he sees a transcendent function working in the psyche with which we can cooperate through engaging in active imagination. (p. 52)

Active imagination means talking back to our shadow, talking to imaginal-fantasies, talking to dream-images. Performing meaningful ritual is a way of talking back and dialoguing with dream-fantasies. Breaking open the psyche is a spiritual act. Becoming spiritual is also becoming more in tune with one's body and the surrounding ecosphere into which that body is thrown. Spirituality is embodied and cosmological. The Holy Ghost of spirit hovers within and around the wounded body.

In the Jewish mystical tradition, broken shards come down to earth; we are those broken shards. Our task in this lifetime is to heal the broken shards, to heal ourselves. *Tikkun* means to heal brokenness. This is a spiritual quest. Healing what is broken is the working out of the numinous. The numinous is the profane. The profane is sacred. Dreams are a sacred landscape. The numinous is everywhere. Broken shards, broken lives are sacred mindscapes too. Broken lives need healing. Spirituality's function is to heal. Many people who become ill and face mortality become more spiritual. Some, on the other hand, lose their sense of the divine.

ARCHETYPE OF THE INVALID: MEET HEPHAISTOS AND THE THIRD SPACE OF DETERIORATION

Chronic illness and invalidism sometimes go hand in hand. Deconstruct the word. In-valid. One's life is thought to be in-valid by those who marginalize the ill. In the academy, one's body is made in-valid by unsympathetic colleagues. One's work as a teacher and scholar becomes in-validated. The multicultural literature talks much about racism and sexism but there is little discussion on discrimination against those who are sick. The chronically ill have to struggle with a deteriorating body. The chronically ill live on the margins. Illness is clearly a stigma in American society. Americans do not make room for the ill.

Unlike intermittent sickness, chronic illness does not go away. How to psychologically manage that? Chronic illness means you will never get better. How to live with that thought? I suggest we live in a third space. Thought is in the inbetween. Thought in the inbetween wavers.

The spirit and body intertwine in the third space. The third space is the mystery that makes us what we are. The third space of chronic illness is a place between here and there, this and that, health and disability. The third space of chronic illness is a space of nowhere. The body moves on in everyday life, yet deteriorates, moves on and then makes lateral deteriorations, sometimes horizontal or vertical deteriorations. The third space is deterioration. The third space is one of anxiety because one never knows whether the body will work right or not. The third space is the space of bodily betrayal.

Every-body betrays, slows down, decays and falls apart. These facts are hard to think about. As we age we decay. Some people get old and never experience illness. They might slow down a bit and turn gray, but they are blessed with good health throughout their lives. And then there are those of us who are not so lucky.

The chronically ill live in a third space. The chronically ill move about between the healthy and the hospitalized. Little is understood about the ways in which the chronically ill suffer. Oliver Sacks (1998) tells us that physicians who rely on case studies forget about the humanness of the case at hand. He states,

> There is no 'subject' in a narrow case history; modern
> case histories allude to the subject in a cursory phrase
> ('a trisomic albino female of 21'), which could as well
> apply to a rat as a human being. To restore the human
> subject at the centre—the suffering, afflicted, fighting

human subject—we must deepen a case history to
a narrative or tale; only then do we have a 'who'
as well as a 'what', a real person, a patient, in relation
to disease—in relation to the physical. (viii)

Sacks has done much to humanize patients. He is a great storyteller and has
introduced many strange stories of neurological disease to lay readers. Sacks
teaches that the brain is stranger than imagined. One of the disturbing things about
reading his work is the discovery that things can always get worse. So many things
can go wrong in a life. It is amazing that any of us function at all. "The man who
mistook his wife for a hat" is the strangest story of all (1998). He literally thought
his wife was a hat. He tried to take off her head and put it on his! Sacks (1998) tells
us that he "saw faces when there were no faces to see: genially, Magoo-like, when
in the street he might pat the heads of water hydrants and parking meters, taking
these to be the heads of children . . ." (p.8). The strangest thing of all is that this
man—at least on one level—did not think there was anything the matter.

Like Sacks, V.S. Ramachandran and Sandra Blakeslee (1998) report some very
strange cases. One very strange case is that of a schoolteacher who thought her arm
"belonged to her brother" (p. 2). Another strange case is of the man who thought
that his parents "had been replaced by duplicates" (p. 2). Injuries of the brain show
us how strange the brain is. There are "phantoms in the brain" in the case of
phantom limbs and pain (Ramachandran & Blakeslee, 1998).

My story is not nearly as serious as the ones reported by Sacks and Ramachandran
and Blakeslee. Brain related injuries really make us think about the notion of alterity.
Most of us do not know alterity at this deeply phenomenological or neurological
level. There are cases of memory and memory loss that boggle the mind. One
patient that Sacks talks about got stuck in 1945 (see "The Lost Mariner", 1998); A.
R. Luria (1968) tells the tale of a man who could remember everything in his famous
case study titled *The Mind of a Mnemonist*. Here, the patient could remember long
series of numbers for decades, he could memorize anything like the names of
streets and which buildings were where-- having not been on those streets or in
those buildings in years. But he could make little meaning out of his life. His
memories were essentially meaningless. And then there is the man who got shot in
the head and forgot everything in *The Man with a Shattered World*. Here, A.R.
Luria (2002) tells the story of this man who tried desperately to remember his
shattered past by keeping a journal. As soon as he would write a sentence he would
forget what he had just written and had to start all over again. This went on for
years. But even more strange were the experiences of his ghost like body. The
patient, in his journal, tells us that,

Sometimes when I'm sitting down I suddenly feel as though
my head is the size of a table—every bit as big—while my
hands, feet and torso become very small. . . . When I close
my eyes, I'm not even sure where my right leg is; for some reason
I used to think (even sensed) it was somewhere above my
Shoulder, even above my head. (cited in Luria, 2002, pp. 42-43)

This might seem funny but it is not funny at all. It is tragic. What ghosts do we harbour in our brains? How much we take for granted. That we know where our legs are, or what the size of our head is in relation to our body is a miracle.

The ghost-demon of illness haunts. The third space of chronic illness is a place of woundedness. The soul-body is wounded. The third space is a wounded-place. To walk around wounded, limping--as it were--is to drag one's heals, to have to push oneself doubly hard to get through the day. Imagine not knowing where your heals were?

Studying side by side lay neurology, traditional psychoanalysis and depth psychology make for mind-blowing discoveries. The study of pathography— because of the very difficulty of the subject matter—should be interdisciplinary. The interdisciplinary nature of this study lends itself nicely to my home field of education and more particularly curriculum studies. As against the work of neurologists, and psychoanalysts of whatever sort, I am mostly interested here in talking about the implications that illness has on teaching and on education generally speaking.

Could you be a teacher if, say, you do not remember where your leg is? Or, could you be a teacher if you thought your wife were a hat? Curiously, the 'man who mistook his wife for a hat' was a teacher!! He was music teacher. Moreover, Sacks (1998) tells us that he was "a musician of distinction" (p. 8). Sacks teaches throughout his work that music helps people with movement disorders get their movement back. Music is about movement, time, rhythm and soul. Sacks also talks about the ways in which people who have no memory, find soul in spiritual or artistic endeavours (see for example "*The Lost Mariner*", 1998).

Neurology and depth psychology—distant bedfellows that they are—teach that stories are key to understanding that which is beyond understanding. Storytelling is what mythology is all about. And it is to these stories that the Jungians suggest we should turn, especially if we are ill. The Jungians talk about finding archetypal stories in ancient literatures. Adolf Guggenbuhl-Craig (1979) remarks that it is difficult to find an archetype of chronic illness in Greek myth. Interestingly enough, the Greeks did not seem to be comfortable with weakness of the chronic sort. Yet, there is a Greek god named Hephaistos who limped, Guggenbuhl-Craig tells us. Hephaistos is an archetype of chronic illness. So it is to Hephaistos I turn. The Jungians suggest that one must have it out with the limping archetype. Why do the wounded limp—metaphorically-- along with Hephaistos? Patients must ask Hephaistos what is going on psychically that may have caused this deterioration. I try to engage Hephaistos in a dialogue but I am not successful. I don't know what Hephaistos wants of me. Perhaps I was born too soon? Perhaps I was born too late? Perhaps I was supposed to be a boy? Perhaps I should have followed my bliss? I am not ready to meet death. Hephaistos, tell me what I need to do. I do not know what to do. Finding an archetypal figure with which to dialogue and study, however, makes the fight, at least, more interesting. There is a bit of solace knowing that the story of the limping god is also my story. I don't feel so alone when I study these myths of illness.

Earlier I talked about the Senex-Puer constellation. I am more Puer than Senex. I certainly identify psychologically with the child archetype more than father time. I am not the Old King or the Old Mother. In my mind, I am a child. And yet I do feel old sometimes. I feel tired as many do who are sick. The illness has made me feel old. But I refuse to believe that I am the Old King Senex. Perhaps I have split off the Old King Senex and he has come back to haunt me. Ah, the return of the repressed.

In any event, Hephaistos is unlike either Senex or Puer. Guggenbuhl-Craig (1979) argues that,

> First [the archetype of the invalid, i.e. Hephaistos] has nothing to do with the child archetype. The child, like the invalid, is weak, but it grows; it becomes an adult, it "kills the father," it has a future. The child is only temporarily weak. Second the archetype of sickness is also something else, because sickness leads to death, or to health, or to invalidity. (pp. 34-35)

The third space of chronic illness is that place between health and death. Chronic illness is living in a straw-man state. At any time you can be knocked over. This is a state where one never wins, where there is no- future. Where life hangs in the balance. A future of no future means constantly being on the lookout for the fall, the demise, the dismissal, the betrayal, the end. A future-of-no-future means that the future is that of chronic limping. Since I have begun to limp alongside Hephaistos, I have come home to Hephaistos. He meets me at the door after a long day's journey into Hades.

Coming home does not only mean taking care of the self, it also means taking care of others. I have taken to taking-care-of- animals. I have taken in three dogs, one is epileptic, one I picked up at a flea market, the other was abandoned under a bridge. It gives me great comfort to care for these animals who are kindred spirits. All three of them had been abandoned or abused in some way. Getting sick feels like being abandoned. It as if by caring for animals I am also caring for my *anima.* Anima is the root of the word animal. Animals have helped me cope. I love my animals like children, they are my children. There is nothing more satisfying than taking-care of my animals. My three dogs are my three kindred souls. Scout, Taylor and Blue, my three sons. The child, the Puer in me, wants to spend time with animals. Perhaps I am trying also to get in touch with my animal nature. When we forget our animal nature, trouble looms. Like my identification with Hephaistos, I identify with my dogs. I identify with their vulnerability and woundedness. They are a symbol of the animal-child within.

Jung (1977) argues that the child archetype, "is therefore a symbol which unites the opposites; a mediator, bringer of healing, that is, one who makes whole" (p. 164). Indeed, the Puer within me wants to 'make whole' by taking care of animals. By taking care of animals I am taking care of myself. My animals make me feel whole. I need this animal refuge from the cold walls of Mother Academy. From the academy I need shelter. My animals shelter me from the coming storm. From any institution, people need shelter.

POST (SCRIPT)

And yet. Healing is always accompanied by an unravelling. Looking back, I try to understand how I wanted so to heal. Part of psyche does heal, but pockets of psyche never do. Ongoing physical struggles. It is all a part of chronic illness. And yet. To get distance from the past and to get distance from the now. Feeling distant and a bit washed out. Moods. Disenchantment. Time. Last week I taught Bachelard in a doctoral seminar on philosophy and education. The focus of the lecture was on the notion of time. Time is the most abstract yet most intimate concept. I think of Wallace Stevens (1972) when lecturing on time as he says, "of introspective exiles, lecturing" (p. 41). Time is an introspective concept. Thinking on time means thinking inwardly. Exiled in time. Time has a way of making us all exiles from the past. Once it is gone it is gone. Some of us are able to get more of the past back— via memory—than others. Memory fades for most of us.

Lecturing. To lecture. Teaching. Words. Teaching through words. Words in time. Timing through words. Thinking about teaching means thinking about words, language, metaphor, time and autobiography. Thinking about teaching means thinking about embodiment. Words. Lecturing. Bathed in words. Speech. Cutting through the emptiness. Speaking through. Lecture as *poeisis*. Teaching art. The art of teaching. If teaching is an art, then the teacher must become artful with words, speech, language, expression. Poeisis.

I return to T.S. Eliot's (1958) 'wounded surgeon.' Wounded teacher healing wounds through words. Love of words. Teachers need teachers. Turning to our teachers means turning to the great ones, the ones who are great with words. Aesthetics. Art words. Wordly, wordfully giving. Silence. Giving pause. Teaching about time means taking time between words. Phrasing and silence. Time unravelling. The unravelled mind. The unravelling lecture. Thinking of Anne Sexton and how unravelled she was while teaching (Salvio, 2007). What is the unravelling teacher? What is it to teach unravelled? Lecturing on time. Poeisis. Allowing ourselves to unravel as time unfolds. Lecturing as exile.

As I read again the early part of this chapter, I think of ways to better articulate black holes. Teaching through a black hole darkly. Teaching is not all light. Perhaps it is not light at all. Time is a serious consideration. Time connects with the ultimate questions: life and death. That's all the time we have for now. Time's up. It is your time. Black holes happen in time and in space. Black holes remind one of a vortex. Teaching in a vortex. Here I am thinking of two related references to vortex in the context of teaching, in the context of life and death. Here I am thinking both of Joan Didion (2005) and Louise DeSalvo (2002). After the death of her husband John, Joan Didion talks about avoiding all the old neighborhoods, all the old freeway intersections, all the old places. Some places were safer than others. She tells us that "[f]or reasons that remain unclear to me the Beverly Wilsher itself only rarely triggered the vortex effect" (2005, p. 113). Didion's 'vortex effect' is my black hole. Didion talks about the feeling of being swept into the confusion of memory and denial. The vortex sucks you into this confusion and brings you down. Black holes do the same thing. The black hole of memory sucks you in and sweeps you into the swirl of memory and denial, into serial music, into the Anne Sextons and Kenneth Patchens of days gone by. Thinking on time pulls you backward into a past life regression of folk art and pain, of poetry and the death of a moth. Some places are safer than others. For Didion the Beverly Wilsher was safer than other places. The vortex is held back by safe places. Safe places are those without memory and association. But how can you escape your own body and its woundedness?

I return again to T.S. Eliot's (1958) 'wounded surgeon.' The wounded teacher cannot escape the vortex of the wounded body, it is right there. The pain is always bringing you down into the black hole. Pain reminds you that the body never fully heals from traumatic injury. Pain reminds that you are a body and that the body is heavy. Rilke (1995) puts it this way, "[b]ut from the sleeper falls (as though from a motionless cloud) the abundant rain of the heavy" (p. 183). An abundance of pain shot through the chest. An abundance of memory through times past. Better times before the illness. Times of teaching before the memory of being struck down by a wounded body. Traumatic injury never fully heals, nor does the mind. I should say the bodymind, for they are not two but how to think of them as one when the pain brings down the body and the mind is caught in the vortex of black holes.

I am thinking here of getting out, how to get out. How the teaching helps to get out of the black holes. White holes spit you out, black holes suck you in. I am thinking here of Louise DeSalvo (2002) as she says that reading helped her to get through the vortex of thinking about her incested past. DeSalvo states,

> Knowing that the opposite of depression is vitality serves as reminder that, for me, no matter how difficult, the act of turning toward whatever causes my pain, of reading about it in works of literature, and of trying to find the words to describe it, helps me modulate the feeling that I am in the middle of a vortex of events that is sucking me under. . . . (p. 7)

Words. Words serve to undo the vortex, the black hole of meaninglessness. And what is teaching? Monkey mind? Teaching is the love of words, language, speech and writing. Hearing words spoken in the classroom, reading from texts, thinking through the words, making meaning of the words--especially profound words— "modulates" that swirling effect, that vertigo, as Louise DeSalvo puts it. How does one teach in a 'season in hell?' (Rimbaud, 1961). This is the stuff that we never talk about. Taboo. Terror. Mortality and fear. Mind unravelling. Taking strength from my Anne Sexton. Years before I became a teacher, I kept my Anne Sexton with me, under my arm. I kept my Kenneth Patchen with me, smoking cigarettes, drinking coffee with pen in hand. I come back to my poets to keep me from falling into the vortex of black holes. It is to the book, the word, the language that I turn. And what is teaching anyway? The love of words, books, language, meaning, the sound of the words like the sound of rain, that heavy rain, that abundance of the heavy rain. Mind unravelling. Black holes and archetypal poets. Illness, impending death makes the mind unravel. Monkey mind. Nobody wants to admit it except the poets. Street lamps and eye strain. Tired teaching. Teaching while tired. Restraint within verse. Restraint within teaching. Care with words. Ever so restrained. Rumi

(1998) says, "[t]he human shape is a ghost made of distraction and pain" (p. 2). Who is this ghost teaching on the subject of time? Being a ghost to your own teachings. To be a ghost to your students. Or are they the ghosts? Ongoing illness ghosts you out. After a while, the mind just becomes ghosted. Nikki Giovanni (2007) says, "[i]'m giving up on language" (p. 167). The poet gives up her words. What kind of teaching is this? Teaching without words. Is that a teaching? Giving pause. In the hesitations and deliberative moments more is said than when babble reigns in the classroom. Ghosted hesitations. Moments of utter stillness. Students wait in that stillness for the next word. But what if that word does not come? What is a teacher without words? A no teacher. A teacher of the great no. Seamus Heaney (1998) says, "[d]awn sniffing revenant, plodder through midnight rain Question me again" (p. 150). A questioning revenant. Plodding through an awful lecture. What if the lecture is awful? Do we ever talk about giving awful lectures when the vortex sucks us up and destroys all thought? These are the things we never talk about. But what good is thought when the thinker is being pulled incessantly into black holes, mind unravelling. The Jungians teach that you must go through the vortex, get sucked into those black holes, give up, and give in to monkey mind. Give up the lie that is logocentrism. Because it is a lie. Mystical feeling, music and art. Not rationality, but emotionality. Intuition. The just so. It is as it is. States of mind not on the test. What is the test teacher? There is no test. I have lost my place in the book. Students can you help me find my place? What page are we on? What page of life are we on? There are no pages in life. Just tatters. Remnants. Pieces and bits. Parts and parcels. Time marching on. Timing going backwards. Worm holes. Worm holes of the mind. Losing that sense of home in the classroom. Getting sucked into those worm holes. Losing the home of the mind. The body is the (un)home. Anne Sexton (1988) says, "[w]ait Mister? Which way is home? They turned the light out and the dark is moving in the corner" (p. 12). Mister, which way to my classroom? Mister which way back? I am lost. I am so lost. After class, wrecked by it all. Trying to hold it together through the lie of logocentrism. Silenced by the logic of nothings. Am I saying anything at all to my students? Do I speak to them in a void? They look at me strangely and laugh. They laugh out of a sense of (un)nerving because the notion of time is too much. Thinking of time, space, place and black holes are just too much. Time means cosmos means black holes and supernova explosions. Because that is what life is, that is what teaching is under the big tent. T.S. Eliot (1958) says famously "April is the cruellest month" (p. 37). But every month is the cruellest month under the sign of a broken body. The broken body has come (un)done. I am thinking here of Pablo Neruda (2004) as he says, "and skeletons of pale horsemen undone" (p. 113). Horsemen pass by, our undone Yeats. Horsemen are always already a reference to our beloved Yeats.

What kind of education are we getting anyway? What kind of education do we give to our children? Not this kind I am sure. Not the kind of Anne Sexton and Kenneth Patchen, not the kind of Louise DeSalvo and Joan Didion. Nobody wants to hear the truth. Nobody wants to talk about mourning and melancholia. Nobody wants to unravel logocentrism. Oh, the postmoderns talk about it, but do they do it, do they really think it? And how can you think about undoing logocentrism when the entire curriculum is built on the lie that is logocentrism? James Agee (2004) speaks to this issue. He states that

> there is no attempt to "teach" a child in terms of his environment, no attempt, beyond the most suffocated, to awaken a student either to "religion," or to "irreligion," no attempt to develop in him either "skepticism" or "faith," nor "wonder," nor mental "honesty" nor mental "courage". . . . nor to open within him the illimitable potential of grief. . . . (pp. 236-237).

It is to all of these things I teach. I try to teach "mental honesty" and "mental courage" and the "potential of grief." I try to write these things as well. But where can you write with mental honesty about the potential of grief in academe? The censors--for the most part--will not stand for this kind of writing or thinking because it undermines the lie that is logocentrism. If we were to be honest--really honest--about our teaching, can we say that we are teaching these things or teaching trivia? Or teaching lies? All the lies my teacher told me. Of course the American curriculum is full of lies. American history--in the state of Georgia-- begins *after* Columbus. Where does your own lie begin? After you were born? Or after your immersion into rationality? Does the lie of teaching begin with lessons of trivia? Does the lie of teaching begin with the dismissal of the out of hand, the out of control, the out of this worldness of the close at hand and the near at hand. Do we teach the near at hand or is that just too real? Do we ever really teach the real? Or do we only teach lies? Do we teach that American history begins *after* Columbus? What about our own histories? Where do they begin? After the breakdown? After the appeal to authority? After the aftermath? Do we simply dismiss the before of genocide (in the case of the Native Americans), do we simply dismiss all tragedy and grief, do we wipe them away, do we erase them from the curriculum? Yes. We do. If we lie about our own history do we not also lie about our subjectivity? We are subjects of a nation, subjects to the nation. Can we not start truth telling? But what kind of truths are we allowed to tell? History, memory, genocide. Matricide, the Holocaust, Viet Nam, Iraq. Virginia Tech, Columbine, 9-11. The big tragedies somehow get either erased or whitewashed in the curriculum. Kenneth Patchen (1941) says, "[m]y soul and I both wish you a good mark in God's little school. Our weeping is for everybody" (p. 253). Let this be a scathing critique of American education. Let us weep for all of our students because they are not being educated at all. Let us all get a "good mark in God's little school." Let us get a good mark in life, let us all get A's in our schools for scandal. The personal is also the political. The personal is also the historical. The historical is also what gets remembered and what gets forgotten. We are part and parcel of that memory and forgetting as the rules of the academe mark us, as the rules forbid our honesty, as the rules forbid real language and real talk and real discussion. Mostly what we have in university are--as Pablo Neruda (2004) might put it, "conversations as worn out as old wood. . . ." (p. 17). American history begins *after* Columbus? All the lies my teacher told me are still being told. When we look around at these places where learning is supposed to take place we can only cringe.

I am thinking here of Robert Lowell (2006) as he says, "I see a dull and alien room, my cell of learning" (p. 154). This cell of learning depresses. Let us open the cell and let all the spiders in--the spiders of history and the spiders of the mind. Lowell (2006) talks of spiders. He says, "[w]e are like a lot of wild spiders crying together but without tears" (p. 143). How can we cry about the Trail of Tears when American history begins *after* Columbus? We have no historical context around which to understand this genocide; we have no historical understanding that Native Americans were here, on this soil, at least 10,000 years before the white man came and ruined everything. How did the white man wipe out 10,000 years of humanity in such a short period of time? And how could he? Our children do not understand this tragedy if American history begins *after* Columbus. But if we are honest and we dig into the lies of the American curriculum, we can begin to dig into the lies of our own subjectivities. The lies of the American teacher are these: she never gets sick, she never gets confused, she never suffers from depression, she never falters in her lectures, she never stumbles, she never stutters, she never hesitates, she never shows weakness of any kind. The classroom is a big lie when all that transpires are trivial lessons. Let us be weak in our classrooms, let us show our humanness. Let us be poets of madness, of darkness. T.S. Eliot (1958) says, "[t]he voice returns like an insistent out-of-tune Of a broken violin on an August afternoon" (p. 9). Let us be this broken, out-of -tune violin in front of our students. Let us be honest once and for all. Let us be like Kenneth Patchen the poet of ghostedness, let us be like my Anne Sexton the poet of the broken body, the poet of multiple breakdowns. Can we not just be honest once in a while? Can we not be crazed once in a while? Can we not embrace the grand pauses in the classroom once in a while? Can we relish the nonsense words once in a while? Can we write crazy once in a while? Can we be allowed to forget what we were saying? Can we ever admit mental illness once in a while? What was Anne Sexton doing anyway? Mother academy tells us that the answer to these questions is 'no'. We cannot be mad in our classrooms; we cannot admit brokenness and we certainly cannot admit mental illness. And so the lie continues. American curriculum begins after the breakdown and under the erasure of that breakdown. The body of the American curriculum is sick. Mother academy is the bad breast.

We must teach through this ill body regardless of what we can or cannot do. Rumi (1998) speaks to the issue of the body. He says, "[a]nd our bodies? [I would add here the body of the curriculum writ large] our body is a cup, floating on the ocean; soon it will fill, and sink. . . ." (p. 13). The body of the American curriculum writ large is filled with lies and sinks. How to keep ourselves from going down with the ship? Can we prevent the shipwreck? Or is it too late? Or are we all shipwrecks? Are we always already shipwrecks? We are part of a broken curriculum, part of a broken body that is the curriculum and many of our bodies are broken because of it. The American curriculum is--as Pablo Neruda (2004) might put it--"a tale of wounded bones" (p. 123). But nobody speaks of this woundedness. We carry on as if nothing is happening. Teaching through the ill body of the curriculum means teaching about this ill body, teaching that--guess what--American history began BEFORE Columbus. And Genocide(s), lynchings, race riots, imperialism(s), fascism(s) are our history. But Americans only like pleasantries and speaking of little nothings. The American curriculum is nothing more than Pleasantville.

As is well known Anne Sexton's life unravelled and so too did Virginia Woolf's. Both ended their own lives. Neither of them could get out of their black holes. For some there is no stopping the body's downward crash. In Michael Cunningham's (1998) *The Hours*, (which is partly about Virginia Woolf), the narrator tells of the ways in which Virginia's body betrays her.

> First come the headaches, which are not in any way ordinary pain. . . . They infiltrate her. They inhabit her rather than merely afflict her, the way viruses inhabit their hosts. (p. 70)

When the body gets sick, it feels as if it has been taken over by some alien force as I mentioned earlier. Here, Virginia's headaches take her over like an alien force, they over take her and do her in finally. Anyone who has ever suffered from debilitating migraines knows this pain. But for Woolf, these were not just headaches. This was the beginning of a psychotic break of which—like Anne Sexton-- she suffered many. The narrator continues here to describe this break.

> When she's crossed over to this realm of relentless brilliance, the voices start. Sometimes they are low disembodied grumblings that coalesce out of the air itself; sometimes they emanate from behind the furniture or inside the walls. (p.71)

Psychosis is the total breakdown of psyche. This is the final unravelling. For both Sexton and Woolf, it was the psychosis that finally did both of them in. Their writing saved them for a time. The writing served to fight against these alien invasions of the bodymind. Writing serves as therapy for many troubled artists— and for troubled academics for that matter. Writings are outlets for psyche to speak, even if coded or veiled. In the case of Woolf, her writings were not transparent. Nobody's writings are. But here I mean that it is hard to tell by reading her fiction that she was a victim of multiple incests and subsequent psychotic breaks. But still, Louise DeSalvo (2002) cracked through Woolf's language and discovered that she was the victim of multiple incests. These incidents were the beginning of her unravelling. Unlike Woolf, Anne Sexton's writing is confessional so the reader knows the ways in which her psyche breaks as she vividly describes these breaks in her poetry.

For readers, the confessional style --especially when we are dealing with issues of the psyche---either annoys or engrosses. We know that Elizabeth Bishop was rather annoyed at the confessional and so too was T.S. Eliot who felt that poetry should be impersonal (Kirsch, 2005). Interestingly enough, Robert Lowell began as a formalist poet but toward the latter part of his career turned inward and was considered the "founder of confessional poetry" (Kirsch, 2005, p. 33). Lowell's inward turn and more confessional style came about because of illness and death in his family. Interesting what illness and death will do to a writer. Adam Kirsch

(2005) points out that Allen Tate was rather disgusted at Lowell's confessional turn. Kirsch explains.

> When Allen Tate first read the poems of Life Stories. . . he was appalled. "All the poems of your family," he wrote Lowell, ". . . are definitely bad. I do not think you should ought to publish them. . . ." (p. 33)

Tate of course was a member of the formalist group of poets like Eliot who felt that poetry should not be about the self, but rather should be about universal symbols. The irony is that for Lowell, what made his name was not his earlier writings, which were formalist. What made him famous was his writing that turned inward to explore his experiences with illness and death. Kirsch (2005) tell us that

> the very features of Life Studies that he [Tate] found distasteful and antipoetic--the private subjects, the prosaic diction-- have proved to be of far more interest to readers. . . . (p. 33)

This reminds me of the turn Wittgenstein made in his writing. He was never really confessional but he did move from the logical to the mystical toward the end of his life and there is speculation that he did so because of his sexuality and his acceptance of it. At any rate, I point these things out because as I mentioned earlier, it became apparent to me that upon farming this manuscript out many publishers had little interest in my story. Clearly a confessional, this pathography unnerved. Nobody wants to hear about you. Take the "I" out of the narrative. Write as if from the third person. Do not under any circumstances talk about yourself or make reference to yourself. I have been told all of these things throughout my academic career. The purpose of writing a pathography is to bring back into the fold the patient's story. Medical studies are technical and scientific; they have little to do with the way in which the patient feels about being sick. In academe especially, we need to hear the voice of the patient and bring that voice back into the discussion. That is what I am attempting to do here. And I know that some will feel that the confessional style is as Tate put it "distasteful." But I am convinced that it is only through the confessional that illness can be understood at a deeply phenomenological and psychological level. A phenomenology of illness is needed especially so that others can understand suffering existentially.

Autobiography in curriculum studies has had a thirty year history as William Pinar introduced this mode of address to the field. I took this mode of address one step further by writing a pathography. This is a deeply personal account of the experience I have had with not only my illness but with others' illnesses as well and the ways in which they have deeply changed me both emotionally and spiritually. Intellectual work must also be emotional. To pretend that one can just split off the emotional is silly. One's subjectivity colors all of one's work, even if that work is written in a more formal style. If one believes that one's "I" can be objective and erased from the narrative, who does the writer become? Nobody? No body? It is the no body that disturbs. The objective gaze has split off intellect from emotion. The objective gaze presupposes that the intellect does not need the body because it is not embodied to begin with. Octavio Paz (1983) has an interesting commentary on the idea of 'nobody' worth quoting here. He says,

> Nobody is the blankness in our looks, the pauses in our conversations, the reserve in our silences. He is the name we always and inevitably forget, the eternal absentee, the guest we never invite, the emptiness we can never fill. He is an omission, and yet he is forever present. (p. 45)

'Nobody' is all of this but more so, the idea of 'nobody' implies a no body. Academe is filled with people who write as if they are out of their bodies or have no bodies or their bodies are not important. I do think that this is the reason why much of academic writing is dreadful. The scholar is an embodied being with feelings; the scholar is an embodied being whose body can breakdown and get sick. It is to the breaking down that we need to turn because it is this that scholars ignore.

Let me return again to my poets. Robert Lowell, like Anne Sexton suffered from debilitating depressions. As a matter of fact, Adam Kirsch (2005)--whose book is appropriately titled *The Wounded Surgeon*--tells us about the lives of many poets who suffered from emotional conflicts. He writes about Robert Lowell, Elizabeth Bishop, John Berryman, Randall Jarrell, Delmore Schwartz and Sylvia Plath. Kirsch states, "these poets [were] mentally ill, or alcoholic, or suicidal" (xi). Unravelling is both bodily and psychical. Poetry, more so than the other arts, is a way of expressing these darknesses. To me, the dark night of the soul is best expressed in terse breakthrough lines. The mystics attempt to get at similar things. So mysticism and poetry do overlap. I have dealt in some detail with mental illness (Morris, 2006) elsewhere so I will not go into it in any depth here. That would be outside the scope of this book. But I do think that mental illness is of a piece with other kinds of illnesses and when one suffers from any chronic illness, mental illness is sure to creep into the story. Depression goes hand in hand with all kinds of other diseases. And when the body breaks down and the mind goes with it, we've got real trouble. James Hillman (1997b) has written one of the most important books in the Jungian literature on suicide called *Suicide and the Soul*. Hillman points out that,

> The tension of body and soul is crystallized most clearly in the problem of suicide. Here, the body can be destroyed by a 'mere fantasy.' No other question forces us so acutely into facing the reality of the psyche as a reality equal to the body. And because all analysis turns on the axis of psychic reality, suicide becomes the paradigmatic experience of all analysis, perhaps all of life. (p. 23)

Throughout this book I have struggled to put body and psyche back together as a piece. We are still children of the Enlightenment so it is difficult to think of two things at once or two things together like body and psyche. Thinking of the problem of suicide changes this. Hillman (1997b) that suicide puts psyche and *physis* back together again. A sick mind kills body and both disappear as one into the grave. If thanatos is a ruling principle and fantasies of death are ongoing, illness can be the trigger for the final decision, for the final cut, for suicide.

Suicidal ideation becomes problematic especially in very serious debilitating illnesses like Parkinson's. And so I worry. There is a history in my family of mental illness, suicidal attempts and suicidal ideation. Not something easy to admit. And perhaps not something to tell the world. "Do I dare disturb the universe? " (Eliot, 1962, p.5) The point of this book is to disturb the universe, especially the universe of the academy. The academy stifles expression of the "I." The academy kills. Must we never speak the truth?

The suicide of the mother must be also the penultimate destruction of the child. It is interesting to me that both Robert Lowell and Anne Sexton wrote about their mothers. Is this yet another taboo in academe? Of course, why should we ever write about our mothers? What do they have to do with social scientific subjects? As an aside here : Although I am a professor of education--which is considered a social science--in no way do I consider myself a social scientist. My love is for the humanities and so that is the base of my work. At any rate, Anne Sexton (1988)-- who had a troubled relationship with her mother-- says, "[o]nly my mother grew ill. She turned from me, as if death were catching. . . ." (p. 30). Robert Lowell (2006) says, "[m]eeting his mother makes him lose ten years, Or is it twenty, Time, no doubt, has ears" (p. 15). Mary Aswell Doll (1995) wrote of "mother matters"--a wrenching story about the death of her mother in her confessional *To The Lighhouse and Back*. Mothers are of course giants in the psyche; they are the figures under which we are mere shadows. Most famously Jamaica Kincaide (1997) wrote *The Autobiography of My Mother*. This book is about the mother's capacity to psychically colonize her daughter. The mother-daughter relation--I think--is particularly fraught. And psychic colonization is a big problem. In psychoanalytic terms we might call this symbiosis. Illnesses make already symbiotic relations more fraught. In one of her poems, Anne Sexton (1988) says that her mother blamed her for getting cancer. It is a rather shocking poem and I do not know if it is to be taken literally or not. But illnesses make people say crazy things sometimes. For Robert Lowell (2005), the deaths of his parents might have been the catalyst for his turn toward the confessional style. Lowell struggled with his father and he felt guilty about the way he and his mother talked about him while he was still alive. He writes about this guilt in one of his poems and asks his father for forgiveness. But it was his mother's death that really did him in. Kirsch puts it this way,

> But if his father's death only seems the last stage in futility, the death of his mother came as a life-altering shock. (p. 26)

It is these "life altering shocks" that change the way we see and write about the world. The primal figures--once they are gone--unmoor. Kirsch tells us that it was only with the illness of his daughter that he discovered "a new compassion for his own parents" (p. 27). When illness hits home, I do think one can become more compassionate, even when relations with those others who are ill are fraught.

If we are teachers, what do we do psychically when we experience one of these life-altering shocks? How is our teaching changed by the death of a primal other? It isn't as if we can teach as if nothing has happened. Although some try. But when something is happening it clearly alters one's classroom practices. I am not saying here, however, that it is okay to act out all of our countertransference relations with our students. This is what Anne Sexton did and her behavior was really rather repulsive--she had no boundaries (for more on this see Salvio, 2007). Acknowledging what is going on psychologically is crucial if one is to be able to teach at all. There will be days when the grief will overwhelm. What kind of teaching comes out of feeling overwhelmed with grief? The teaching may become split off and crazy. But if the teacher goes on as if nothing is happening trouble looms. You can only slide on the surface for so long. In the end, you will crash and burn.

THE CADUCEUS: TEACHER AS DIVINER

Socrates believed that the Oracle of Delphi taught lessons. When in trouble consult the Oracle. Socrates taught unpopular lessons. Socrates, for me, is an archetypal teacher. He is, for me, a sort of diviner because he taught the unpopular. He worked his magic by asking unpopular questions. Teaching through the ill body means asking unpopular questions. Let Socrates be our guide.

They killed Socrates finally. They killed him because he asked too many unpopular questions.

The ill teacher must ask unpopular questions of the body-soul. The ill teacher must raise philosophical questions of life and death. Academicians do not like their feathers ruffled. The academy kills us in many ways. It kills the spirit, as it asks us NOT to ask too many unpopular questions. To follow orders, to conform. The great mediocrity of university life. Is this the goal of the professorate? The Oracle thinks not. Chronic illness forces one to follow the Socratic method of unpopularity because what is at stake is bigger than pettiness and mediocrity. What is at stake is life and death. The Socratic model is one of asking questions that raise eyebrows.

I go to my inner archetypal Oracle and ask for help. I ask Hephaistos what to do next. I ask for guidance. I ask what the future-of-no-future holds. The Oracle says to me, move on, move on, move. The Oracle asks me to think about symbols. One of the symbols in my dreams are snakes. Ever since childhood I have dreamt of snakes. I fear snakes. In Georgia, poisonous snakes are a real and present danger. But my internal snakes are not the snakes in my backyard, these are the snakes of my psyche. Snakes are symbols of good or evil, symbols of virility or temptation, symbols of day or night, symbols of wholeness or fragmentation. What are psychic snakes meant to do? How to make use of psychic snakes?

In the context of medicine, the snake is considered a symbol of healing. Consider the Caduceus. Look at any bottle of medicine and you will see two snakes intertwined around a rod (perhaps a divining rod). We learn from Jungian scholar Ginette Paris (1991) that the Caduceus symbolizes balance and even "divinity" (p. 96). She states,

> Sometimes the staff represents the axis of the universe, and the two serpents, the contrary forces that swirl around it. The organization of these forces around an axis bring equilibrium, because without organization there is chaos. The caduceus thus becomes a symbol of peace, as opposed to war, of course, but also as opposed to chaos, disorder and destruction. This peace is attained by balancing contrary forces. . . . (p. 96)

In order to attain balance and peace three elements are necessary. These three elements are: two snakes and a rod. Two snakes and a rod bring balance where there is instability. Three is a mystical number, a ghosted number. The holy ghost is the third thing. Three is Odd, it is Other. Three is a crowd, the third is odd man out. Third base is almost a home run but not quite. Three is that third space. Two snakes and the rod around which they are intertwined symbolize the third space of illness. Dreams of snakes may be symbols of balance. The postmoderns talk about chaos as if it were a state to be achieved. That's fine in argument, but nobody really likes chaos. Nobody likes anxiety and uncertainty. Do they? I do not like chaos. I experienced too much chaos as a child. I experience too much chaos being sick.

Psyche tells me to allow the snakes to lead me out, to educate me, to guide me through the wilderness that is illness. Dreams of snakes are fearful and shocking. They attack, they pounce and they bite. I am continually in a state of shock. Perhaps the snake is the unconscious caduceus archetype trying to send messages. The snakes are sitting [if snakes can sit?] on a divining rod, a magical rod that can predict the future-of-no-future. The snakes are my teachers, my diviners. What message do they send? Genette Paris (1991) suggests that, "[a]s for the serpent, doubled on the caduceus, it is one of humanity's oldest representations of divinity. . ." (p. 96). The symbol of medicine—the caduceus—is also the symbol of divinity. This seems a strange mix. Can modern medicine take part in the divine I wonder? Is there something deeply soulful about medicine? Doctors are supposed to heal. Is healing not a soulful act?

A Snake eating its own tail is the symbol of wholeness. How to go about eating one's tail? Eating. That is my trouble. The trouble with eating. I suppose the gods of the underworld are telling me to eat my own tail. I sure would have trouble doing so because half the time I can't eat anything at all. The inability to eat might symbolize the psychological inability to take in external surroundings. Maybe I simply cannot take in Mother Academy. To me she is the Bad Breast, the Phallic Mother, the Sadistic Superego. Mother Academy pushes away her sick children. In fact, most of society pushes away those who are sick. Robert Sardello (1983) teaches that,

> Disease, despite all the advances of technological medicine, remains one of the great mysteries of life. We, the unhospitalized, relatively healthy, relate to disease as we do to death. It is something that happens to someone else; or it is something reserved for the future--maybe one day I will have cancer. And, so not to become obsessed with the fear of disease lurking everywhere, we give disease a place on the borderline of culture--the hospital or the clinic. Passing through the gates separating the community of the city from the hospital marks an initiation ceremony in which invisible fears, are transformed into visible enemies. (p. 146)

The chronically ill who are not hospitalized pose a special threat to the healthy because we live in the community, we live among the healthy. And this becomes a threat. We are too close to home for the healthy. We are your next door neighbor. We are the enemy within the city walls. We are not locked away behind the gates of the hospital. In Jewish life, it has been noted time and time again that when Jews assimilated into European society during the fin-de-siecle, they became even more of a threat to their anti-Semitic counterparts because the anti-Semites couldn't tell who they were. Ironically, hostilities against Jews worsened in Europe the more Jews assimilated into society (Morris, 2001). Likewise, those who are sick might become more feared as they are better able to assimilate into the culture of the healthy. The healthy would rather put us behind the gates of the hospital, do away with us, cleanse society of all of its inferiors. America is a culture of cleanliness. Being ill is thought to be polluting. Sardello (1983) argues that ideally the city should welcome its infirm with open arms and integrate the ill into society. But this is not the case. The inhabitants of the city of the healthy would like nothing better than to kick us out. Sardello (1983) asks,

> Do we not risk discarding our humanity and the living body of the city when we take what is worn, weak, and hurting and demand that it be restored to its former condition or excluded permanently? (p. 163)

Yes, Sardello is right when he says we risk our humanity when we cast out the weak. But Americans have always cast out the weak. And so too have Europeans. That is why we have hospitals, prisons and schools. These are places where we put people so we do not have to deal with them. Patients, prisoners and students are all vulnerable. We like to put our vulnerable away. Schools were initially invented to keep young adults off the streets and out of trouble. Schools have never been places of education, but rather they are holding cells. We fear our young people today. So we lock them up in schools. Police searches, metal detectors and random drug tests. What people fear they get rid of. We fear illness, so we hospitalize patients, we fear criminals so we lock them up in jails and we fear students so we lock them up in schools.

ILLNESS: AN INTOLERABLE WOUNDEDNESS

As I travel into the fifth year of my illness, I begin to understand that this condition is with me to stay. There has been little progress. And yet there has been progress. I can eat and yet I have to be careful how I eat. I have had to re-educate myself completely. Meals are out of the question. There is no room for meals in the underworld of the stomach. When I cannot tolerate food, liquids make do. I have been living on coffee much of the last year. Starbucks loves me. Coffee fills me up and drives me. Symbolically liquids and solids make for interesting alchemical discussion. Marie Louise von Franz (1980a) points out that for many ancient alchemists, liquids and solids were considered to be the same thing. She explains:

> It is a very great paradox that liquid--the unformed water of life--and the stone--the most solid and dead thing-- are, according to the alchemists, one and the same thing. That refers to those two aspects of the realization of the Self: Something firm is born, beyond the ups and downs of life, and at the same time is born something very living which takes part in the flow of life, without inhibitions of consciousness. (p. 174)

Food-- the solid dead thing about which the alchemists speak-- makes me sick. Food is my enemy. Every (non)meal is a dead thing, a rock, a hard place, a feeling of terrible and merciless satiety. The solid dead thing--food-- is a murderer, a 'soul murderer' as Schreber (2000) might have said.

The alchemists got it exactly wrong. The solid dead thing of food is indeed NOT the same thing as liquid. Liquid is the gentle flow of life, liquid is the saving grace, the water from which dreams spring. Liquids move through the stomach differently than solids. I can attest to this. For people with gastroparesis this is fact, not fiction. What is fiction is that solids and liquids are one and the same, for they are not.

The stomach is the heart of Being. Is it not? It is the center of our bodies, it is the engine, the driving force, and it's got a mind. Stomachmind. Stomachmind is like monkeymind. Stomachmind is the mad mind. When the engine refuses to take in fuel, the rest of the body suffers. Exhaustion is the first sign that the body is not getting enough fuel. Most Americans do not understand this condition because they are, for one thing, fat. Yesterday on the evening news I saw a story about pace makers for the stomach for fat people. To me, this is disgusting. The pace maker for the stomach should be primarily for people who cannot eat, it is used primarily as a medical device for gastroparesis. The pace maker for the stomach helps to electrically stimulate nerves in the stomach when natural electrical impulses no longer work. Some argue that gastroparesis is caused by nerve damage. Monkeymind stomach has no more nerves. They monkey has gone to sleep.

Using this device—the gastric pace maker-- as a cosmetic one is revolting. The pace maker would be a last resort for me, if I get worse. Implanting such a device is dangerous. It could mean death. There are times when I wish I had a pace maker in my stomach. Like any other illness, cycles of badness recur. For months at a time donuts are about all I can eat. Donuts pass through my stomach easily, they are full-proof food for me. Unlike donuts, real food causes early satiety and tremendous discomfort.

I am sick of being sick. It is sickening being sick all the time. Bad times are here to stay. What to do in these bad times? How can I make use of bad times? I learn from von Franz (1980a) that ancient alchemical texts teach that philosophers pass through cycles in order to grow. Von Franz (1980a) states that

> there are many different texts in alchemy in which it is said that the philosopher's stone has to circulate. Usually that is connected with time symbolism, for they say the philosopher's stone has to pass through winter, spring, summer, and autumn, or it has to go through all the hours of the day and night. (p. 166)

The philosopher lives through many seasons, yes. Thinking that comes with great difficulty is always done in winter. Summertime is the season of ease and play, spring is the season for new ideas, and autumn is the season of dying thoughts. It is always winter in my stomach. My stomach only circulates through different kinds of winter(s). It is a cold, dark place. It is a place packed with snow, ice and slush. It is a place that is always packed. I am almost always full, whether I eat or not. This is the perpetual winter of my life. Here, there is no growth, but only shrinkage.

James Hillman (2004) points out that really nobody 'grows' psychically. Rather, he suggests that psyche shrinks! We shrink back to what we were meant to be before we lost our way. We become—he suggests—what we already are. Growth, then, is a problematic idea for psyche. We strip away the masks throughout life to become what we were meant to be. That is not progress, but regress. In winter, psyche regresses to its most basic state.

The stomach is always a place of drama. The drama of the stomach is one of pain and torment. It is a Greek tragedy. Things are never quite worked out in the stomach. There is always already a remainder in the stomach. That is both literally and figuratively true. And thoughts are always already generated from undigested food. Undigested food-thoughts plague the psyche. Something is indigestible in my psyche. In fact, the underworld of the psyche is composed mostly of undigested images. Many Jungian depth psychologists agree that archetypal material becomes manifest primarily when undigested material overwhelms. (Von Franz 1980 a&b; Hillman2004; Sardello, 2002; McNeely,1991; Stein, 1983) Undigested psychic material appears mostly in dream-images such as dragons, worms, drowning, mudslides, blood, death, vomiting. This is the stuff of Greek drama. James Hillman (2004) reminds us that according to Jung, "[t]he unconscious produces dramas, poetic fictions; it is a theater" (p. 36). The dream-theater's characters are different manifestations of the psyche. All of the dream-characters are you. Both Freud and Jung agreed on this point.

Interestingly enough, however, you are not the director of your dream-images. Dreams do not have a director. Dreams have a mysterious origin. Dreams are the drama of no director. Dreams are a film in search of a film maker. Robert Sardello (2002) suggests that "the world [and this includes the world of dreams] is experienced as a sacred drama. We have dramatic form whenever there is the experience of polarities, opposites, contradictions held in irresolvable tension" (p. 50). There is nothing 'nice' about dreams. Dreams tell it like it is. Dream-stories are the stuff of myth. Dreams are the stuff of rape, of death, murder, man-eating animals, two headed beasts, swimming monkeys, devouring dragons, trampling horses. Dreams appear in technicolor. Some composers say they hear songs in their dreams. I dreamt that my puppy was my grandmother. My puppy was my grandmother sitting at the kitchen table when I was very little. This is the stuff of psychosis. We all have psychotic tendencies (Morris, 2006).

When the life of consciousness is in a constant state of discomfort and tension, archetypal dramas tend to be heightened. One's psyche is activated when life becomes difficult. James Hillman (2004) says "we are composed of agonies" (p.40). Life is agony, especially when one is chronically ill. Moreover, it is an agony not to able to articulate what chronic illness feels like. Phenomenologically, it is nearly impossible to articulate to others what it is like to live with this condition. There are no exterior signs of illness. I am on the thin side. But there are lots of thin people who are not sick. There are many kinds of disabilities that are not visible. When sickness is not visible, people misunderstand. Looking fine does not necessarily mean that you are fine. Looks do not equal health. What you see is not what you get. And it is this that people misunderstand.

Martin Buber is helpful here. Buber (1958) built his entire career on the term "mismeeting". He felt always misunderstood by his mother because she abandoned him when he was very young. He felt that he never really 'met' his mother in a psychological way. He never had an I-thou relation with her. So he sought what he called I-thou meetings the rest of his life. When one gets sick, life becomes a series of 'mismeetings.' People do not know how to 'meet' with the ill, people do not know what to say or how to relate or whether to relate at all. The first response to illness for many is to run away. People run from illness because they are afraid of catching it; they are afraid--deep down--that one day they might get it. 'Mismeetings' cause much tension. Much of the time, people don't even try to understand. Moreover, they just don't care. We live in a very uncaring world.

I am one of the lucky ones. I have a loving partner. I have a handful of close friends who do care. I've got people with whom I confide, people who are genuinely concerned. But these kinds of people are rare. We are so steeped in the everyday business of paying bills and attending to household chores that other peoples' problems are of little concern. But what about paying attention to the house of the soul and to the house of the soul of the Other?

I had a dream that couldn't be more clear. This dream had the clarity, in fact, of a Zeus-like prophecy. A voice in the dream said to me in a command from mount Olympus "YOU HAVE UNFINISHED BUSINESS." This is the Zeus within ordering me to take care of my psychic house, of my spiritual well-being. Interestingly, Donald Cowan (1995) says of Zeus that he is

the spiritual faculty in all of us that knows, intuitively-- not with the practical wisdom of an Athena, not with the inventiveness of a Prometheus, not with the lyric idealism of Apollo, but with a Zeusian clarity that allows things to be what they are in themselves. (p. 13)

It is difficult to allow things to be what they are especially if they are bad. Commands of the inner voice are often not heeded. But one must heed the call of illness and integrate illness into the everyday. The Jungians teach that we need to pay attention to those things which we've neglected in our unconscious, those archetypes which need tending to. Murray Stein (1983) puts it this say,

[P]sychopathological symptoms [or in this case symptoms of physical illness] are manifestations of "neglected archetypes." From this it follows that the 'cure' for psychopathological symptoms includes remedying this state of neglect, and this means discovering which archetype ('god') has been neglected and 'honoring it' (p. 65)

Honoring illness, rather than pushing it away, might be helpful. By honoring illness, one makes a place for it, lets it breath and speak. Honoring chronic illness and letting it be what it is means not glossing it over by thinking that it will get better or go away. Honoring illness also means identifying with archetypal symbols. Identifying, say, with the myth of Icarus, might allow one to amplify the fall into illness. Icarus flew too close to the sun and fell into the sea. A dialogue with Icarus is in order. His father told him not to fly too high. Icarus did not heed his father's call.

I had a dream that my finger was cut so deeply that it was splitting apart. A friend in the dream would not let me go to the emergency room to get stitches because we had to attend a conference. I kept telling him how controlling he was and how much I needed stitches. Without the stitches my finger might fall off. This is the stuff of drama, of theater. The controlling friend might be my ongoing struggle with the controlling aspects of my superego. My superego will not let me heal fully, will not let me get fully stitched up. My psyche is cut deeply into parts, perhaps it is split off. Being split off suggests psychic woundedness. There are psychic wounds so deep that they will never go away. Psychic wounds manifest eventually in physical problems. Alice Miller (2005) teaches that the body never lies. What truth does the body teach? Are the truths the body teach archaic? My stomach is a tomb. And this tomb is made of lead. Marie Louise von Franz is especially helpful here. Von Franz (1979) states,

> Therefore one reads in old texts that "lead contains a dangerous spirit which makes people manic, maniac, crazy. Beware of the spirit of lead in the work." That is not only a psychological truth. Lead is a symbol and is connected with Saturn, with the spirit of depression, symbolically. But the hook for the projection that lead is the devil, that it contains the devil and a mania-producing spirit is also a concrete chemical fact. (p. 16)

Lead in the head is connected with lead in the stomach. Depression feels heavy, weighty, toxic. Early satiety feels heavy, weighty and toxic as well. The leadened stomach is one without electrical currents, without the ability to move the food along. The stomach gets me depressed. Eventually the depression alters the stomach. So here you have a vicious cycle.

My case is not an isolated one. Many people suffer from chronic illnesses of all sorts. Hillman (2004) explains that "[t]here is no part of my personal record that is not at the same time the record of a community, a society, a nation, an age" (p. 45). My story has already been told by the Greeks. My story is as old as the Greeks; it is a repetition of what has already been told. My story is the story of Orpheus descending, of Hephaistos limping, of Odysseus's journey to Hades. My personal god is Saturn who is the god of "mutilated people" (von Franz, 1980b). The only way I can theorize around illness, is to draw on my own auto-ethnography. I could have written a completely theoretical piece without bringing my story into it. But I would have felt disingenuous if I would have done this. It is easier to theorize without brining the self into it because then you do not have to deal with your own problems. The point of writing is to deal with problems and share those problems with others. Some would rather not read such personal thoughts. A conservative approach to scholarship is one where the self has no place in the narrative. I think this is absurd. Jung teaches otherwise. Did he not write an autobiography? Did he not make his breakdown public?

CHAPTER 9

THE FIGHTING SPIRIT AND THE ACTIVE IMAGINATION

So the question remains. What are we to do? We must fight. My fighting spirit has kept me alive. Jungians 'fight' psychic wounds by utilizing what they call active imagination. Marie Louise von Franz (1979) explains.

> Jung sometimes defined the introverted psychological tradition in alchemy as the art of active imagination with material. We generally think of active imagination as talking to our own personified complexes, and trying in our imagination and fantasies to personify certain of our complexes and then have it out with them. . . . (p. 18)

To have it out with our complexes means to fight back, to wrestle with psyche. Fighting the dragons of the unconscious means acknowledging them. Taking on snakes, floods, falling elevators, sinking in quicksand means acknowledging the existence of what is bad within us. To have it out with complexes means not ignoring them.

The experience of getting sick might allow one to heal others. Von Franz (2000) talks about the healing aspects of being wounded.

> For instance, Philoctetes, written about by Kerenyi in his paper "Hero Iatros," which means the healing hero. There he has collected all the Greek material on the healing gods and demons: Asclepius, Chiron, and so on, all of whom are according to certain versions, wounded and therefore healing. One has to be wounded in order to become a healer. This is the local image of a universal mythological motif, which is described in Eliade's book about the initiation of medicine men and shamans. Nobody becomes either one or the other without first been wounded. . . . (pp. 111-112)

I certainly do not claim to be a healer or a shaman! I only hope that telling my story might help others cope. Hopefully, this book will help others to at least become more empathetic toward people who get sick.

VEGETATIVE STATES

In a state of wellness all the road signs are clearly marked. In a state of illness there are no road signs. This is a state unlike any other. In fact, illness is a state without roads, a state beyond states. States of mind altered. Indeed, one state of mind when illness strikes is that of vegetation. Vegetation is connected with the Egyptian god Osiris. Marie Louise von Franz (1979) explains.

> [T]he Egyptian's communal life was concentrated in the archetypal image of the God Osiris. Osiris, in contrast to the order, ruling sun God, was the suffering God. He represented the passive, suffering aspect of nature and of the psyche. Histories of religion always depict him as the God of vegetation, but vegetation as a symbol of his being: it is that which does not move, which does not have its own volition, which is the greatest suffering thing on this earth. . . . (pp. 3-4)

This dead state of psyche feels like vegetation. Vegetation is like lead, it is heavy. Osiris, the god who vegetates, is the god to which I turn. I ask for advice and compassion. I psychically identify with Osiris when I simply must remain still. Long days and longer nights. Days when no writing comes. Days when I cannot leave the house. Days when sitting is about all I can do. In the early days of my illness, I did this a lot. Some days I "have it out" (von Franz, 1980b) with Osiris. To have it out with the gods also means asking them what it is that they want from us. Having it out with Osiris. During vegetative days, one day is like the next, time never seems to move. What day is it? Is it Tuesday or Wednesday? What does it matter? Every day is like every other day, horrible. Agony. Every day is Sunday.

In a state of confusion--which is brought on by feeling like a vegetable-- one might "have it out" with Poseidon. Daniel Russ (1995) comments that Poseidon represents "celebration of flux, fusion, and confusion" (p. 45). Not only this, Poseidon, Murray Stein (1983) tells us, was one of the most important gods for Jung. Stein (1983) says "Poseidon Earthshaker, Lord of the Deeps. For Jung, this god was the psyche itself, which was for him a numinous daimon of creativity. . ." (p. 126). As Jung teaches, confusion may be related to creativity. One creates out of confusion. Writing is an attempt to make sense of chaos. Otherwise why would one write?

Poseidon is not only the god of confusion, but he is also the god of locomotion (Russ, 1995). Daniel Russ (1995) tells us that "[w]hile Poseidon has with many gods the deep connection with the bull, it is Poseidon's distinction to be the giver and tamer of wild horses" (p. 46). Russ says that "[h]e first gave man [sic] horse power, freeing us for locomotion on a massive scale" (p. 48). Locomotion is the exact opposite of vegetation. Both locomotion and vegetation are part and parcel of the human condition. When one is vegetative for months, locomotion beckons. The soul needs movement and speed. Dreams are the site of movement. Dreams do speed by. Images come and go quickly. Tending to the quickness of dream-images helps psyche balance out vegetative states.

It is interesting that people tend to thrive in states of opposites. Vegetation-locomotion. Robert Sardello (2002) comments that soul-making occurs "between polarities." He says that

> There is no imagination in dogmatic steadiness, so the soul is not satisfied. Soul always finds its expression between polarities. We know we are not in soul when paradox, irony, tension, drama, are absent. (p. 56)

We are a bundle of contradictions, yes? I know I am. I say one thing and do something else. I say I won't do this and then do it. I say I won't read Jung and then read Jung. Human beings are highly complicated. To be contradictory is to be human. Those who seem to live in steadiness, those who seem to be totally sure of themselves, those who seem never to contradict themselves are actually--as Sardello points out--not living.

To make something, *homo faber*. To do something. To find meaning. To live. To find energy. Energy is the underlying principle of the soul. This is what Aristotle called *Energia*. The principle of movement. But when one is sick, finding enough energy to get up in the morning and make coffee is a drama. Try getting out of bed.

Or taking a shower. That is a monumental event. Finding the energy to write a few pages, finding the energy to play an instrument or talk with students or meet with colleagues becomes terribly difficult. How to continually find enough energy to live on. How to get energy back once it's lost. Energy comes from the heart of being, from the depths of the unconscious. Energy is the source of the will-to-live. Deldon Anne McNeely (1991) argues that "[a]rchetypal energies deriving from the Self keep us moving, not transfixed. Tensions may bring outrage, grief and love" (p.52). Energy, then, comes not from places of light , but from places of darkness. From vegetation comes locomotion. Locomotion returns to vegetation. This is the basic dialectic of life. Without vegetation there would be no need for locomotion. Maybe there is energy in vegetation but it is repressed or it is trapped. Marie-Louise von Franz (1980b) tells us that

> As Jung points out at the end of "On the Nature of the Psyche," the concept of energy is originally derived from the primitive concept of energia or mana, which simply means the extreme impressiveness of something. Therefore the original concept of energy was more the idea of psychological intensity. (p. 66)

What is it that presses in upon psyche? What impresses? What presses in upon the soul? These are primal questions. What impresses me is music. Wood and steel particularly. Somehow guitars speak directly to me. I am guitar crazed. Searching for the perfect soul-instrument. The cello, too, speaks to my soul. The piano is my old friend. I have often felt that I have been called to play music. Music impresses me. It gets pressed out of me. Soul-speaking through music. The need to play music is stronger than ever now because of my illness. I feel called to play.

Pan, the god of the flute said 'play again,' play for the state of your soul, play for your soul. This is what presses in on me, impresses me. Words have always come second to me. I struggle with words. Scholarship is hard work for me because writing does not seem natural for me. Maxine Kumin (1981) tells us that Anne Sexton revised some of her poems twenty times. She was a great poet. I am not a great poet. But I feel that I too need to revise my papers many, many times. But still I do not feel that I get the words the way they should be, for I am not a great writer. In fact, I do not consider myself to be a writer at all. I am an academic who struggles with words. I struggle so with words.

Playing music is what I've always done. Music making comes natural for me. Paradoxically, if it weren't for the illness, I would have never returned to music. For twenty years I did not play. I was dead to music. But now things have changed. The illness made me think about what is most important in my life. Music is probably the most important aspect of my life. Since I got sick, I felt a tremendous urge to get back to my music. I'm glad that I did get back to my music for I think it has helped me through the worst of times.

TEACHING THROUGH THE ILL BODY

So what is it that the body teaches through illness? It teaches us the basics. It teaches us that life is holy and that the soul needs nourishment. What impresses upon our soul and nourishes our soul allows us to live in the now. Jean Shinoda Bolen (1996) states that,

> The Greeks had two words for time: Kairos and Kronos. When we participate in time and therefore lose our sense of time passing, we are in Kairos; here we are totally absorbed in the present moment. . . . (p. 86).

When one is engaged in soul-work, in doing what one truly loves, time passes quickly. Sometimes this happens during periods of writing. But for me, it happens most often when playing an instrument. Music is meant to be played by our soul-ear. Tonight I am teaching Derrida's (1998) *Ear of the Other*. Derrida teaches that we must listen to the Other. Really listen. There is no other way to teach but through the 'Ear of the Other.'

Jungians understand what listening means and what it means to be Other-to the self. Sickness makes one Other. That Other becomes an image. Jungians teach, in other words, that Otherness must be freely associated with the use of images. Greg Mogenson (1995) argues that for Jungians,

> Psychic images. . . refer to the images that animate objects, not to the objects as they are defined by physical categories, not, that is to say, to the objects as objects. Viewed imaginatively, objects are as well living images. . . . (p. 98)

For non-musicians, guitars might be dead objects. They have no practical function. Rock stars smash guitars. People do not usually pay much attention to the beauty of the instrument, the way it looks, feels, smells and sounds. One guitar is pretty much like another one for the non-musician. But for a guitarist, the instrument takes on animate qualities. It speaks, dances, sings, resonates and ex-presses soul if one allows it to. For me, the guitar is very much alive. The vibrations of the guitar do something to my Self, to the archetypal Self. The vibrations are indeed healing. The sounds heal a wounded body and psyche. The vibrations pass through the body right into the bones-of-being. And there is something spiritual about this passing-through feeling that one gets while playing. Slyviane Agacinski (2003) remarks that

> Having become strangers to the ancient dreams, it remains for us to consider "passingness," to accept the lightness of what passes. . . . Freud invited us to embrace the Verganglichkeit--the passingness of things. . . . (p. 12)

'Passingness' does not mean obliviousness. Passingness means being-there in the moment. One must be fully present and fully engaged in order to allow things to pass through. Music only passes through the body if one is deeply attuned to it. 'Passingness' does not mean being passive either. To make connections with the lifeforce, things must pass and flow. Jungians make much of the notion of flow. Robert Sardello (1995), in a discussion of Hermes, talks of the importance of flow. He states,

> Ancient mythology of Hermes presents a picture of modern hermetic consciousness. This consciousness consists of the capacity of "seeing through." The invisible flow of back and forth connections, relating one thing to

another, is seen through the visible diversity of phenomena making a kinship of all beings. (p. 150)

The back and forth flow of relating to others is key to good relationships. But there is also a flow one gets in relation to objects. To flow with objects means to animate objects. Schizophrenics are particularly good at this, but they get lost inside objects. Intact egos do not get lost inside objects but do not animate objects enough. Animated objects--like guitars--are conduits to the soul. Musical instruments are vehicles that allow soul-speaking.

Our lives would be much richer if we could use our imaginative capacities to find flow with objects. Objects are books, instruments, radios and so forth. Computers. Pens. Guitars. Artists animate objects. Cans of soup. How to become the artists of our own lives. That is the question here. An artist feels a sense of flow with an object. A canvass, an instrument, a camera, a pencil, the word. We say that the best writing flows. The best music flows. It just seems to pour out of the musician. The soul must find its flow connection with its soul-work, with its objects. Object-relations can be about real objects not just people. Object relations can literally mean objects--literally. And why shouldn't we think about what objects mean to us? Is there a philosophy of objects? Is there an ontology of objects? Maybe the psychology of objects has yet to be written. Winnicott, as we know, talked about transitional objects. But I think there is more to it than that.

Again the paradox. An object is a block, a hard thing, a solid. In order to flow, the soul has to find a way to connect to the block of matter, a hard thing, a solid. The human spirit must find a way to animate the object by infusing life into it. How that is done is hard to say. Objects take on a particular meaning when one is ill. They can become menacing reminders of one's inability to flow during vegetative states. Objects become albatrosses. Objects torment. Objects can be demonic. When one is very very sick, connecting with objects becomes impossible. As much as I wanted to play guitar during the early days of my illness, I could not. I was simply in too much pain. Not being able to play pains.

When one gets sick, sounds are too loud, smells are too intense and light hurts the eyes. Walking is a chore. The body becomes an object; It becomes an inanimate object. The body becomes heavy and immobile. Objectified. When the body becomes an object for medical inspection what does that mean? To become objectified is to become transmogrified into a mere thing. One must wait until states of flow return. Robert Sardello (2002) states,

> The interior space of the heart is all dynamic motion, a flow of the subtle soul connects with moral feeling, emotion and feeling and the many subcurrents they create--the forces of passion, desire, longing, waiting, loving. This dynamic of flow also holds the soul experiences of mourning, sorrow, woundedness, hurt and absence. (p. 62)

Thus, flow is not all light but darkness too. Flow means embracing the human condition in its entirety. Teaching through the ill body means teaching through the dark and the light, the good and the bad.

Teaching through the ill body has been a torment to write. I end this narrative a little tired and a little sad. It is time for me to pick up my guitar and play.

FINAL POST (SCRIPT). BROKEN BODY OF THE BODHISATTVA: THE TEACHINGS OF MEMORY

Postscripts are built on memory. This book has been an attempt to get at illness from competing time(s). The first part of each section of the book was written in the heat of the moment--in the now of the early days of the illness. The post (scripts) were written from distant memory of those early days. I deliberately repeat this in each chapter so as to remind the reader of what I am doing throughout the book. Hopefully the post (scripts) have been an ongoing thread to help readers understand that the book was written along a continuum of time(s). Edward Casey (1991) says that memory is like a "polyform time with many turning centers" (p. 282). Time is actually time(s) that are de-centered, not centered, as Casey suggests. Time(s) are decentered because psyche is decentered. Memory is decentered and out of whack all the time. There is no real continuum of memory, it is more like a broken picture puzzle. We can never put all the pieces back in the puzzle because half of them get lost or simply disappear. Even when writing in the heat of the moment, one becomes forgetful. Memory is a funny thing. As soon as an event happens it is a memory and that memory is subject to change. Michel de Certeau (1988) says,

> The oddest thing is no doubt the mobility of this memory in which details are never what they are: they are not objects, for they are elusive as such; not fragments, for they yield the ensemble they forget; not totalities, since they are not self-sufficient; not stable, since each recall alters them. (p. 88)

Because memories are unstable they are never what they seem to be. However, this does not make them any less real. Memories are part fantasy and partly based on events. But it is fantasy that drives our inner lives. Our lives are tied together by fantasy and by the fantastic. If we think otherwise, we are deluded. Some memories of illness are so hideous that they are forgotten and put into the dustbins of psychic history. Like the ripping of the fabric of time, Robert Lowell (2006) says that sickness is the "ripping up [of] memory" (p. 308). Most memories are indeed ripped up and thrown away. And after years of life gone by, most of the past is just a blip, a faded family album.

The body does not remember what it feels like to experience intense pain after it is over. The embodied memory of those intensities vanish. And when one is in pain, articulation of that pain is nearly impossible. And yet we must try to articulate pain even though we cannot. As the pain recedes, so too does the memory. This book was written as a testimony to that pain. Pain isolates. Reading of others' pain helps one feel less isolated. Pain breaks the body and the psyche. Poets address the issue of pain better than academics. Pain is best addressed metaphorically. Anne Sexton (1988) says, "I confess I am only broken by the source of things" (p. 17). John Berryman (1969) says, "[m]y framework is broken" (p. 129). Gerard Manley Hopkins

(1961) says, "[s]ickness broke him" (p. 34). Pablo Neruda (2004) talks about the moon which "delivers up its shipwrecks" (p. 113). Adrienne Rich (1989) puts it this way: "Their life, collapsed like unplayed cards" (p. 191). Being sick is being broken in both soul and body. Body betrays. To deal with this betrayal means turning it into words or music or art or mysticism. Otherwise, sickness wins. Otherwise there is no otherwise. To turn sickness into music, art, words, poetry, prose, mysticism does not mean making it happy or making it okay or making a happy ending of it. To turn sickness into poetry means making meaning out of it. Meaning making might depress. But depression is better than suicide. Art is born of depression. Who are our happy artists? If they are happy, perhaps they are not creating art. On this note, painter Mark Rothko (2004) says that,

> It is significant that such emotionality in relationship to the individual is found only in a tragic emotionality. . . . Let us just briefly state that pain, frustration, and the fear of death seem the most constant binder between human beings. . . . (p. 35)

Rothko's paintings haunt and speak to the most mystical part of psyche. But it seems that his negative emotionality got the better of him as he eventually took his own life. What gifts of color he gave to humanity while he was alive. His art has always particularly moved me because looking at one of his paintings is like being bathed in color and spirit. His paintings heal and wound because of their strange austerity. His paintings speak to the deepest part of human spirituality. It is not an accident that some of his work is found in a chapel, aptly named the Rothko Chapel in Houston. Sickness may break you and make you feel shipwrecked but art heals. This healing, again, is not a happy ending healing, it is, rather, the "diving into the wreck" as Adrienne Rich (1989, p. 147) puts it.

American education runs counter to diving into the wreck of illness. History is about victors. But being sick is not about being a victor it is about being a victim. The voices of the losers are squashed out of history because historians do not think that they are reliable. Pathographies attempt to put those voices back into the historical record. An individual's memory is part of that historical record. Public schooling in America has little to do with the individual and her sufferings. Standardized knowledges know not of bodily brokenness. A broken body is not in any way standard. Public schooling in this country is a shame and a disgrace. We have lost our way. As politicians stole the last election (namely Bush and his cronies), so too have they stolen our educational system and ruined it. So what do we do? I suggest we turn again to thinking about teachers. Teachers should not be puppets of a corrupt state. Being a puppet is not being a teacher. The true sense of the word teacher is wisdom figure. I tried to get at this in the early part of this chapter. Here I would like to add a few final remarks.

The ill body as teacher. This teacher turns toward wisdom traditions, toward the poets, the mystics, the artists. Why does the ill body need wisdom traditions? For sustenance and guidance. Why turn toward Buddhism or any other wisdom tradition? Because the symbol of the Buddha gives one strength to continue.

> There has never been such a thing as "Buddha," so do not understand it as a Buddha. "Buddha" is a medicine for emotional people; if you have no disease, you should not take medicine. (Cleary, 1997, p. 263)

Buddha is not a person. Buddha is a symbol. It is not a symbol of hope--for there is no concept of hope in Buddhism. Buddha is a symbol of suffering and the release of that suffering. Release of suffering comes from nonattachment to things and the release of suffering comes from compassion toward the Other and being-toward-the-other. I spoke of compassion previously but it is worth mentioning again here. The Bodhisattava is that figure of compassion. Mystical forms of religious experience--especially in Mahayana Buddhism--are to be shared with others, not kept secret. Most mystics do not close themselves off in huts, they go out into the world to help others. This is a point many misunderstand. Mysticism should not be the height of selfishness and solipsism--it should be the beginning of movement out toward the other. Moshe Idel (1988) says of Jewish mysticism that,

> Mystical union, or communion, thus serves as a vehicle used by the individual in order to better serve the community. (p. 53)

Again, this point is worth repeating. When one suffers from debilitating illness, the worst thing one can do is shut oneself off from the community. This isolation becomes dangerous and can lead to suicide. One of the reasons I wrote this book was to share my experiences with others so as to become a part of other peoples' lives. Pathography or autobiography is not only about the self it is about the self's relation to the other through storytelling. Storytelling is a lost art in America because children are schooled out of their own stories. The stories that children tell are thought to be irrelevant to the standardized curriculum. So, children grow up erasing their subjectivities and lose their sense of self. Children grow up without a sense of self. They grow up in a world of fear. Schooling experience only leads to "[t]he fear of nameless dread" (Waska, 2002, p. 57). Schooling is a dreadful experience for children. This dreadful experience then gets carried over into college and university where there is only more dreadful experience. Schooling at all levels has become soulless. Teachers teach to the test. Teachers put fear in students from the time they are in kindergarten. This fear can make children sick. And so we must find our teachers elsewhere. Peter Matthiessen (1978) says, ""[w]hen you are ready," Buddhists say, "the teacher will appear" (p. 316). With few exceptions, I have always found my teachers outside of school. My teachers are the artists, poets and mystics.

The most profound moments in a life turn on death and traumatic experiences. It is to these experiences that the poets and mystics speak. While still a Ph.D. student, my father suddenly died. He died four weeks before I defended my dissertation. His death was a horror to me. I was teaching at the time at Xavier University in New Orleans. It was a Sunday when I got the phone call. Monday, I started my new job as an Assistant Professor of Theology at Xavier. I decided to go on because I could not stop for my father's death. Emily Dickenson (1961) says, "[b]ecause I could not stop for Death, He kindly stopped for me" (p. 269). I did not stop my life by not teaching and by not defending my dissertation. But eventually my father's Death did stop me emotionally. There is no way to prepare for the death of a primal figure. And certainly schooling helps little. In times of great stress and crisis I return to my mystics, artists and poets as I did during those years of grief that I suffered over the loss of my father. One gets to a point where melancholia turns to mourning and mourning turns to memory and the tears finally stop. There comes a point--as John Berryman (1969) puts it--when "[i]'ve had enough of this dying" (p. 136). And then you move on. Things fade and the tears stop. When I got sick, memories of my father's illness came flooding back. From illness to illness. When my mother got sick, I began to remember the early days of my illness. And so illness swirls amidst memories of primal others. Life is a mess. School does not teach us about the mess, it only seems to tidy up the edges with fill in the blank tests.

This book--*Teaching through the ill Body*-- has been attempt to explore the interconnections between the ill body, art, poetry, language and music. As there are repetitive themes in the book, so too are there repetitive forms of illness. Experience of chronic illness is a constant theme and variations. Repetition is the heart of the illness experience. The over and over again of episodes reflect the over and over again of lived experience. Repetition is life, life is repetition.. Teaching is repetition as well. The best teachings are the repetitions. Repetition in this book has been deliberate. This is another no-no in academe. God forbid you repeat yourself!! But illness is about repeating; it is about repeating sorrow, pain, frustration, despair. Chronic illness is a continual repeating of these themes. Freud knew that repetition is the very stuff of the death drive. Repetition compulsion is what makes us crazy. But it is to this craziness we must turn. Memory by its very nature is repetitive. Dreams are repetitive. It is curious to me why academics want to wipe away this natural tendency to repeat. Academe wants clean, clear lines, fill in the blank lives, clear research agendas. But life is just not that way. Wisdom traditions teach that the repetitive chant leads toward the divine. The heartbeat repeats. Memory is a repeat of childhood with a new and different twist. And history does in fact repeat itself. Poets repeat phrases to make a point, to emphasize and illuminate. Rothko's paintings are repetitions on a theme. The Bodhisattva repeats the same message over and over: go into the community and be with others, help others.

In times of great turmoil and stress, I return again and again to the same writers, the same poets and the same ideas. I have returned to my Anne Sexton, my Kenneth Patchen, my Mark Rothko, my Steve Reich and to Buddhism. To make sense of the darkness, these artists, poets and Wisdom figures give me strength. Some are driven crazy by the eternal return: Nietzsche. Others learn from it.

In closing here, I want to finally thank my doctors who saved my life. I want to thank my loving partner for being there through it all. And I want to thank my parents who have taught me through their ill bodies.

REFERENCES

Agacinski, S. (2003). *Time passing: Modernity and nostalgia*. New York: Columbia University Press.

Agee, J. (2004). From let us praise famous men. In R. Coles (Ed.), *Teaching stories: An anthology on the power of learning and literature* (pp. 233–256). New York: The Modern Library.

Anzaldua, G. (2002). Now let us shift... the path of conocimiento... inner work, public acts. In G. Anzaldua & A. L. Keating (Eds.), *This bridge we call home: Radical visions for transformation* (pp. 540–578). New York: Routledge.

Auden, W. H. (1958). *Selected poetry of W. H. Auden*. New York: The Modern Library.

Ayers, W., & Quinn, T. (2001). Series foreword. In W. H. Watkins (Ed.), *The white architects of black education: Ideology and power and America, 1865–1954* (ix–x). New York: Teachers College Press.

Bachelard, G. (1988a). *The flame of a candle* (J. Caldwell, Trans.). Dallas, TX: The Dallas Institute.

Bachelard, G. (1988b). *The right to dream* (J. A. Underwood, Trans.). Dallas, TX: The Dallas Institute.

Bachelard, G. (1990). *Fragments of a poetics of fire*. Dallas, TX: The Dallas Institute.

Bachelard, G. (1994). *On poetic imagination and reverie* (C. Gaudin, Trans.). Dallas, TX: Spring Publications.

Bachelard, G. (2000). *The dialectic of duration* (M. Mcallester Jones, Trans.). Clinamen Press.

Bachelard, G. (2002). *Air and dreams: An essay on the imagination of movement* (E. R. Farrell & F. Farrell, Trans.). Dallas, TX: The Dallas Institute.

Bataille, G. (1988). *Inner experience* (L. A. Boldt, Trans.). New York: SUNY Press.

Baudelaire, C. (1982). *Les fleur du mal*. Boston: David R. Godine Publishers.

Beckett, S. (1958). *The unnamable*. New York: Grove Press.

Bergman, I. (1978). *Autumn sonata*. Film. A.B. Svensk Filmindustri.

Berlin, I. (1997). *The proper study of mankind: An anthology of essays*. New York: Farrar, Strauss & Giroux.

Berry, P. (1982). *Echo's subtle body: Contributions to archetypal psychology*. Dallas, TX: Spring Publications.

Berryman, J. (1969). *Dreamsongs*. New York: Farrar, Straus & Giroux.

Bloch, E. (1999). *Essays on the philosophy of music* (P. Palmer, Trans.). New York: Cambridge University Press.

Bolen, J. S. (1996). *Close to the bone: Life-threatening illness and the search for meaning*. New York: Simon & Schuster.

Borges, J. L. (1964). *Labyrinths: Selected stories and other writings*. New York: A New Directions Book.

Bowles, P. (1998). *The sheltering sky*. New York: Harper Perennial.

Bradbury, R. (1996a). *Fahrenheit 451*. New York: A Del Ray Book, Random House.

Bradbury, R. (1996b). *The October country*. New York: Ballantine Books.

Bradbury, R. (1997). *Something wicked comes this way*. New York: Avon Books.

Bradbury, R. (2001a). *Dandelion wine*. New York: William Morrow/Harper Collins.

Bradbury, R. (2001b). *The illustrated man*. New York: William Morrow/Harper Collins.

Britzman, D. (1998). *Lost subjects, contested objects: Toward a psychoanalytic inquiry of learning*. New York: SUNY Press.

Britzman, D. (2003). *After-education: Anna Freud, Melanie Klein, and psychoanalytic histories of learning*. New York: SUNY Press.

Brown, N. O. (1966). *Love's body*. New York: Vintage.

Broyard, A. (1992). *Intoxicated by my illness and other writings on life and death*. Columbine, NY: Fawcett.

Buber, M. (1947/2002). *Between man and man* (R. Gregor-Smith, Trans.). New York: Routledge.

Buber, M. (1958). *Meetings: Autobiographical fragments*. New York: Routledge.

REFERENCES

Burroughs, W. (2003). *Junky*. New York: Penguin.

Campo, R. (1997). *The desire to heal: A doctor's education in empathy, identity, and poetry*. New York: W.W. Norton.

Camus, A. (1972). *A happy death*. New York: Vintage.

Carson, R. (1990/1962). *Silent spring*. New York: Houghton Mifflin.

Carter, A. (2003). *Nights at the circus*. London: Vintage.

Casey, E. (1991). *Spirit and soul: Essays in philosophical psychology*. Dallas, TX: Spring Publishers.

Cassell, E. J. (1991). *The nature of suffering and the goals of medicine*. New York: Oxford University Press.

Chodron, P. (2005). *No time to lose: A timely guide to the way of the Bodhisattva*. Boston: Shambhala.

Chopra, D. (2003). *The spontaneous fulfillment of desire: Harnessing the infinite power of coincidence*. New York: Harmony Books.

Cicchetti, J. (2003). *Dreams, symbols, and homeopathy: Archetypal dimensions of healing*. Berkeley, CA: North Atlantic Books.

Cleary, T. (Ed.). (2005). *Classics of Buddhism and Zen: The collected translations*. Boston: Shambhala.

Coles, R. (Ed.) (2004). *Teaching stories: An anthology on the power of learning and literature*. New York: The Modern Library.

Cowan, D. (1995). Zeus: The form of things. In J. H. Stroud (Ed.), *The Olympians* (pp. 1–13). Dallas, TX: Spring Publications.

Cunningham, M. (1998). *The hours*. New York: Picador.

Dali Lama. (2003). *Advice on dying and living a better life* (J. Hopkins, Trans.). New York: Atria Books.

De Certeau. (1988). *The practice of everyday life*. Berkeley, CA: The University of California Press.

Deleuze, G., & Guattari, F. (1994). *What is philosophy?* (H. Tomlinson & G. Burchell, Trans.). New York: Columbia University Press.

Deleuze, G., & Guattari, F. (2002). *A thousand plateaus: Capitalism and schizophrenia* (B. Massumi, Trans.). Minneapolis, MN: Minnesota Press.

Delpit, L. (1995). *Other people's children: Cultural conflict in the classroom*. New York: The New Press.

Derrida, J. (1998). *The ear of the other: Otobiography, transference, translation*. Lincoln, NE: The University of Nebraska Press.

Derrida, J. (1991). From Plato's pharmacy. In P. Kamuf (Ed.), *A Derrida reader: Between the blinds* (pp. 112–142). New York: Columbia University Press.

Derrida, J. (1993). *Memoirs of the blind: The self-portrait and other ruins* (P.-A. Brault & M. Nass, Trans.). Chicago: The University of Chicago Press.

Derrida, J. (1995). *The gift of death* (D. Wills, Trans.). Chicago: The University of Chicago Press.

Derrida, J. (2002). *Who's afraid of philosophy? Right to philosophy I* (J. Plug, Trans.). Stanford, CA: Stanford University Press.

Derrida, J., & Stiegler, B. (2002). *Echographies of television* (J. Bajorek, Trans.). Malden, MA: Blackwell Press.

DeSalvo, L. (2002). *Vertigo: A memoir*. New York: First Feminist Press. City University of New York.

Dewey, J. (1981). Experience as aesthetic. In J. J. McDermott (Ed.), *The philosophy of John Dewey. Two volumes in one* (pp. 525–554). Chicago: The University of Chicago Press.

Dewey, J. (1989) *On education*. Chicago: Chicago University Press.

Dickenson, E. (1961). Because I could not stop for death. In M. Mack, L. Dean, & W. Frost (Eds.), *Modern poetry* (p. 269). Englewood Cliffs, NJ: Prentice Hall.

Didion, J. (2005). *The year of magical thinking*. New York: Alfred Knopf.

Doll, M. A. (1988). *Beckett and myth: An archetypal approach*. Syracuse: Syracuse University Press.

Doll, M. A. (1995). *To the lighthouse and back: Writings on teaching and living*. New York: Peter Lang.

Doll, M.A. (2000). *Like letters in running water: A mythopoetics of curriculum*. Mahwah, NJ: Lawrence Erlbaum and Associates Publishers.

Duff, K. (1993). *The alchemy of illness.* New York: Bell Tower.

Easton, C. (1989).*Jacqueline Du Pre: A biography.* New York: Da Capo Press.

Eckhart, M. (1941). *Meister Eckhart. A modern translation* (R. B. Blakney, Trans.). New York: Harper Perennial.

Eco, U. (1994). *Six walks in the fictional woods.* Cambridge, MA: Harvard University Press.

Eigen, M. (1993). *The electrified tightrope.* Northvale, NJ: Jason Aronson, Inc.

Eigen, M. (1996). *Psychic deadness.* Northvale, NJ: Jason Aronson.

Eigen, M. (1998). *The psychoanalytic mystic.* New York: Free Association Books.

Eigen, M. (2001). *Ecstasy.* Middletown, CT: Wesleyan University Press.

Eigen, M. (2004). *The sensitive self.* Middletown, CT: Wesleyan University Press.

Eigen, M. (2005). *Emotional storm.* Middletown, CT: Wesleyan University Press.

Eliot, T. S. (1958). *The complete poems and plays 1909–1950.* New York: Harcourt, Brace & Company.

Eliot, T. S. (1962). *T.S. Eliot. The wasteland and other poems.* New York: A Harvest Book.

Feuntes, C. (2001). Introduction. In *The diary of Frida Kahlo: An intimate portrait* (pp. 7–24). New York: Harry N. Abrams Press.

Fourster, E. M. (1920). *Where angels fear to tread.* New York: Vintage.

Fox, M. (1988). *The coming of the cosmic Christ.* New York: Harper and Row.

Fox, M., & Sheldrake, R. (1997). *Natural grace: Dialogues on creation, darkness, and the soul in spirituality and science.* New York: Doubleday.

Frank, A. W. (1991). *At the will of the body: Reflections on illness.* New York: Houghton Mifflin Company.

Frank, A. W. (2004). Emily's scars: Surgical shapings, technoluxe, and bioethics. In *The Hastings Center Report* (Vol. 34, no. 2, pp. 18–29).

Frank, A. W. (2005). *The wounded storyteller: Body, illness, and ethics.* Chicago: The University of Chicago Press.

Freud, S. (1961). *The interpretation of dreams* (J. Strachey, Trans.). New York: Science Editions, Inc.

Freud, S. (1996). *Three case histories: The wolf man, the rat man and the psychotic Doctor Schreber.* New York: Touchstone.

Garrison, J. (1997). *Dewey and eros: Wisdom and desire in the art of teaching.* New York: Teachers College Press.

Gay, K., & Whittington, C. (2002). *Body marks: Tattooing, piercing, and scarification.* Brookfield, CT: Millbrook Press.

Gaynor, M. (2002). *The healing power of sound: Recovery from life-threatening illness using sound, voice, and music.* Boston: Shambala Press.

Gilman, S. (1995). *Picturing health and illness: Images of identity and difference.* Baltimore: The Johns Hopkins Press.

Gilman, S. (2003). Art, healing, and history. In J. Morgan (Ed.), *Pulse: Art, healing and transformation* (pp. 44–49). Boston: Ila & Steidl Publishers.

Giovanni, N. (2007). *The collected poetry of Nikki Giovanni 1968–1998.* New York: Harper Perennial.

Gunther, J. (2007). *Death be not proud.* New York: Harper.

Greene, M. (1995). *Releasing the imagination: Essays on education, the arts, and social change.* San Francisco: Josey-Bass.

Green, A. (1999). *The work of the negative.* New York: Free Association Press.

Groddeck, G. (1961/1923). *The book of the it.* New York: Vintage Press.

Groddeck, G. (1977). *The meaning of illness: Selected psychoanalytic writings.* New York: International Universities Press, Inc.

Guggenbuhl-Craig, A. (1979). The archetype of the invalid and the limits of healing. In *Spring* (pp. 29–41).

Guggenbuhl-craig. (1980). *Eros on crutches: Reflections on amorality and psychoapathy.* Irving, TX: Spring Publications.

Hanh, T. N. (2006). *Understanding our mind.* Berkeley, CA: Parallax Press.

Hanh, T. N. (2007). *Chanting from the heart: Buddhist ceremonies and daily practices.* Berkeley, CA: Parallax Press.

REFERENCES

Haraway, D. (1996). *Modest-witness, second-millennium: Femaleman meets oncomouse: Feminism and technoscience.* New York: Routledge.

Harding, M. E. (1973). *The i and the not i: A study in the development of consciousness.* Princeton, NJ: Bollingen Series Princeton.

Hawkins, A. H. (1993). *Reconstructing illness: Studies in pathology.* Purdue University Press.

H.D. (1983). *H.D.: Collected poems 1912–1944.* New York: A New Directions Book.

Heidegger, M. (1962). *Being and time* (J. Macquarrie & E. Robinson, Trans.). New York: Harper and Row.

Heaney, S. (1998). *Open ground: Selected poems. Seamus Heaney 1966–1996.* New York: Farrar, Straus & Giroux.

Henderson, J. L. (1995). Reflections on the history and practice of Jungian analysis. In M. Stein (Ed.), *Jungian analysis* (pp. 3–28). Illinois, IL: Chicago & LaSalle.

Heschel, J. (2004). *A passion for the truth.* Woodstock, VT: Jewish Lights Publishing.

Hesse, H. (2001). *Steppenwolf.* London: Penguin.

Hillman, J. (1975a). *Loose ends: Primary papers in archetypal psychology.* Zurich, Switzerland: Spring Publications.

Hillman, J. (1975). *Re-visioning psychology.* New York: Harper & Row.

Hillman, J. (1979a). Senex and puer: An aspect of the historical and the psychological present. In *Puer papers* (pp. 3–53). Dallas, TX: Spring Publications.

Hillman, J. (1979b). Peaks and vales: The soul/spirit distinction as basis for the differences between psychotherapy and spiritual discipline. In *Puer papers* (pp. 54–74). Dallas, TX: Spring Publications.

Hillman, J. (1979c). *The dream and the underworld.* New York: Harper Perennial.

Hillman, J. (1985). *Archetypal psychology: A brief account.* Dallas, TX: Spring Publications.

Hillman, J. (1997a). Culture and the animal soul. In *Spring 62: A Journal of archetype and culture Fall & Winter* (pp. 10–37).

Hillman, J. (1997b). *Suicide and the soul.* Putnam, CT: Spring Publications.

Hillman, J. (2000). *Pan and the nightmare.* Wood stock, CT: Spring Publications.

Hillman, J. (2004). *Healing fiction.* Putnam, CT: Spring Publications.

Hillman,J. (2007). *The thought of the heart and the soul of the world.* Putnam, CT. Spring Publications.

Hopkins, G. M. (1961). Felix Randal. In M. Mack, L. Dean & W. Frost (Eds.), *Modern poetry.* Englewood Cliffs, NJ: Prentice Hall.

Hunt, L. (2000). Strategic suffering: Illness narratives as social empowerment among Mexican cancer patients. In C. Mattingly & L. Garro (Eds.), *Narrative and the cultural construction of illness and healing* (pp. 88–107). Berkeley, CA: The University of California Press.

Idel, M. (1988). *Kabbalah: New perspectives.* New Haven, CT: Yale University Press.

James, W. (1890/1918a). *The principles of psychology* (Vol. 1). New York: Dover.

James, W. (1890/1918b). *The principles of psychology* (Vol. 2). New York: Dover.

James, W. (1998). *Pragmatism and the meaning of truth.* Cambridge: Harvard University Press.

Johnson, R. A. (1986). *Inner work: Using dreams and active imagination for personal growth.* San Francisco: Harper & Row.

Jung, C. G. (1958). *The undiscovered self* (R. F. C. Hull, Trans.). Boston: Little, Brown & Company.

Jung, C. G. (1963). *Memories, dreams, reflections* (R. & C. Winston, Trans.). New York: Pantheon Books.

Jung, C. G. (1976). *The collected works of C. G. Jung Volume 18. Bollingen Series XX* (R. F. C. Hull, Trans.). Princeton, NJ: Princeton University Press.

Jung, C. G. (1974). *Dreams.* (R. F. Hull, Trans.). Princeton, NJ: Princeton University Press.

Jung, C. G. (1977). *The archetypes and the collective unconscious* (R. F. C. Hull, Trans.). Princeton, NJ: Princeton University Press.

Jung, C. G. (2002). Consciousness slipped from its natural foundation. Excerpts. In M. Sabini (Ed.), *The nature writings of C. G. Jung* (pp. 67–76). Berkeley, CA: North Atlantic Books.

Jung, C. G. (2002).The primitive knows how to converse with the soul Excerpts. In M. Sabini (Ed.), *The nature writings of C. G. Jung* (pp. 92–98). Berkeley, CA: North Atlantic Books.

Kaufmann, W. (1968). *Philosophic classics: Thales to Ockham.* New Jersey: Prentice Hall.

Kearney, M. (2000). *A place of healing: Working with suffering in living and dying.* New York: Oxford University Press.

Keats, J. (1959). *John Keats: Selected poems and letters.* Boston: Houghton Mifflin.

Kerouac, J. (1957). *On the road.* New York: Penguin Books.

Kerouac, J. (1976). *The dharma bums.* New York: Penguin Books.

Kierkegaard, S. (1845/1973). Stages on life's way. In R. Bretall (Ed.), *A Kierkegaard anthology* (pp. 175–189). Princeton, NJ: Princeton University Press.

Kierkegaard, S. (1971). *Either/or* (Vol. 1). Princeton, NJ: Princeton University Press.

Kincaid, J. (1997). *The autobiography of my mother.* New York: Plume.

Kirsch, A. (2005). *The wounded surgeon: Confessions and transformations in six American poets.* New York: W.W. Norton.

Klein, M. (1946). *Envy and gratitude and other works 1946–1963.* London: Karnac.

Kleinman, A. (1988). *The illness narratives: Suffering, healing and the human condition.* New York: Basic Books.

Kristeva, J. (1989). *The black sun.* New York: Columbia University Press.

Kumin, M. (1981). Foreword: How it was. In *The complete poems of Anne Sexton* (xix–xxxiv). Boston: Houghton Mifflin Company.

Lamm, L. J. (1993). *The idea of the past: History, science, and practice in American psychoanalysis.* New York: New York University Press.

Le Guin, U. (2001). *The lathe of heaven.* Great Britain: Gollancz/Orion publishing.

Levinas, E. (1985). *Ethics and infinity* (R. Cohen, Trans.). Pittsburgh, PA: Duquesne University Press.

Levinas, E. (1998). *Collected philosophical papers.* Pittsburgh, PA: Duquesne University Press.

Levinas, E. (2000). *Otherwise than being or beyond essence.* Pittsburgh, PA: Duquesne University Press.

Levinas, E. (2001). *Existence and existents* (A. Lingis, Trans.). Pittsburgh, PA: Duquesne University Press.

London, J. (1994). In a far country. In E. Labor (Ed.), *The portable Jack London* (pp. 11–25). New York: Penguin.

London, J. (2003). *The call of the wild and white fang.* London: Barnes and Noble Classics.

Lorde, A. (1997). *The cancer journals special edition.* San Francisco: Aunt Lute Books.

Lowe, S. M. (2001). Essay. In *The diary of Frida Kahlo: An intimate portrait* (pp. 25–29). New York: Harry N. Abrams Press.

Lowell, R. (2006). *Robert Lowell: Selected poems. Expanded edition.* New York: Farrar, Straus & Giroux.

Luria, A. R. (1968). *The mind of a mnemonist: A little book about a vast memory.* Cambridge, MA: Harvard University Press.

Luria, A. R. (2002). *The man with a shattered world: The history of a brain wound.* Cambridge, MA: Harvard University Press.

Macdonald, J. B. (1995). *Theory as a prayerful act: The collected essays of James B. Macdonald* (B. J. Macdonald, Ed.). New York: Peter Lang Publishers.

Mann, T. (1996). *Magic mountain.* New York: Vintage.

Matthiessen, P. (1978). *The snow leopard.* New York: Penguin.

McDougall, J. (1989). *Theaters of the body: A psychoanalytic approach to psychosomatic illness.* New York: W. W. Norton.

McNeely, D. A. (1991). *Animus aeternus: Exploring the inner masculine.* Toronto, Canada: Inner City Books.

Mercury, M. (2000). *Pagan fleshworks: The alchemy of body modification.* Rochester, VT: Park Street Press.

Merleau-Ponty, M. (1964a). *The primacy of perception.* Northwestern University Press.

Merleau-Ponty, M. (1964b). *Signs.* Northwestern University Press.

Merton, T. (1983). *No man is an island.* New York: Harcourt Brace Javanovich.

REFERENCES

Merton, T. (1988). *The ascent to truth*. New York: A Harvest Book.

Merton, T. (2007). *Echoing silence: Thomas Merton on the vocation of writing* (R. Inchausti, Ed.). Boston: New Seeds.

Miglietti, F. A. (2003). *Extreme bodies: The use and abuse of the body in art* (A. Shugaar, Trans.). Milano, Italy.

Miller, A. (2005). *The body never lies: The lingering effects of cruel parenting*. New York: W.W. Norton.

Miller, J. P. (2000). *Education and the soul: Toward a spiritual curriculum*. New York: SUNY.

Milner, M. (1957). *On not being able to paint*. Boston: Houghton Mifflin.

Mogenson, G. (2004, Fall). The afterlife of the image: On Jung and mourning. In *Spring 71 Orpheus: A journal of archetype and culture* (pp. 89–111).

Moore, T. (1983). *Rituals of the imagination*. Dallas, TX: The Pegasus Foundation.

Moore, T. (1992). *Care of the soul: A guide for cultivating depth and sacredness in everyday life*. New York: HarperCollins.

Moore, T. (2004). *Dark nights of the soul: A guide to finding your way through life's ordeals*. New York: Gotham Books.

Morris, D. (2000). *Illness and culture in the postmodern age*. Berkeley, CA: The University of California Press.

Morris, M. (2001). *Curriculum and the holocaust: Competing sites of memory and representation*. Mahwah, NJ: Lawrence Erlbaum and Associates Publishers.

Morris, M. (2006). *Jewish intellectuals and the university*. New York: Palgrave.

Neruda, P. (2004). *Pablo Neruda: Residence on earth*. New York: A New Directions Paperbook.

Nettles, S. (2001). *Crazy visitations: A chronicle of illness and recovery*. Athens, GA: The University of Georgia Press.

Paris, G. (1991). *Pagan grace: Dionysos, hermes, and goddess memory in daily life*. Dallas, TX: Spring Publications.

Patchen, K. (1941). *The journal of Albion moonlight*. New York: A New Directions Paperbook.

Paz, O. (1985). *The labyrinth of solitude*. New York: Grove Press.

Pinar, W. F. (1994). *Autobiography, politics and sexuality: Essays in curriculum theory, 1972–1992*. New York: Peter Lang.

Pinar, W. F., Reynolds, W., Slattery, P., & Taubman, P. (1995). *Understanding curriculum: An introduction to the study of historical and contemporary curriculum discourses*. New York: Peter Lang.

Pinar, W. F. (2000). Strange fruit: Race, sex, and an autobiography of alterity. In P. Trifonas (Ed.), *Revolutionary pedagogies: Cultural politics, instituting education, and the discourse of theory* (pp. 30–46). New York: Routledge/Falmer.

Pinar, W. F. (2004). *What is curriculum theory?* Mahwah, NJ: Lawrence Erlbaum and Associates Publishers.

Plato. (2003). Phaedo. In *Plato: The last days of Socrates* (H. Tredennick & H. Tarrant, Trans. (pp. 116–199). New York: Penguin Classics.

Poe, E. A. (1976). *The science fiction of Edgar Allan Poe*. New York: Penguin.

Preston, E. (1990). Mind and matter in myth. In K. Barnaby & P. D'Acierno (Eds.), *C. G. Jung and the humanities: Toward a hermeneutics of culture* (pp. 11–23). Princeton, NJ: Princeton University Press.

Prigogine, I. (1997). *The end of certainty: Time, chaos, and the new laws of nature*. New York: The Free Press.

Proust, M. (2003). *Remembrance of things past*. New York: The Modern Library.

Radley, A. (1998). *Making sense of illness: The social psychology of health and disease*. London: Sage Publications.

Ramachandran, V. S., & Blakeslee, S. (1998). *Phantoms in the brain: Probing the mysteries of the human mind*. New York: Quill. HarperCollins.

Rexroth, K. (1984). *Kenneth Rexroth: Selected poems*. (Ed.), Bradford Morrow. New York: A New Directions Book.

Rich, A. (1984). *The fact of a doorframe: Poems selected and new 1950–1984*. New York: W.W. Norton.

Rilke, R. M. (1962). *Letters to a young poet* (M. D. Herter Norton, Trans.). New York: W.W. Norton.

Rilke, R. M. (1967). *Duno elegies* (J. B. Leishman & S. Spender, Trans.). New York: W.W. Norton.

Rilke, R. M. (1985). *The notebooks of Malte Laurids Brigge* (S. Mitchell, Trans.). New York: Vintage.

Rilke, R. M. (1995). *Ahead of all parting: The selected poetry and prose of Rainer Maria Rilke* (S. Mitchell, Ed. & Trans.). New York: The Modern Library.

Rimbaud, A. (1957). *Illuminations* (L. Varese, Trans.). New York: A New Directions Paperback.

Rimbaud, A. (1961). *A season in hell and the drunken boat*. New York: A New Directions Paperback.

Rorem, N. (2000). *Ned Rorem: The later diaries 1961–1972*. Fairfield, PA: Da Capo Press.

Rothko, M. (2004). *The artist's reality: Philosophies of art*. New Haven, CT: Yale University Press.

Royce, J. (1988). *Josiah Royce: Selected writings* (J. E. Smith & W. Kluback, Eds.). New York: Paulist Press.

Royer, A. (1998). *Life with chronic illness: Social and psychological dimensions*. Westport, CT: Praeger.

Russ, D. (1995). Poseidon the god of confusion. In J. H. Stroud (Ed.), *The Olympians* (pp. 43–51). Dallas, TX: Spring Publications.

Sacks, O. (1996). *An anthropologist on mars: Seven paradoxical tales*. New York: Vintage.

Sacks, O. (1997). *The island of the colorblind*. New York: Alfred Knopf.

Sacks, O. (1998a). *A leg to stand on*. New York: A Touchstone Book.

Sacks, O. (1998b). *The man who mistood his wife for a hat an other clinical tales*. New York: A Touchstone Book. Simon & Schuster.

Sacks, O. (2000). *Seeing voices*. New York: Vintage.

Sacks, O. (2007). *Musicophilia: Tales of music and the brain*. New York: Alfred Knopf.

Salvio, P. (2007). *Anne Sexton: Teacher of weird abundance*. Albany, NY: SUNY.

Sanders, C. R. (1989). *Customizing the body: The art and culture of tattooing*. Philadelphia: Temple University Press.

Santayana, G. (2006). *The sense of beauty*. Pasadena, CA: Kessinger Publishers.

Sardello, R. (1983). The suffering body of the city: Cancer, heart attack, and herpes. In *Spring* (pp. 145–164).

Sardello, R. (1992). *Facing the world with soul: The reimagination of modern life*. Hudson, NY: LindisfarrePress.

Sardello, R. (1995). Some new aspects of hermes. In J. H. Stroud (Ed.), *The Olympians* (pp. 137–151). Dallas, TX: Spring Publications.

Sardello, R. (2002). *The power of the soul: Living the twelve virtues*. New York: Hampton Roads Publishing.

Schreber, D. P. (2006). *Memoirs of my nervous illness*. New York: NYRB Classics.

Sedgwick, E. (1999). *A dialogue on love*. Boston: Beacon Press.

Sedgwick, E. (2003). *Touching feeling: Affect, pedagogy, performativity*. Durham, NC: Duke University Press.

Seneca. (1969). *Seneca: Letters from a stoic: Epistulae morales and lucilium*. (R. Campell, Trans.). New York: Penguin.

Sexton, A. (1988). *Selected poems of Anne Sexton*. New York: Houghton Mifflin.

Silin, J. (2003). *Sex, death, and the education of children: Our passion for ignorance in the age of AIDS*. New York: Teachers College Press.

Simon, R. I. (2000). The torch of the past: The pedagogical significance of a transactional sphere of public memory. In P. P. Trifonas (Ed.), *Revolutionary pedagogies: Cultural politics, institutions, education, and the discourse of theory* (pp. 61–80). New York: Routledge.

Singer, J. (1990). On William Blake: Reason versus imagination. In K. Barnaby & P. D'Acierno (Eds.), *C. G. Jung and the humanities: Toward a hermeneutics of culture* (pp. 162–173). Princeton, NJ: Princeton University Press.

REFERENCES

Slattery, D. P. (2004). *Grace in the desert: Awakening to the gifts of monastic life*. San Francisco: Jossey-Bass.

Smith, D. G. (2006). *Trying to teach in a season of great untruth: Globalization, empire and the crisis of pedagogy*. Rotterdam/Taipei: Sense Publishers.

Smith, E. L. (1990). Descent to the underworld: Jung and his brothers. In K. Barnaby & P. D'Acierno (Eds.), *C. G. Jung and the humanities: Toward a hermeneutics of culture* (pp. 251–264). Princeton, NJ: Princeton University Press.

Smith, L. (2000). *Kenneth Patchen: Rebel poet in America*. Bottom Dog Press.

Solomon, A. (2001). *The noonday demon: An Atlas of depression*. New York: Scribner.

St. John of the Cross. (2003). *Dark night of the soul* (e. Allison Peers, Trans.). Mineola, NY: Dover Publications.

Stein, M. (1983). *In midlife: A jungian perspective*. Dallas, TX: Spring Publications.

Stevens, W. (1972). *Wallace Stevens. The palm at the end of the mind: Selected poems and a play*. New York: Vintage.

Sontag, S. (1977). *Illness as metaphor and AIDS and its metaphors*.

Tamargo, R. J. (2001). Foreword. In S. M. Nettles (Eds.), *Crazy visitation: A chronicle of illness and recovery*. The University of Georgia Press.

The Rumi Collection. (1998). K. Helminski (Ed.). Boston.

Thomas, D. (2003). *Dylan Thomas: Selected poems 1934–1952*. New York: A New Directions Book.

The Tibetan Book of the Dead. (2005). New York: Penguin.

Tolstoy, L. (1886). *The death of Ivan Ilych and other stories*.

Toombs, S. K. (1993). *The meaning of illness: A phenomenological account of the different perspectives of physician and patient*. The Netherlands: Kluwer.

Tuan, Y. (1977). *Space and place: The perspective of experience*. Minneapolis, MN: University of Minnesota Press.

Ulanov, A. B. (1995). Spiritual aspects of clinical work. In M. Stein (Ed.), *Jungian analysis* (pp. 50–78). Illinois, IL: Chicago and LaSalle.

Underhill, E. (1990). *Mysticism: The preeminent study in the nature and development of spiritual consciousness*. New York: Doubleday.

Von Franz, M. L. (1979). *Alchemical active imagination*. Irving, TX: Spring Publications.

Von Franz, M. L. (1980a). *Alchemy: An introduction to the symbolism and the psychology*. Toronto, Canada: Inner City Books.

Von Franz, M. L. (1980b). *On divination and synchronicity: The psychology of meaningful chance*. Toronto, Canada: Inner City Books.

Von Franz, M. L. (2000). *The problem of the puer aeternus*. Toronto, Canada: Inner City Books.

Waska, R. T. (2002). *Primitive experience of loss: Working with the paranoid-schizoid patient*. London: Karnac.

Wear, D. (1989). What literature says to pre-service teachers and educators. *Journal of Teacher Education, XXXX*(1), 51–55.

Wear, D. (1991). A reconnection to self: Women and solitude. In J. Erdman & J. Henderson (Eds.), *Critical discourse on curriculum curriculum issues* (pp. 168–184). Chicago: Mid-West Center for Curriculum Studies.

Wear, D. (Ed.). (1993). *The center of the web: Women and solitude*. Albany, NY: SUNY.

Wear, D., & Bickel, J. (Eds.). (2000). *Educating for professionalism: Creating a culture of humanism in medical education*. Iowa City, IA: University of Iowa Press.

Weaver, J. (2001). Silence of Method. In M. Morris & J. Weaver (Eds.), *Difficult memories: Talk in a (post) Holocaust era* (pp. 157–170). New York: Peter Lang.

Weil, S. (2006). *Gravity and grace*. New York: Routledge.

Wexler, P. (1996). *Holy sparks: Social theory, education and religion*. New York: St. Martin's Press.

Wexler, P. (2000). *Mystical society: An emerging social vision*. New York: Westview Press.

Wheeler, M. (2004, March). Signal discovery. In *Smithsonian* (pp. 30–32).

Whitman, W. (1958). *Leaves of grass*. New York: The New American Library.

Wilson, E. (1998). *Jacqueline du Pre: Her life, her music, her legend.* New York: Arcade Publishing.

Wittgenstein, L. (1958). *Philosophical investigations.* New York: Prentice Hall.

Woolf, V. (2002). *On being ill.* Ashfield, MA: Paris Press.

Yeats, W. B. (1989). *The collected poems of W. B. Yeats* R. J. Finneran, Ed.). New York: Collier Books, Macmillan.

TRANSGRESSIONS: CULTURAL STUDIES AND EDUCATION

Breinigsville, PA USA
30 March 2011
258837BV00002B/2/P